Betty Crocker

HOSTESS

COOKBOOK

Illustrated by   *Deirdre Stanforth*

GOLDEN PRESS NEW YORK

FIRST EDITION   FIRST PRINTING

Contents

Dear Hesitant Hostess,

If you're like most women, giving a party means many things to you. It provides an opportunity to entertain close friends, to let people you like discover each other. It offers you a chance to prove your prowess as a cook, to display your talent for decorating, to demonstrate your diplomacy, to give your children firsthand knowledge of the social world. Most important, it's a special way of saying, "I like you."

But let's face it, a party that accomplishes all these things doesn't just happen. Like a fine theatrical performance it calls for careful plotting, some rehearsal and, of course, personal artistry. And, like any dramatic appearance, it may produce a little unnecessary stage fright. That's what this book is all about.

On the following pages you'll find full stage directions for dozens of parties, with menus and scores of recipes. Browse through them, choose a party in character for you and then learn your part, from overture—the invitation—to curtain line —"We're so glad you could come."

All the behind-the-scenes details are spelled out for you. You'll find information for planning and presenting all kinds of parties, ideas for decorating and for fun and games, tips for coping with emergencies and special problems. And for most of the dinner parties, there's a tested plan for the orderly preparation of your party menu plus helpful suggestions for serving it.

So don't let inexperience, shyness or a tiny kitchen stop you. Pick a party, and start planning it now. One star performance will lead to another and another, each a little easier and perhaps a bit more elaborate than the last. May every one be a smash hit!

Cordially,

Betty Crocker

A Handbook
for the Hostess

Planning the Party

What Kind of Party?

There are literally dozens—perhaps hundreds—of different kinds of parties. And every one of them has the potential of fun. There are formal and informal parties, parties indoors and parties outdoors, and parties that move freely from living room to lawn and back again.

A party may involve a full-scale meal, a between-meals meal—morning coffee, afternoon tea, late evening supper—or merely part of a meal, such as dessert and coffee. Or the food may be no more than light refreshment, an assortment of chips, dips, olives and nuts to go along with beverages.

The party may be in honor of *somebody*—a bride, a baby, a birthday person, a new neighbor, an out-of-town visitor, or a friend's houseguest. It may be in honor of *something*—a holiday, a housewarming, a bon voyage. Or it can be a celebration just for celebration's sake—because it's June and the weather is lovely, because it's January and the weather is awful.

Of course every party is not for *everybody*. A formal dinner for twelve is a joy in a large dining room with an experienced maid to serve it, a nightmare in a small living-dining room with a novice at the helm. On the other hand, the same small living-dining room can be the scene of a delightful get-together of the same twelve people, if the same novice hostess provides a few hearty dishes on a buffet and lets everyone help himself.

So your first step when planning a party is to decide what you can handle gracefully with the space and equipment and experience that you have. A small party, elegant or casual, is ideal for occasions when you really want to talk. It gives you and your guests a chance to get acquainted with a newcomer, to catch up with friends you seldom see, or to hear about or tell about travels. For this kind of entertaining, be sure there's a comfortable place for each guest to sit and a table within easy reach.

A big party, on the other hand, allows people to talk in small groups, discover new acquaintances, and do their own mixing. In a group of twenty or more, you'll find most people standing by choice, so the chair and table requirements are greatly reduced. However, if you value your rugs and table-tops, do be sure that no one is far from an ashtray and a coaster.

Medium-size parties, groups of about sixteen, seem to be the most difficult to handle unless they're out of doors, so it's a good idea to save these gatherings for summer. Concentrate on making your indoor parties either small enough to be intimate or large enough to break happily into smaller groups.

Who Goes With Whom?

When you've decided how many people you are going to entertain, the next question is which ones. Obviously, you're not going to invite two mortal enemies to the same party. (If you want to play peacemaker, choose another time to get the feuders together.) But there's more to making up a successful guest list than merely separating the Hatfields from the McCoys.

Some of the most successful parties bring very unlikely people together. Two persons or two couples that you'd have sworn would have nothing in common strike up a surprisingly enthusiastic acquaintance. A couple of men who have been nodding for years on the commuter train suddenly find a mutual interest in stamp collecting or skin diving. Two women who seem temperamentally poles apart amaze you by taking to each other instantly. A young bachelor for whom you have thoughtfully provided a pretty girl spends his whole evening in fascinated conversation with your husband's middle-aged cousin. All this is great fun, but bizarre combinations are best risked at a large party. Then if enthusiasm fails to develop, each person can move easily into another conversation group.

At small parties it's a good idea to invite people who have something in common. They don't all have to know each other—it's often more interesting if they don't—but if *you* know that all are about the same age and all sports lovers or all enthusiastic about civic projects, the chances of their hitting it off are just that much greater.

Whatever the size of the party, make it easy on yourself by including some people who'll carry part of the entertainment load for you. We all have friends like this—men and women who talk easily and amusingly, who don't seem to have a shy bone in their bodies, and who admittedly like playing to an audience. One or two such guests are your best insurance that while you're getting dinner on the table your party isn't going to die on its feet. But don't have *all* your entertaining friends at one gathering; too many life-of-the-party types can be overwhelming.

One final note of caution: *Never* make the mistake of trying to sweep away all your obligations with one pay-off party. Have your "must" guests, a few at a time, with others you think they'll enjoy—even if it means waiting a little longer than you'd like to return an invitation.

The Pleasure of Your Company...

The way you invite guests to a party should give them an indication of the kind of party to expect. If it's a very significant occasion—a bridal dinner or a silver anniversary or a party honoring a distinguished guest—the invitations will imply this formality. Not only will they be issued at least two or three weeks in advance, but they will most likely be written rather than telephoned.

Most of the parties you'll be giving probably aren't going to be that formal, and the telephone is often the best way to give and get all the information necessary. Of course, a written invitation, though a bit more formal, is always in good taste. Ten days to two weeks before the party, call the people on your guest list and invite them, clueing them in on your plans. "It's Dave Rogers' birthday, and I'm asking everybody to bring a gag gift" or "Wear low heels because if the weather's decent we're going to cook outdoors" or "The Moffats are having a houseguest that weekend, so I thought I'd dress up a little." However casual the invitation, don't be vague about the date or the hour. "Two weeks from Friday" can lead to confusion, and "late in the afternoon" can mean four o'clock to one person and six o'clock to another. So be explicit. "Friday, the twenty-sixth, at five" leaves no room for misunderstanding.

If the party is small, try to reach all the guests the same day, so no one will feel he's been an afterthought. If you're having a large cocktail party it may be wise to mail invitations—a little note or a printed invitation card with time and place filled in —so that all will arrive at the same time. In the past, invitations to an open house or cocktail party didn't require an acknowledgment, but today almost everyone wants to know how many guests to expect.

If the invitations are made by telephone, chances are you'll get your acceptances or regrets right then —though a wife will probably want to check with her husband to be sure he hasn't made other plans. If so, she should call you back the next day. If the invitations are mailed, you'll have to wait a little longer for a final countdown of guests, but all such invitations should be answered as promptly as possible. It's thoughtless of anyone to keep a hostess waiting for a reply for more than a day or two. If other plans threaten to conflict, the guest should either decline right away or explain the situation to the hostess—"Mother is coming to town either Friday or Saturday and hasn't let us know which day. We'd hate to miss the party Friday night if she decides not to come till Saturday, but I'm afraid we won't know until next week." In this case you can tell the guests that they'll be welcome at the last minute if Mother decides to come on Saturday, or, if you're feeling particularly expansive, you can include Mother in the invitation if she arrives in time.

When guests are visiting you for the first time, and the instructions for getting to your house are complicated, put them in writing or draw a map. If you're off the beaten path, or have a hard-to-find driveway, your friends will appreciate really clear directions. It's even worth driving the route from the main highway yourself, looking for conspicuous landmarks to identify each turn, or measuring mileages exactly. Once you have the foolproof directions on paper, be sure you keep a copy to duplicate for all future parties.

What to Serve?

The food you serve your guests will depend on many factors—the type of party, the time of day and time of year, the ages and preferences of the people you're inviting, and to some extent on your budget, your equipment and your cooking know-how. Further on in this book you'll find meal plans and recipes for practically any occasion and any cook. But regardless of the specific recipes you choose, there are some general rules about meal planning that any hostess would be wise to commit to memory. Although most of the following points pertain to dinner parties, you'll see they can be adapted to other types of parties as well.

• Never experiment with a new dish for a party. If you've found a recipe that sounds exciting, give it a test run on the family before presenting it to guests. This may mean investing a few extra dollars in a dress rehearsal, but if it spares you the embarrassment of failure or the disappointment of a less-than-smashing success, it's worth the small tab.

• Take advantage of do-ahead dishes. Bake cakes, cookies and pastries ahead of time. Mix salad dressings beforehand. Wash and dry salad greens early in the day and refrigerate them in plastic bags. Many hors d'oeuvres and casserole dishes can be assembled a day early and simply baked or reheated at party time. Most ice-cream desserts can be put together early in the day and kept in the freezer. Just be sure to remove them in time to soften a bit before serving. If you're lucky enough to have a large freezer, take advantage of it and freeze ahead as many of your party foods as possible.

• Plan no more than one dish that calls for split-second timing. Avoid top-of-the-range and broiler cooking as much as possible, as well as sauces and soufflé desserts that demand the full attention of the cook at zero hour. Generally speaking, a flexible casserole dish that includes meat or chicken or seafood, and perhaps a vegetable or two, is the safest main dish. The casserole plus a salad and a made-ahead dessert will allow you to devote your just-before-serving minutes to a sumptuous hot bread or simply to adding the finishing touches to the table.

Equally hostess-perfect would be an *all*-oven dinner with foods that can be baked or roasted at the same temperature. (See Dinner's in the Oven, page 30.)

• If your kitchen counter space is limited (and whose isn't?), avoid foods that must be arranged and served separately. Serve a tossed salad in one big salad bowl and save individual molded salads for a very small group.

• When the meal is to be eaten without benefit of a table—from trays or plates held in the guests' laps—choose foods that don't require a knife for cutting. This means meats or seafood already cut into bite-size pieces or foods like ground meat, tuna or sweetbreads that can be easily broken with a fork.

• Ease the serving problem for a crowd by using large dinner plates that will accommodate all the foods in your main course. For such service, steer clear of "runny" foods—casseroles with thin gravy, overdoses of salad dressing, stewed tomatoes and the like.

• Be sure your menu provides contrast in flavor, color and texture. Balance a spicy food with a bland one, a white food with a bright red or a dark green garnish, a soft texture with a crisp one. Condiments provide easy ways to introduce contrast in flavor. A hot mustard, a sharp vinegar, piquant horseradish sauce add instant pick-up to foods low-key in flavor. If the main dish is highly flavored, balance it with the blandness of sour cream or the sweetness of mint sauce or a jelly. Color-balance the white of mashed potatoes and the brown of roast meat with radishes, carrots, shiny green or ripe olives, kumquats, spiced crab apples or minted pears. Give an essentially soft dish or menu crunch with potato chips, celery, nuts, French fried onions, toasted bread crumbs or water chestnuts.

• Include one spectacular in every party menu. A beautiful mold, an exotic vegetable combination or a flaming dessert will cast an aura of glamor over the most commonplace meat-and-potatoes meal.

• Never serve the same dinner to the same people more than once. It takes only a minute or two to jot down a menu in a notebook or hostess diary and thus avoid a carbon copy of the party six months or a year hence.

Ready and Waiting

It doesn't take a genius to figure out that the more tasks you can take care of well in advance of the party, the more relaxed and composed you'll be at zero hour. Several days before the party, run down this list to see which pre-party steps apply to your entertaining plans. Then do them!

• Arrange your schedule so that all housecleaning chores are completed well ahead of time and your rooms look just the way you want them to the day before the party. Once-over dusting and pillow-plumping are all that should remain for party day.

• Write out your menu—down to salt, pepper and butter. Check each recipe to make sure you have every ingredient. Never, never shop the day of the party! Study your menu with an eye to do-ahead dishes—and do them ahead.

• Using your menu as a guide, take inventory of everything you'll need for serving. Unsheathe your big serving pieces and wash or polish them before the big push begins.

• Take down your glasses and make sure there are enough—hopefully extras if you're planning a cocktail party or open house. Check the silver. Does it need polishing?

• Inspect the china—plates, cups, saucers, platters—for chips. If you're planning a sit-down dinner, it's nice to have all the china match. But you can still have a lovely table by using two patterns and making every other place setting a different one. If you're serving buffet style, you can mix patterns in crystal and linen as well as china.

• Select the containers you'll need for the flower or fruit arrangements you plan to use. If you're splurging on greenhouse flowers, you might want to take your favorite vase or bowl to the florist and let him arrange the blooms right in your container.

• Cast a careful eye on your party linens for dust streaks or wrinkles. If a cloth or place mats need pressing, do it on the morning of the party and put the linens right on the table.

• Inspect your closet space. Be sure you have plenty of hangers for guests' coats.

• Make a powder room check. You'll probably want to have new cakes of soap and boxes of tissues.

• Decide what you're going to wear and see that it's cleaned and pressed. Choose a simple costume—no billowing sleeves or skirts and nothing too tight. Fashion points can be a handicap in the kitchen.

• Don't forget ice cubes—more than you think you'll need. Freeze a good supply a couple of days in advance and store them in several plastic bags. You can take them out of the freezer in batches then, not all at once.

• Assemble ashtrays and, if necessary, coasters. There should be an ashtray, maybe two, on every table, chest and sideboard—in fact, on every surface. Have a good supply of match folders, too. You may, if you like, provide a variety of cigarettes.

Decorator Touches

There's no law that says you have to decorate for a party, but most hostesses find that a few gala touches add immeasurably to the feeling of festivity. In party decorations, anything goes—anything pretty and bright, anything artful or attractive or even amusing. And the wherewithal is everywhere.

• Use flowers, plants, blossoming fruit tree branches, or fall leaves.

• Use candles lavishly—tall tapers in three-branched candelabra on the sideboard or mantel, single candles in old-fashioned saucer holders as the tiny centerpieces for card-table service, yellow beeswax candles in an arrangement of vegetables and strawflowers.

• Use fruits in wonderful monochromatic combinations—strawberries, apples, tomatoes, cranberries, red grapes or plums; perhaps mixed with pieces from your collection of cranberry or Bavarian glass and displayed dramatically. Arrange a symphony in orange, with persimmons, peaches, oranges, kumquats, nectarines or apricots heaped in a brass bowl. Or combine avocados, artichokes, acorn squash and cucumbers in a green basket with a bunch of green grapes tied to the handle.

• Use spray to enhance anything shapely. Frost fir branches with white, gild a pineapple, spray artichokes silver, or put a sheen on dull vegetables or walnuts with a clear plastic spray.

• Use unusual containers—casseroles, soup tureens, umbrella stands, demitasses, stemmed goblets.

• Use imagination. Pile fruit on a cake stand, twine ivy around driftwood, fill hurricane lamps with cherries, glass marbles, holly sprigs or paper flowers.

• Use a theme. Let all the world inspire you. Go Hawaiian, with sunny travel posters on the wall and a lei for each guest. The possibilities are unlimited. Or salute a holiday, and let the obvious help your imagination along. (You will find a whole chapter of holiday parties and decorating ideas, beginning on page 141.)

1

2

Setting the Scene

3

4

1. *Enjoy design in your table accessories.* China, crystal and silver create a pleasing effect when the design elements are repeated from one to the other as shown here.

2. *Two for one.* A simple switch of linens and accessories creates an entirely different mood for your table.

3. *A patio party offers adventure.* Here's your chance to set a table in a way you might not dare indoors. Use bold colors and splashy prints; feature paper products or non-breakable dishes.

4. *It's a thrill to set a formal table.* Go ahead; get out all of your silver and china, your best damask tablecloth and polish the candelabra wedding gift. Show off! It's fun!

5. *A centerpiece needn't be in the center.* In fact, placed at the end of the table, it may be larger and ever so much more dramatic than would be possible if placed between facing guests.

6. *Be bold with patterns.* You may, you know, if such boldness is tempered with the use of other plain or co-ordinated table accessories. Here is a cheery brunch table that shows both striped and flowered patterns.

7. *Set the pace with runners.* Run them down the length of your table to replace a multitude of place mats. Or cross two runners over the table to seat four guests, one at each end of the runners.

The Party Table—Setting and Service

One of the most exciting and rewarding aspects of preparing for company is the setting of a lovely table, perfect for the party-to-come. Most of all, you want your party to have the appearance of freshness and good taste. The prime way to achieve this effect is through a beautiful setting—spotless tablecloth, sparkling crystal and polished silver. When all of your arrangements look as if you have taken a bit of trouble, the atmosphere says "Welcome!" to guests as soon as they enter.

Just how your table or buffet is arranged depends on many factors—the kind of party you're giving, the guests you're expecting (how many and who they are), the limitations of your furniture and, of course, on the food you'll be serving. Whatever the occasion, make sure your table setting expresses the real you—and the way you like to see things done. After all, it is your table! Make it understated or elaborate, cool and relaxed or colorful and vibrant. Anything goes—*if* it doesn't interfere with food and service.

Build up a wardrobe of tablecloths, runners, mats and napkins; collect unusual serving pieces, one-of-a-kind centerpieces and colorful table accessories. Then use them. Let the photographs on the preceding pages inspire you and instruct you in setting a memorable party table.

Sit-down Service

The table setting for a sit-down luncheon or dinner presupposes plenty of room for your guests to be seated comfortably. The silver, placed one inch from the edge of the table, is arranged so that the pieces to be used first are farthest from the plate, the forks to the left, the knife and spoons to the right. A seafood fork, however, is usually placed to the right of the spoons. The butter plate is set above the forks, the butter knife in either a vertical or horizontal position. If salad is to be served *with* the main course, the salad plate is placed to the left of the forks. (In this case, the salad fork may be placed at either side of the dinner fork.) Above the knife the glasses are arranged in the order of their use, with wine glasses to the right of the water glasses. If you're serving coffee at the table, the coffee cup is placed slightly above and to the right of the spoons.

Traditionally, the napkin is placed in the center of the dinner plate, unless the first course is already on the table when guests are seated. If that is the case, the napkin goes to the left of the forks.

Dessert service may be on the table throughout the meal, or you may bring it to the table with the dessert course.

SERVICE OR DINNER PLATE

APPETIZER

SOUP

MAIN COURSE

SALAD

DESSERT

Here we have illustrated the progression of a fairly formal six-course dinner. And although this is probably more elaborate than most of your party meals will be, see how smoothly it moves from the first course to the last.

The best way to serve a sit-down meal, be it dinner or luncheon, is the most convenient way. The host may serve each plate from a stack at his place, passing to the left. Or he may serve just the meat course and let the hostess serve the vegetables or pass them to the guests. And it's perfectly acceptable to arrange the plates individually in the kitchen and serve them two at a time.

Before offering dessert, clear the table of all serving dishes, salt and pepper sets, plates and the silver that won't be used for the dessert course. The hostess presides over the serving of dessert and coffee at the table. But often, after-dinner coffee is served in the living room instead of at the dinner table. Arrange the coffee server, cups, napkins, cream and sugar on a tray and serve from the coffee table or from a tea cart, if you have one.

However you choose to serve your dinner, don't make a production out of it. It should be done in the most natural way. Throughout this book you will find many helpful serving ideas accompanying the menus and recipes.

Buffet Service

The arrangement of a buffet is a matter of common sense and convenience. If the meal is to be served on a sideboard or table pushed against the wall, the arrangement illustrated below is the most logical. Begin at one end of the table with plates, then move on in order to meat or main dish, vegetables, salad, breads, condiments, silver and finally napkins. Guests should finish at the end of the table nearest the door to eliminate congestion.

For a larger crowd, place the table in the center of the room and duplicate service on both sides. Two lines of guests may serve themselves at the same time.

For a sit-down buffet, the dining-room table is set just as it would be for a sit-down dinner *except* the plates and food are on the sideboard or serving table. A card-table buffet operates on the same principle, except that the dining-room table can be used as the buffet table. Card tables set up in the living room or on the patio have the silver, glasses and napkins in place. And don't forget the salt and pepper shakers, at least one pair for each table.

Buffet service is somewhat simplified by the happy fact that guests serve themselves. Water, however, is usually served by the hostess, who pours from a pitcher after the guests have been seated. This cuts down on the hazard of spills as guests move around the room and take their seats. The hostess must also keep an eye on the buffet table, refilling serving dishes as the need arises.

Just before the guests have finished, the hostess clears the buffet and arranges the dessert plates and silver on the table. After the guests are through, the dessert is brought on. The hostess may pour coffee at the buffet and serve it to her guests with dessert, or she can offer it after dessert. The latter approach is far easier for guests to manage if they are not seated at a table.

Above all else, remember—the most important thing is for *you* to be relaxed; don't worry about all the rules. You want to create a comfortable atmosphere. Once you have, you and your guests will just naturally enjoy every minute.

Fun-and-Games Department

If your party is a cocktail party or an open house, there will probably be no room and little time for any kind of planned entertainment. But if you're inviting guests for lunch or dinner, something in the fun-and-games department may be indicated.

Some parties, like the bridge party or the small dance, are specifically planned *around* entertainment. But even with no such prior arrangements, many a flagging get-together has been brought back to merriment with either of these activities. Charades and Twenty Questions are reliable party rescuers, too, and almost everyone knows how to play these games.

A memory test can be fun, too. Assemble 20 or 25 small items on a tray and permit your guests to study the array for a full minute. Take the tray away and ask each guest to write down as many of the items as he or she can remember. Be sure to have a supply of joke prizes for the winners.

Any quiz brightens the lull that often sets in after eating. All you need is enough pads and pencils to go around, and a series of questions to read aloud. Guests write down their answers and "grade" their own papers. Such quizzes often appear in magazines and newspapers, so you might clip them whenever you come across an interesting one. Or you might make up your own questions, basing them on some special interest you know your guests have in common.

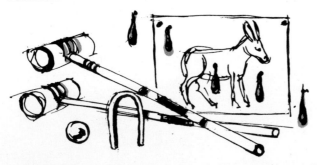

Children's games will often captivate a group of adults. Pin the Tail on the Donkey can be riotously funny. If the weather's nice, a croquet game set up in the backyard can prove to be a star attraction.

Practically everybody likes to sing. With a piano or guitar and a modest talent, you have all the party insurance you need. Old favorites are sure to please, but try something different occasionally—Christmas carols in July, old college songs. Sing-along albums come to the aid of the party, too.

Music to sing to is one thing; music for listening, another. If you have a recorded symphony or opera score, save it. Instead of heightening the party mood, a long opus has been known to kill conversation permanently. Soft, light background music, on the other hand, is always welcome and never interferes with conversation.

If you have photographic equipment, use it. Show slides or movies if you're *sure* all your guests want to see them. Or assign the classic roles of a melodrama to your guests and let them improvise as you shoot. (You can show the film the next time the same crowd gets together.) If you have a Polaroid camera, take shots of everyone for on-the-spot souvenirs.

The really smart hostess is one who senses the mood of a party and is able to change her plans when the situation calls for it. Don't prolong a game if only half the guests seem to be enjoying it. Most important, don't start one if everyone is having a good time talking. Save your entertainment ammunition for a time when you really need it.

Presenting the Party

Caring for Company

Once the doorbell signals the arrival of your first guests, all your attention should be focused on your company—on their comfort and enjoyment.

• Unless you're having a very large party, everyone should be introduced to everyone else. The hostess usually makes the introductions, but the host can help out, too. Or, if you're entertaining without benefit of a husband, a close friend may pinch-hit for you if you have to leave the room. When the group is small, simply introduce the new arrivals to your other guests in whatever order they happen to be seated or standing. At a larger party, where guests have already broken into small clusters, present the newcomers to a nearby group. Join in the conversation for a minute or so yourself, dropping little clues that might help the cause: "Mrs. Wilton was asking about the nursery school. I told her you'd sent Jackie there last year and could tell her all about it." But stifle any impulse to grow effusive. "Dr. Graham is the most *fascinating* person I know" would be enough to leave everyone tongue-tied with embarrassment.

• If you're serving cocktails, be sure to provide at least one non-alcoholic beverage. Then, if a guest doesn't want one of your stronger potions, he or she can elect fruit punch or ginger ale without calling attention to the choice.

• Don't prolong the pre-dinner cocktail hour *more* than an hour, even if one of your guests is late. If dinner is planned for seven-thirty and the Joneses still haven't arrived, go ahead and serve it. There's no reason to penalize your prompt friends for the laggard ones. When the tardy Joneses do appear, say without apologies, "I knew you'd want us to go ahead," and let it go at that.

• Never urge food on anyone. Offer it, but don't press. If someone refuses a second helping—or even a first one—accept the refusal without comment. Any further remarks on the subject are likely to make everyone uncomfortable.

• Keep tabs on the heat and ventilation. Nothing puts a party to sleep faster than a too-warm or air-less room. It's a wise idea to turn down the thermostat for any party. If you're having a dinner party and serving it in the dining room, keep a window open in the living room during the meal. The room will be fresh and cool when you return to it.

• Keep an ear peeled for argument—especially if your guests don't know each other very well. If you're all old friends and you know that Fred and Larry have fought the battle of the last election every week for a year, ignore it. But if you've brought people together for the first time and voices begin to rise over politics, religion or any other controversial subject, create a distraction. Turn on the phonograph and invite one of the combatants to dance with you. Solicit advice on what you should do about the zinnia bed or the curtains in the children's room. Do anything that will separate the antagonists, conversationally and physically.

• Stay with your guests as much as possible. Avoid making unnecessary trips to the kitchen; and when you do have to check on something, as you undoubtedly will, make your stay brief. Even after a big dinner party, just stack the dishes in the dishwasher or on a counter (you can cover them with a gay plastic cloth), close the door and quickly return to the scene of the party.

• When the party begins to break up, send your guests on their way graciously but with dispatch. The guest who says goodnight for three quarters of an hour is a stock comic figure, but a host or hostess can be responsible for an equally long-drawn-out leave-taking. This is not the time to plan a future meeting or to open a new topic of conversation. Just accept all thanks with "It was fun having you."

Special Situations

Two-by-Four Parties

It's a cliché to say that no one has as much room as he used to—but there's still a considerable difference between entertaining in the average small house and in the postage-stamp apartment. Even if your entire "castle" consists of one room you can have merrily memorable parties—if you use your head.

Be realistic. There are a number of things you can't do in a 15 by 15 room. You can't have thirty or forty guests with any degree of comfort—but perhaps you can have fifteen for cocktails. You probably can't have a sit-down meal for more than four —and even that may be a problem. On the other hand, you can have a delightful buffet for ten if you stick to a few delicious, hearty dishes, and have *plenty* of each. (You'll find a perfect example in our Old Italy Buffet on page 56.)

Be inventive. In a tiny apartment conventional service is difficult if not impossible, so look for unconventional ways to serve. If there's a foyer or a sleeping alcove, set up a card table or two for buffet service. Or serve from low bookcase tops or chests. Top a sturdy small table with a larger solid piece— even a bedboard—covered with a cloth, and use as a tabletop. Let guests eat from individual stack tables or seat them on big floor cushions around the coffee table.

Avoid clutter. Instead of vases full of flowers or decorations that take up surface space, pin paper flowers to the curtains or swag ropes of artificial greens around a window or mantel. If you're short on closet space, hang your guests' coats on the shower rod in the bathroom.

Try the two-party system. For those who limit their entertaining to weekends—and find that they don't have too many free ones—ask a few friends to Friday night supper, a few more to Sunday dinner. Choose a menu appropriate for both occasions and cook just once for the two parties. Decorations will do double duty. Any leftover party extras like flowers or relishes or mints can make a second appearance. And you've a day between for cleanup and rest.

Hostess on Her Own

No one will deny that the greatest asset any hostess can have is an obliging husband. But lacking this advantage, it's still possible for a girl on her own to earn her stripes as a party-giver.

First, choose a menu that requires the absolute minimum of last-minute time in the kitchen—for either cooking or serving.

Second, avoid a roast or bird that needs to be carved. This is really man's domain, and you'll look more graceful serving if no surgery is involved.

Third, if you're having cocktails, set up a bar in the living room with glasses, ingredients, shakers and ice on a table, chest or bookcase.

Now delegate. Ask whichever one of your men guests you know the best—your beau, your brother-in-law, the husband of your best friend—to act as bartender. Most men enjoy this role, but may hesitate to assume it without a specific go-ahead from you. If you have to leave the room, ask the woman guest you know best to take over such hostessly duties as door-answering, introductions and peanut-passing.

What to Do with the Children

Party-giving in a household with small children can present certain problems, but it's also an ideal way to introduce your youngsters to the pleasures and politenesses of entertaining. So do make children part of the party, but in small doses.

• Allot enough time to feed junior members of the family well before your guests arrive.

• Spell out the ground rules in advance. Explain carefully what courtesies you expect — shaking hands, saying "How do you do, Mrs. Leonard," standing when a guest comes into the room—or whatever *you* consider the necessary amenities. If a youngster forgets, a quiet reminder is permissible; if that doesn't work, forget it. You'll embarrass the child and the guests by making an issue of it.

• Assign simple duties to each child—opening the door, showing guests where to put their coats, passing potato chips or peanuts.

• Never allow a youngster to take over the stage at an adult party. No reciting, no dancing, no singing or performance of any sort—unless grandparents are the only guests, in which case all rules are suspended.

• Be firm about curfew. The youngsters should retire to their bedrooms when the guests go in to dinner, if not before. However, there's no harm in extending their treat a little by sending along some cookies or allowing an extra half hour of TV.

The Care and Feeding of Dieters

Every year more people seem to be going on different kinds of diets—low-cholesterol, low-sodium, low-fat, sugar-free and reducing diets in addition to the traditional religious dietary restrictions. Actually any diet is the responsibility of the dieter, and no hostess is expected to know that a casual acquaintance is allergic to cheese, nor to serve eleven guests an unsalted meal because one person is on a low-sodium diet. However, it is a mark of special thoughtfulness to give such attention as you can to these restrictions.

• For weight-watchers, provide a low-calorie beverage along with your cocktails and some raw vegetables with the canapés. Whenever possible serve a rich sauce or a whipped cream topping separately, so a dieter can use his own judgment—and willpower.

• If someone is on a strict medical diet, make real capital by asking him (or her) and spouse to dinner, alone or with another couple, planning a party dinner within the restrictions. For example, on page 38 you will find a menu designed to fit the needs of someone on a low-cholesterol or low-fat diet. Attractively served, this dinner can compete with any gourmet feast.

• Never urge a dieter to go off his diet "just this once," or to "try just a little—it can't possibly hurt you." If the diet is a medical one, it *can* possibly hurt him; if it's a reducing diet, he's not going to thank you for putting temptation in his way.

Short-order Entertaining

Normally a party's a planned occasion, and you can give yourself as much time for preparation as you want. But every so often, you will find yourself cast in the role of hostess with no advance notice. Your husband returns from a football game accompanied by friends he ran into at the half. Out-of-town relatives surprise you with a visit. Or your college roommate calls from the station saying she has three hours between trains and, impulsively, you insist that she spend them with you.

This kind of spur-of-the-moment entertaining is a real test of hospitality. The most important considerations are not how the house looks, or whether there's a centerpiece on the table, or what you can find to eat—but rather the feeling of welcome you give your surprise guests, and the relaxed manner with which you treat the visit. Of course, you're way ahead of the game if you happen to have the makings of a nice meal on your pantry shelf—and on pages 106-111 you'll find suggestions for such emergency menus and recipes. But whether or not you are well prepared, remember these two rules.

• Don't apologize for anything. That means the food, the house and the way your hair looks. Even if company catches you doing the laundry in your blue jeans, don't say a word. An apology can too easily sound like a rebuke.

• Do let the guests help if they offer. Let Cousin Anne put the baby to bed and Cousin Fred pick up more hamburger buns. Let Janet-from-the-football-game set the table while Stu-from-the-football-game reads to the older children. Ask your former roommate to make the salad or the coffee so you two can chat as you work. And if there's time afterward, let everyone help with the dishes. The nicest gift you can give to unexpected guests is the assurance that they haven't put you out—even if they have.

Weekend Company

A guest you invite for the weekend is usually someone you know rather well, and such company expects to share part of your regular schedule, to help out a bit in a maidless household, to fit into whatever plans you've made. However, even a very dear friend or a member of your family is entitled to certain courtesies and a bit of preferential treatment. For your guest's convenience and your own, observe the following rules and adapt them to your plans.

• Be completely clear about the time span your invitation covers. "Jack will be coming out on the 5:17 Friday and will look for you at the station. There's only one decent train back on Sunday. It leaves here a little after eight so I'm planning an early dinner."

• Give your company a clue to your activities so they'll know what clothes to bring. "The party Saturday night is likely to be a bit dressy, but otherwise we live in slacks and bathing suits."

• Make the most private bed and bath arrangements you can for your guest. If you don't have a guest room, ask a member of the family to take the living room couch for a night or two.

• Plan at least one special event—but don't make a marathon party of the visit. One party at home is really about all the average hostess can manage comfortably, so if you're having a Saturday night buffet for ten, let Sunday dinner be a family affair.

• Do allot some time to chat privately with your guest—but you needn't be entirely idle as you talk. Save some undemanding chore—stemming beans or doing some mending — for talk time. Or take your friend along for the drive when you do an errand.

• Let your company help out with the things that are really helpful. Unless you have a servant, it is taken for granted that the guest will make his or her own bed and tidy up the bedroom. And there's no reason at all for refusing offers of table-clearing, dish-drying or dog-walking. On the other hand, if you honestly prefer to do the cooking without assistance, be candid about it.

• Don't expect perfection. While you may be able to handle a three-hour party flawlessly, two days of everything going as planned is a lot to ask. So by all means *try* to keep the children quiet if your company wants to sleep late, and *hope* that the weather will hold for the barbecue, and that the tennis matches or the boat races will be exciting. But if you strike a few small snags during the weekend, laugh them off. An overanxious or overapologetic hostess can do more to spoil the guest's weekend than any number of minor mishaps put together.

The Welcome Guest

Just as the hostess has an obligation to provide a good time for each and every guest, the guest, too, has certain duties. And though these duties are certainly fewer, they are no less important.

Accept invitations promptly and with pleasure. If you must decline, explain why. Having said you'd come to a party, don't retract your acceptance except for an emergency. Certainly not for a later invitation.

Arrive promptly—but not early. To be 15 minutes late is perfectly permissible; to be 15 minutes early can be close to catastrophic.

Take care when parking. Don't bottle up earlier guests in the host's driveway, and don't block the neighbors' drives.

Don't be too helpful. Bustling about, peering into the kitchen, offering too much assistance implies that the hostess is incapable of handling the party herself.

Be entertained and entertaining. Seek out a shy person and talk to him while the hostess is busy. Be a good audience for an extroverted guest. Add a bit of gaiety on your own, or a bit of appreciation for someone else's stories or jokes. Above all, have a good time and show it. You won't, you know, if you arrive at the party "worn out" from the day's activities.

Don't outstay your welcome. If the normal hour for departure has come and the party's still going full tilt, don't hesitate to be the first to take leave. Your hosts will probably bless you secretly if others follow your lead.

Extend your thanks, warmly but briefly, at the door. Don't carol gay goodnights from the curbside. The neighbors are probably asleep.

Do call to say thank you again. Nothing pleases a hostess more than an appreciative rehash of her party, the day after.

Dinner Parties

Everybody loves a dinner party! It's such a friendly way to entertain, and to be entertained. Good food and good conversation in the warmth of a comfortable home just naturally result in a good time—for guests, host and hostess alike. And there is such a variety from which to choose—from casual to elegant, small to crowd-size. On the following pages we offer samples of all types, to present just as we planned them or to adapt to your own needs.

First we offer you four Gay Supper Parties. Perfect for the young at heart, these spirited menus seem to shout for gay decorations and unconventional table settings. They're splendid dinner parties per se, and ideal pre- or post-event parties. Yes, these little suppers are right for almost any occasion.

Geared for groups of four or six, our five Easy Little Dinners have their own special advantages. Because your guest list is small, you can cater to guests' preferences. Bake hot rolls or a favorite cake for dessert—a treat your guests will enjoy and remember. Or, plan a festive dinner within the regimen of a dieter—he'll love you for it. And easy dinners? Well, that goes without saying, especially when you follow the tested preparation plans.

Our Classic Company Dinners are, indeed, classic—in choice of food, in table setting and in service. Here's an opportunity to serve a great big roast, elegantly garnished, and to come forth with a truly spectacular dessert. Choose from among these menus when you really want to make your mark —perhaps with the in-laws or with your husband's business associates.

For a pleasant change of pace or for entertaining many people at one time, Buffet Suppers really fill the bill. Mix china, linens and serving pieces; you won't disturb the decor. You can mix people more freely, too. Invite one or two older (or younger) couples or group together distant cousins. Our menus will please all of them. And hostessing a buffet supper will please you, too.

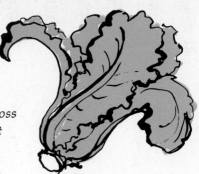

Spaghetti Supper

Italian Spaghetti with Meat Sauce
Salty Breadsticks
Marinated Artichoke Hearts   Zucchini Toss
Fruit and Cheese Tray with Anise Toast
Coffee

A spaghetti supper is easy and fun for both cook and guests. It's especially appreciated by the young crowd, for whom the atmosphere of easy informality insures a good time. Done up right with a red and white checkered cloth, candles stuck in wine bottles and all the traditional Italian trappings, it's still almost unbeatably inexpensive.

Our spaghetti sauce is full-bodied and thick with meat, suggesting that it took hours to assemble— but, in fact, it's based on a spaghetti sauce mix for- tified with a few extra seasonings. If you want to make the breadsticks yourself, go ahead, but you can also buy them ready-made. Another time-saver: buy a small jar of marinated artichoke hearts; or, if you'd *rather* do it yourself, marinate cooked arti- choke hearts (canned or frozen) in Italian dressing.

Serving suggestions: Better let the host serve both spaghetti and sauce as it takes a bit of practice. Salads are on the table when you sit down; every- thing else can be passed.

PLAN FOR PREPARATION

Day before: 1. *Prepare spaghetti sauce.* **2.** *As sauce simmers, prepare dough for breadsticks; bake Anise Toast.* **3.** *Prepare Garlic Dressing. Wash, dry and chill salad greens.* **4.** *Bake breadsticks.*

Day of party: 1. *Set table.* **2.** *Arrange Fruit and Cheese Tray. (Do not add the soft cheese until just before serving so that it is chilled.)* **3.** *Tear salad greens into bowl; slice vegetables for salad and add to greens; refrigerate.* **4.** *Reheat spaghetti sauce and breadsticks.* **5.** *Prepare coffee.* **6.** *Cook spaghetti.* **7.** *Toss salad with dressing; place in individual bowls or on plates; set on table.* **8.** *Set out bowl of artichoke hearts.* **9.** *Pour water.*

Permanent Party Gear

Spaghetti tongs are a great aid and comfort when serving the slippery strands. Once you've used them you'll wonder how you ever managed without them.

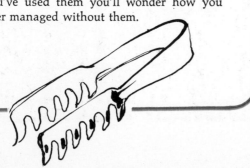

ITALIAN SPAGHETTI WITH MEAT SAUCE

2 pounds ground beef
1 medium onion, finely chopped
1 green pepper, finely chopped
2 cans (15 ounces each) tomato sauce
2 cans (12 ounces each) tomato paste
1 can (7½ ounces) pitted ripe olives,
   drained and sliced
2 envelopes (1½ ounces each) Italian-style
   spaghetti sauce mix with mushrooms
3 cups water
1 tablespoon sugar
1 teaspoon crushed oregano leaves
2 cloves garlic, crushed
1 bay leaf, crumbled
16 ounces Italian-style spaghetti
Parmesan cheese

Cook and stir ground beef, onion and pepper until meat is brown and onion is tender. Stir in remaining ingredients except spaghetti and Parmesan cheese. Simmer uncovered 1½ hours, stirring occasionally. Place in covered container; refrigerate overnight. Cook spaghetti as directed on package. Heat sauce; serve over hot cooked spaghetti and sprinkle with Parmesan cheese. *8 servings.*

Do-ahead Note: The sauce can be made well in ad- vance and frozen.

SALTY BREADSTICKS

1 package active dry yeast
¾ cup warm water (105 to 115°)
2½ cups Bisquick
¼ cup butter or margarine, melted
Salt or garlic salt

Dissolve yeast in warm water. Mix in Bisquick; beat vigorously. Turn dough onto surface well dusted with Bisquick. Knead until smooth, about 20 times. Divide dough into 16 equal parts. Roll each piece between hands into pencil-like strip, 8 inches long. Spread part of butter in oblong pan, 13x9x2 inches. Place strips of dough in pan. Brush tops with remaining butter; sprinkle with salt. Cover and let rise in warm place (85°) until light, about 1 hour.

Heat oven to 425°. Bake breadsticks 15 minutes or until light golden brown. Turn off oven; allow breadsticks to remain in oven 15 minutes longer to crisp. *Makes 16 sticks.*

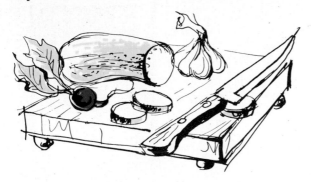

ZUCCHINI TOSS

1 head lettuce, torn into bite-size pieces
1 head romaine, torn into bite-size pieces
2 medium zucchini, thinly sliced
1 cup sliced radishes
2 tablespoons sliced green onions
3 tablespoons salad oil
Garlic Dressing (below)

Toss salad greens, zucchini, radishes and onion with salad oil just until leaves glisten. Toss with Garlic Dressing. *6 to 8 servings.*

Garlic Dressing

2 tablespoons tarragon vinegar
1½ teaspoons salt
1 clove garlic, crushed
Dash each ground black pepper and monosodium glutamate

Mix all ingredients thoroughly.

ANISE TOAST

2 eggs
⅔ cup sugar
1 teaspoon anise seed
1 cup Gold Medal Flour (regular or Wondra)

Heat oven to 375°. Grease and flour a loaf pan, 9x5x3 inches. Beat eggs and sugar in small mixing bowl until light and fluffy. Add anise seed; gradually mix in flour. Push batter into prepared pan. Bake about 20 minutes, or until wooden pick inserted in center comes out clean. (Pan will be only ¼ full.) Remove from pan and cut loaf into ¼-inch slices. Place slices on buttered baking sheet; bake 3 to 4 minutes, or until slices are browned on bottom. Turn slices; bake 3 to 4 minutes longer, or until slices are browned on other side. *Makes 32 slices.*

FRUIT AND CHEESE TRAY

Mix-matching fruit and cheese for dessert is such an easy, adventuresome and spectacular way to end a meal. Start with your prettiest plate or wooden platter or a tiered compote. Arrange on it a variety of cheeses, choosing those that will give you different flavors and textures. As a guide, select at least one soft, one semisoft and one hard cheese; some mild and some sharp. And be sure to include at least one cheese you or your guests haven't sampled.

Fill in the tray with tart apples, pears, oranges and graceful grapes. To complement the soft cheese —especially cream or Neufchâtel—add strawberries or raspberries if in season. Dates, prunes, fresh figs and walnuts in the shell will spark the tray. Crackers, anise toast or other plain cookies, perhaps wine also, complete the dessert.

Serving can be very simple—just provide an individual dessert plate for each person and small knives for cutting fruit and spreading soft cheese. Remember to serve all cheeses, except for the soft unripened ones, at room temperature.

Cheese Chart

SOFT CHEESES

Brie—Creamy ripened cheese with an edible thin brown and white crust. Mild to strong flavor.

Camembert—Soft, ripened cheese with a creamy yellow interior and edible crust. Pleasantly pungent.

Cream—White, smooth, mild; unripened type. Available plain and as pimiento, pineapple and other varieties. Also comes whipped—plain and flavored. An unripened cheese; serve slightly chilled.

Liederkranz—Soft, creamy yellow. Pungent in flavor; similar to a mild limburger.

Neufchâtel—Soft, white, mild. Similar to cream cheese. An unripened cheese; serve slightly chilled.

SEMISOFT CHEESES

Bel Paese—Light yellow Italian cheese; mild and smooth.

Blue—Blue veined, white and crumbly; robust flavor. A first cousin to Roquefort.

Brick—Mild flavor; creamy yellow with tiny holes.

Gorgonzola—Italian blue-veined cheese; sharp flavor.

Gruyère—Nutlike flavor; light yellow color. Similar to Swiss cheese but with smaller "eyes" and sharper flavor.

Port du Salut—Mild flavor; creamy yellow. Cheese made by Trappist monks in France.

Roquefort—French blue-veined cheese; sharp flavor.

Stilton—English blue-veined cheese; sharp flavor.

HARD CHEESES

Cheddar—Mild to very sharp flavor.

Edam or Gouda—Firm, mild, red-coated rounds; a colorful addition to the cheese tray.

Fontina—Round Italian cheese with mellow flavor.

Swiss—Mild, nutlike flavor and distinctive holes or "eyes."

From left to right...

Top row: Cream, Neufchâtel, Camembert, Brie, Liederkranz
Second row: Roquefort, Port du Salut, Blue, Brick, Gorgonzola
Third row: Stilton, Fontina, Bel Paese, Gruyère, Swiss
Bottom row: Gouda, Cheddar, Edam

Mexican Medley

"Sangría" Punch   Taco Appetizers
Enchilada Casserole
Tossed Salad with Guacamole Dressing
Chilled Crinkle-style Beets
Almendrada with Quick Custard Sauce
Coffee or Hot Chocolate

For world travelers (actual or armchair) and friends with venturesome palates, a hot and spicy south-of-the-border menu can be the party high spot of the year. Do make sure that no one on the guest list is on a bland diet, and then go all out with piquant foods. Feature a big basket of Mexican paper flowers as decoration. (You can make them easily by using sheets of red, pink and orange tissue paper folded lengthwise to a width of about two inches, then rolled loosely, snail fashion. Pin at the bottom and fluff out into petals.) And if someone plays the guitar, urge him to bring it along to accompany a folk-song fest.

Serving suggestions: Pass appetizers and the festive fruited punch in the living room. Have individual bowls of salad on the dining table. The host serves the Enchilada Casserole; the bowl of beets is passed. At dessert time, serve the custard sauce in a separate pitcher—you won't want your guests to miss the colors you selected for the mold.

PLAN FOR PREPARATION

Day before: 1. *Prepare casserole; cover and refrigerate.* **2.** *Prepare Almendrada; chill. Prepare custard sauce; chill.* **3.** *Wash, dry and chill salad greens. Prepare dressing; cover and chill.* **4.** *Chill cranberry cocktail, grape juice and beets.*

Day of party: 1. *Set table.* **2.** *Section oranges and slice radishes; cover tightly and refrigerate.* **3.** *Bake tacos.* **4.** *Prepare punch; serve with tacos.* **5.** *Meanwhile, bake casserole.* **6.** *Prepare coffee or chocolate.* **7.** *Arrange chilled beets in bowl; set on table. Pour water.* **8.** *Toss salad.*

"SANGRÍA" PUNCH

Chill 1 quart cranberry cocktail and 1 cup grape juice. At serving time, pour chilled juices over cracked ice. Top with maraschino cherries, lemon slices and orange slices. *Makes 5 cups.*

TACO APPETIZERS

Prepare 2 packages (5½ ounces each) frozen cocktail tacos as directed on package for crisp tacos. To each baked taco, add a small leaf of lettuce, chopped tomato and onion, if desired. *6 servings.*

ENCHILADA CASSEROLE

1½ pounds ground beef
1 medium onion, chopped
1 can (15½ ounces) refried beans
½ teaspoon salt
¼ teaspoon pepper
1 cup salad oil
12 canned or frozen tortillas
1 tomato, peeled and chopped
Cheese Sauce (right)

Heat oven to 350°. Cook and stir ground beef and onion until meat is brown and onion is tender. Stir in beans, salt and pepper. In another skillet heat oil until hot enough to sizzle. Quickly dip each tortilla in hot oil *just* until it is softened. Place about ⅓ cup meat mixture on each softened tortilla; top with chopped tomato and roll tightly. Arrange tortillas seam side down in oblong baking dish, 13½x9x2 inches. Pour Cheese Sauce over tortillas. (At this point casserole may be refrigerated.) Bake uncovered 20 to 25 minutes, or until cheese is bubbly in center. Garnish with pitted whole ripe olives and green pepper rings, if desired. *6 servings.*

Cheese Sauce

¼ cup butter or margarine
¼ cup Gold Medal Flour (regular or Wondra)
½ teaspoon salt
¼ teaspoon paprika
2 cups milk
1 can (15 ounces) enchilada sauce
¾ cup sliced pitted ripe olives
4 drops Tabasco
1½ cups shredded natural Cheddar cheese
    (6 ounces)

Melt butter over low heat in heavy saucepan. Blend in flour and seasonings. Cook over low heat, stirring until mixture is smooth and bubbly. Remove from heat. Stir in milk and enchilada sauce. Heat to boiling, stirring constantly. Boil 1 minute. Add olives, Tabasco and cheese; stir until cheese melts.

TOSSED SALAD
WITH GUACAMOLE DRESSING

2 heads lettuce, torn into bite-size pieces
2 oranges, pared and sectioned
1 cup sliced radishes
½ cup chopped green pepper
Guacamole Dressing (below)

Combine lettuce, orange sections, radishes and green pepper in bowl. Just before serving, pour Guacamole Dressing over salad; toss lightly to mix fruit and vegetables. *6 servings.*

Guacamole Dressing

2 avocados, peeled and pitted
1 medium onion, finely chopped
1 green chili pepper, finely chopped
1 tablespoon lemon juice
1 teaspoon salt
½ teaspoon coarsely ground pepper
Mayonnaise or salad dressing

Beat avocados, onion, chili pepper, lemon juice, salt and pepper until creamy. Spoon into dish; spread top with a thin layer of mayonnaise. Cover and chill. Stir gently just before tossing with salad. *Makes 2 cups.*

ALMENDRADA

A light, fluffy pudding, delicate in flavor. The tinted layers symbolize the Mexican flag.

1 envelope (1 tablespoon) unflavored gelatin
½ cup unsweetened pineapple juice
4 egg whites
¼ teaspoon salt
¾ cup sugar
½ teaspoon vanilla
¼ teaspoon almond extract
Green food coloring
⅓ cup chopped blanched almonds
Red food coloring
2 tablespoons coarsely chopped maraschino
    cherries
½ teaspoon grated lemon peel
Quick Custard Sauce (below)

Soften gelatin in pineapple juice. Stir over low heat to dissolve gelatin. Cool. Beat egg whites with salt until frothy; gradually beat in sugar. Continue beating until soft peaks form. Add dissolved gelatin; beat until thick and of a marshmallow consistency. Beat in vanilla and almond extract. Divide mixture into 3 parts. Tint 1 part light green with green food coloring and stir in almonds; tint 1 part pink with red food coloring and stir in maraschino cherries; stir lemon peel into remaining mixture. Spoon white mixture into loaf pan, 9x5x3 inches. Top with green layer, then pink layer. Refrigerate overnight or until set. Unmold, cut into slices and serve with Quick Custard Sauce. *6 servings.*

Quick Custard Sauce

Prepare 1 package (about 3½ ounces) vanilla pudding and pie filling as directed on package except—increase milk to 3 cups. Chill.

Fondue Party

Fondue Bourguignonne   Fondue Sauces
Fresh Mushroom Salad with French Dressing
Rye Bread
Riviera Peaches   Coffee

Guaranteed to break the ice for even the shyest group is a party where guests do their own cooking. Perfect strangers are chatting merrily in minutes as they spear their own meat cubes, then cook and dunk them. And it's easy on both host and hostess, for all the preparations are made well in advance—and there's no carving to do.

Serving suggestions: Place the fondue pot in the center of the table with the meat arranged on two lettuce-lined plates at either end. Bowls of sauce may circle the pot or can be placed on a lazy Susan for passing; either way, they should be readily available so that guests can spoon their choices onto their own plates. For a pleasing variety, balance the sauces among tomato, butter and creamy types.

Strong note of caution: The hot oil in which the meat is browned must be handled with the greatest care. Do keep a careful watch to see that everyone is treating it with respect, and never allow a child to be nearby while this meal is being served.

PLAN FOR PREPARATION

Day before (or morning of party): 1. *Wash, dry and chill salad greens.* **2.** *Butter and wrap bread, if desired.* **3.** *Prepare sauces; refrigerate.*

Day of party: 1. *Prepare desserts and chill.* **2.** *Cube meat.* **3.** *Set table.* **4.** *Set out sauces.* **5.** *Heat bread.* **6.** *Prepare coffee.* **7.** *Arrange cubes of meat on plates.* **8.** *Pour water.* **9.** *Heat oil.* **10.** *Toss salads.*

FONDUE BOURGUIGNONNE

Trim fat from 2 pounds beef tenderloin or tenderloin tips and cut into bite-size (1 inch) cubes; cover and refrigerate until serving time. Prepare as many of the sauces (at right and on next page) as you wish to serve; refrigerate.

About 15 minutes before dinner, mound pieces of meat on bed of greens. Measure salad oil (¼ butter, if desired) in sufficient quantity to fill a metal fondue pot or *deep* chafing dish to depth of 1 to 1½ inches. Heat the oil on range top until hot enough to brown a bread cube in 1 minute. CAREFULLY place pot on stand on table and ignite denatured alcohol burner or canned cooking fuel.

To eat beef fondue, spear cube of meat with long-handled fondue fork; dip into hot oil and cook until meat is crusty on outside and juicy and rare inside. Dip cooked meat into a sauce of your choice. *4 servings.*

FONDUE SAUCES

Anchovy Butter

Drain 1 can (2 ounces) anchovy fillets. In small mixer bowl beat ½ cup softened butter, the anchovy fillets and ⅛ teaspoon pepper until smooth. Refrigerate. Let come to room temperature before serving. *Makes ¾ cup.*

Garlic Butter

Whip ½ cup softened butter until fluffy. Stir in 1 tablespoon snipped parsley and 1 clove garlic, crushed. Refrigerate. Let come to room temperature before serving. *Makes ½ cup.*

Blue Cheese Sauce

Combine ½ cup dairy sour cream, ¼ cup crumbled blue cheese, 1 teaspoon Worcestershire sauce and ¼ teaspoon salt. Refrigerate. *Makes ¾ cup.*

Horseradish Sauce

1 cup dairy sour cream
2 tablespoons horseradish
½ teaspoon lemon juice
¼ teaspoon Worcestershire sauce
⅛ teaspoon salt
⅛ teaspoon pepper

Combine all ingredients; refrigerate. *Makes 1 cup.*

Sauce Remoulade

1 cup mayonnaise
¼ cup finely chopped green onions
1 hard-cooked egg, finely chopped
2 teaspoons prepared mustard
2 teaspoons snipped parsley

Combine all ingredients; refrigerate. *Makes 1¼ cups.*

Curried Fruit Sauce

2 cups dairy sour cream
1 can (8¾ ounces) crushed pineapple, drained
1 unpared medium apple, chopped (about 1 cup)
1 teaspoon curry powder
½ teaspoon garlic salt

Combine all ingredients; refrigerate. *Makes 3 cups.*

Hot 'n Spicy Sauce

1 cup chili sauce
½ cup chopped onion
3 tablespoons lemon juice
2 tablespoons salad oil
1 teaspoon brown sugar
2 teaspoons vinegar
1 clove garlic, crushed
½ teaspoon Tabasco
¼ teaspoon dry mustard
¼ teaspoon salt

Combine all ingredients in small saucepan. Heat to boiling; simmer 5 minutes. Serve warm or cool. *Makes 1¼ cups.*

Pleasant Party Afterthoughts

· Send leftover cookies or cupcakes home to your guests' children. You might even bake some extras with the children in mind. Save small bakery or florist's boxes for this.
· Telephone a guest the next day to say thank you if she or he was particularly helpful or entertaining.
· Send a floral centerpiece home to an ill or elderly person.
· If you take pictures at your parties, send prints of the better shots to your guests.

FRESH MUSHROOM SALAD WITH FRENCH DRESSING

½ pound fresh mushrooms, washed, trimmed and sliced
1 head lettuce, torn into bite-size pieces
1 head romaine, torn into bite-size pieces
French Dressing (below)

Combine mushrooms, lettuce and romaine; toss with French Dressing. Serve in bowl lined with romaine leaves, if desired. *4 to 6 servings.*

French Dressing

½ cup salad oil or olive oil (or combination)
2 tablespoons vinegar
2 tablespoons lemon juice
½ teaspoon salt
¼ teaspoon dry mustard
¼ teaspoon paprika

Beat all ingredients with rotary beater or shake well in tightly covered jar. Keep in covered jar in refrigerator. Just before serving, shake to blend. *Makes ¾ cup.*

RYE BREAD

Heat oven to 400°. Spread slices of 1 loaf (1 pound) rye or pumpernickel bread with ¼ cup soft butter. Reassemble loaf. Wrap securely in aluminum foil. Heat 15 to 20 minutes. *4 servings.*

RIVIERA PEACHES

8 fresh or canned peach halves (drained, if canned)
⅓ cup red raspberry jelly
1 pint pistachio ice cream

Place 2 peach halves in each sherbet glass. Melt raspberry jelly; pour over peaches. Refrigerate several hours. At serving time, top with scoop of ice cream. *4 servings.*

Variation: Follow recipe above except—use bottled brandied peaches and stir 1 tablespoon of the syrup into melted raspberry jelly.

Swiss Treat

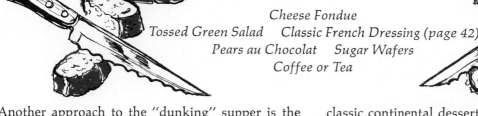

Cheese Fondue
Tossed Green Salad   Classic French Dressing (page 42)
Pears au Chocolat   Sugar Wafers
Coffee or Tea

Another approach to the "dunking" supper is the cheese version. This kind of party is fun for any informal group but especially appropriate for skiing and winter sports enthusiasts; it's also made-to-order for a light supper or midnight snack. Bolster the alpine theme with Swiss travel posters, and after supper run through your skiing movies.

The menu couldn't be simpler—a cheese fondue, a marvelous tart-crisp salad and a quick version of a classic continental dessert are the only ingredients. Although some of the easy preparations can be made ahead, it's also possible for a wife with a job to start supper from scratch after work and have it on the table by seven thirty.

Serving suggestions: The fondue pot is centered on the table with salads at each place and baskets of bread handy to everyone. Guests take turns spearing bread and twirling it in the cheese.

CHEESE FONDUE

Here is a simple "Americanized" version of the traditional Swiss ceremonial specialty. To eat this rich cheese dunk, one guest at a time spears a chunk of bread with his long-handled fondue fork, dips, stirs and twirls the cheese around the bread before lifting it out. Then the next guest takes over, as the fondue must be stirred constantly.

8 ounces sharp natural Cheddar cheese, shredded
1 package (8 ounces) natural Swiss cheese,*
    shredded
2 tablespoons flour
½ teaspoon salt
¼ teaspoon pepper
1 clove garlic
1 can (12 ounces) beer
Dash Tabasco
French bread, cut into 1-inch cubes (half rye
    bread, if desired)

Mix cheeses, flour, salt and pepper in large bowl. Rub cut clove of garlic around bottom and sides of an earthenware fondue casserole, blazer pan of chafing dish, electric frypan or heavy skillet. Pour in beer and heat slowly; gradually stir in cheese mixture, adding only a cup at a time and stirring after each addition until cheese is melted and blended. (Do not allow mixture to become too hot.) Stir in Tabasco. Serve immediately over very low heat, stirring constantly. (If fondue becomes too thick, stir in a little additional heated beer.) *4 servings.*

*The Swiss cheese should be aged at least 6 months.

PLAN FOR PREPARATION

Day before (or morning of party): 1. *Chill cans of pears.* **2.** *Wash, dry and chill salad greens.* **3.** *Prepare salad dressing.* **4.** *Shred cheese; wrap tightly and refrigerate.*

Day of party: 1. *Assemble Pears au Chocolat.* **2.** *Set table.* **3.** *Cut bread; pile into two small baskets; cover with napkins.* **4.** *Prepare coffee or tea. Pour water.* **5.** *Cook Cheese Fondue.* **6.** *Toss salad.*

TOSSED GREEN SALAD

1 large head lettuce
1 bunch leaf lettuce
½ small bunch endive
½ small bag spinach (2 cups torn)
Classic French Dressing (page 42)

Use choice part of greens; discard stems and cores. Tear greens into bite-size pieces (do not cut). Have them dry and cold. Before serving, toss with Classic French Dressing. *4 generous servings.*

PEARS AU CHOCOLAT

Chill 2 cans (1 pound each) pear halves. For each serving, place 2 well-drained pear halves together with 1 tablespoon of our chocolate satin ready-to-spread frosting in cavity. Stand pears upright in dessert dishes. Refrigerate. At serving time, melt ¼ cup chocolate frosting in top of double boiler or in custard cup set in boiling water. Pour melted chocolate over pears. *4 servings.*

Dinner's in the Oven!

Olive Surprise Roast
Cheesy Potato Casserole   Buttered Broccoli
Garden Relish Mold   Poppy-seed French Bread
Cardinal Parfaits   Brownie Nuts
Coffee

Want to look free as a breeze when the guests arrive? It's simple (and surprisingly economical, too) when meat, potatoes and bread are all happily cooking together in the oven. The mouth-watering mainstay of this dinner is an easy-on-the-pocket-book rump roast, spectacularly stuffed with olives. This goes in the oven in late afternoon to be joined later by a cheese-rich potato casserole and still later by poppy-seeded French bread. Almost everything else can be made a full day ahead if you like. And when the doorbell rings, you're a lady of leisure.

Serving suggestions: Here's a chance for the host to shine—this dramatic-looking roast deserves to be carved at the table. The salads should be in place when you sit down, and either you or your husband may serve the vegetables. Don't try passing the potato casserole—if it's as it should be, it will be too hot for guests to handle. The colorful Cardinal Parfait and a brownie or two go on each dessert plate—though there's no harm in having extra brownies on a serving plate for passing. The men are certain to want seconds.

PLAN FOR PREPARATION

Day before: 1. *Prepare gelatin salad; wash, dry and chill salad greens.* **2.** *Prepare parfaits; freeze.* **3.** *Bake brownies.*

Day of party: 1. *Prepare roast and place in oven.* **2.** *Set table.* **3.** *Prepare potato casserole; set aside.* **4.** *Turn salads onto plates; refrigerate.* **5.** *Prepare bread; set aside.* **6.** *Bake potato casserole.* **7.** *Prepare coffee; heat bread.* **8.** *Cook broccoli.* **9.** *Pour water; place salads on table.* **10.** *Make gravy.*

OLIVE SURPRISE ROAST

4-pound rolled rump roast
1 jar (4½ ounces) small pimiento-stuffed olives, drained
Fat
1 large onion, sliced
1 can (10½ ounces) condensed tomato soup
1 soup can hot water
Tomato Gravy (below)

Heat oven to 325°. With point of knife make about 5 deep crisscross gashes in a circle as far in as the middle on each end of roast. Open gashes with finger or spoon; push about 5 olives into each gash. Brown roast on all sides in small amount of fat in Dutch oven on medium heat, about 20 minutes. Arrange onion slices over top of roast. Stir together soup and water; pour over roast. Cover tightly and place in oven; cook 2½ hours. Remove meat from pan. To serve, cut cord from roast; place meat seam side down on platter for easier slicing. Accompany with Tomato Gravy. *6 servings.*

Tomato Gravy

Shake ¾ cup cold water and ⅓ cup Gold Medal Flour (regular or Wondra) in covered jar. Stir flour mixture slowly into 3 cups hot meat broth. Cook, stirring constantly, until mixture thickens and boils. Boil and stir 1 minute. *Makes 3 cups.*

CHEESY POTATO CASSEROLE

Enough of our mashed Potato Buds (dry) for
   8 servings
½ teaspoon garlic salt
1 tablespoon snipped parsley
1 cup shredded sharp Cheddar cheese
   (about 4 ounces)
1½ cups Country Corn Flakes, crushed
2 tablespoons soft butter or margarine
½ teaspoon dry mustard
½ teaspoon paprika
¼ teaspoon salt

Prepare Potato Buds as directed on package for 8
servings except—decrease salt to ½ teaspoon and
add ½ teaspoon garlic salt. Stir parsley and cheese
into potatoes. Turn mixture into 1½-quart casserole.
Mix remaining ingredients; sprinkle over potatoes.
Bake in 325° oven 20 minutes. *6 servings.*

BUTTERED BROCCOLI

Prepare 2 packages (10 ounces each) frozen broccoli spears as directed on package. Season broccoli
with ¼ cup butter. *6 servings.*

GARDEN RELISH MOLD

1 package (3 ounces) lime-flavored
   gelatin
1 cup drained shredded pared cucumber
1 cup thinly sliced celery
3 tablespoons thinly sliced green onions
½ teaspoon salt
Crisp salad greens

Prepare gelatin as directed on package. Chill until
partially set; fold in vegetables and salt. Pour into
4 to 6 individual molds or 1-quart mold. Chill until
set. Unmold on salad greens. Serve with mayonnaise or dairy sour cream (thinned with milk), if
desired. *4 to 6 servings.*

POPPY-SEED FRENCH BREAD

Slice 1 loaf (1 pound) French bread diagonally, not
cutting all the way through. Combine ½ cup soft
butter and 1 teaspoon poppy seed. Spread bread
slices with butter mixture. Place loaf on baking
sheet and heat in 325° oven about 15 minutes or
until piping hot and crusty. *6 servings.*

CARDINAL PARFAITS

1 tablespoon sugar
2 teaspoons cornstarch
2 tablespoons orange juice
1 package (10 ounces) frozen raspberries,
   partially thawed
1 teaspoon grated orange peel
1 quart orange sherbet

In small saucepan stir together sugar and cornstarch.
Blend in orange juice. Stir in raspberries and orange
peel. Cook, stirring constantly, until mixture thickens and boils. Boil and stir 1 minute. Chill. Layer
orange sherbet and raspberry sauce in parfait glasses.
Freeze until firm. Remove from freezer to soften
slightly before serving. If desired, top with whipped cream. *6 servings.*

BROWNIE NUTS

Bite-size brownie confections with a nut atop each.

Prepare Fudgy Brownies as directed on our fudge
brownie mix package (1 pound) except—omit nuts
from batter. Spread batter in pan; place 36 or 48
toasted whole almonds, walnut halves or salted assorted nuts in rows on batter. After baking, cut into
squares with a nut in center of each. *Makes 36 or
48 bite-size brownies.*

Chicken Dinner with a Difference

Snowcapped Asparagus
Almond-fried Chicken
Potatoes in Olive Sauce   Tomato-Pickle Platter
Brown 'n Serve Rolls   Butter
Orange Chiffon Cake
Coffee   Tea

When you're not certain of guests' preferences in food, play it safe with a tried-and-true menu. This doesn't mean the meal must be trite. Far from it. Here for example is a traditional dinner with a whole repertory of delicious variations. Although the basic ingredients are familiar, there's a surprise element in every dish—chicken, yes, but chicken made exotic with an unexpected coating of toasted almonds; asparagus to be sure, but the spears are "tied" in bundles with pimiento and served icy cold as an out-of-the-ordinary appetizer; potatoes, with olives as a hidden asset, and so on through dessert.

Serving suggestions: Arrange asparagus on salad plates and place on top of dinner plates. When the first course is finished, remove the salad plates and bring in chicken, potatoes, tomatoes and rolls for guests to pass. At dessert time, cake is cut and served at the table.

PLAN FOR PREPARATION

Day before: 1. *Prepare and partially bake rolls.* **2.** *Bake and frost cake.*

Day of party: 1. *Cook asparagus and chill.* **2.** *Cook potatoes; cool.* **3.** *Place chicken in oven.* **4.** *Set table.* **5.** *Arrange tomato platter and asparagus plates; refrigerate.* **6.** *Cube potatoes and assemble ingredients for sauce; set aside.* **7.** *Heat rolls.* **8.** *Prepare coffee or tea. Heat potatoes.* **9.** *Pour water.*

SNOWCAPPED ASPARAGUS

2 packages (10 ounces each) frozen asparagus
  spears or 3 pounds fresh asparagus
½ cup mayonnaise or salad dressing
1 tablespoon milk
Pimiento strips

If using frozen asparagus, cook as directed on package. If using fresh asparagus, break off tough ends. Wash asparagus and remove scales; tie stalks in bunches. Cook upright in boiling salted water in narrow deep pan or coffeepot 10 to 20 minutes. Drain asparagus and chill. Arrange chilled asparagus in "bundles" on individual salad plates. Mix mayonnaise and milk; mound on asparagus. Trim with pimiento strips. *6 servings.*

ALMOND-FRIED CHICKEN

Two 2½-pound broiler-fryer chickens,
  cut into pieces
Salt
1 cup Gold Medal Flour (regular or Wondra)
2 teaspoons salt
¼ teaspoon pepper
2 teaspoons paprika
2 eggs, slightly beaten
3 tablespoons milk
2 cups finely chopped blanched almonds
2 tablespoons butter or margarine
2 tablespoons shortening
¼ cup butter or margarine, melted

Heat oven to 400°. Do not use chicken wings; remove skin from remaining pieces. Salt chicken; coat with a mixture of flour, 2 teaspoons salt, the pepper and paprika. Combine eggs and milk; dip chicken into egg mixture. Roll in almonds. In oven, melt 2 tablespoons butter and the shortening in jelly roll pan, 15½x10½x1 inch. Place chicken bone side down in pan. Drizzle with melted butter. Bake 1 hour. *6 servings.*

POTATOES IN OLIVE SAUCE

6 pared medium potatoes, cooked and drained
2 cups dairy sour cream
¼ cup finely chopped onion
2 tablespoons finely chopped pimiento-stuffed
    olives
1 teaspoon salt
½ teaspoon pepper
½ teaspoon paprika
1 tablespoon snipped parsley
4 pimiento-stuffed olives, sliced

Cut cooled potatoes into ½-inch cubes. Combine in skillet with sour cream, onion, chopped olives, salt and pepper. Heat over medium heat, stirring frequently, until cream bubbles and potatoes are heated through. Garnish with paprika, parsley and sliced olives. *6 servings.*

TOMATO-PICKLE PLATTER

Place a small bowl in center of platter or plate. Fill with drained chilled bread-and-butter-style pickles. Slice 4 chilled tomatoes; circle around bowl. Sprinkle crushed basil leaves over tomatoes. *6 servings.*

BROWN 'N SERVE ROLLS

1 package active dry yeast
¾ cup warm water (105 to 115°)
¾ cup lukewarm milk, scalded then cooled
¼ cup sugar
2¼ teaspoons salt
¼ cup shortening
4½ cups Gold Medal Flour* (regular or Wondra)

In mixing bowl dissolve yeast in warm water. Stir in milk, sugar, salt, shortening and half the flour. Beat until smooth. Stir in remaining flour. Turn onto lightly floured board and knead until smooth and elastic. Place in greased bowl; cover and let rise in warm place (85°) until double, about 1½ hours. Punch down, turn onto lightly floured board and divide into 24 equal pieces. Form into smooth balls. Place in greased muffin pans or about 3 inches apart on greased baking sheet. Cover with towel and let rise until almost double, about 45 minutes.

Heat oven to 275°. Bake 20 to 30 minutes. Remove from pans and allow to cool at room temperature. Wrap in plastic wrap or aluminum foil or place in plastic bag. Store in refrigerator, or freeze. When ready to serve, brown in 400° oven 7 to 10 minutes. (Bake only half the rolls to serve 6.) *Makes 24 rolls.*

If using Self-Rising Flour, omit salt.

ORANGE CHIFFON CAKE

Light as angel food, rich as butter cake.

2¼ cups Softasilk Cake Flour or
    2 cups Gold Medal Flour* (regular or Wondra)
1½ cups sugar
3 teaspoons baking powder
1 teaspoon salt
½ cup salad oil
5 egg yolks (with Softasilk) or 7 egg yolks
    (with Gold Medal Flour), unbeaten
¾ cup cold water
2 tablespoons grated orange peel
1 cup egg whites (7 or 8)
½ teaspoon cream of tartar
Orange Butter Icing (below)

Heat oven to 325°. Stir together flour, sugar, baking powder and salt in bowl. Make a "well" and add in order: oil, egg yolks, water and orange peel. Beat with spoon until smooth. Measure egg whites and cream of tartar into large mixer bowl. Beat until whites form very stiff peaks. Pour egg yolk mixture gradually over beaten whites, gently folding with rubber scraper just until blended. Pour into *ungreased* tube pan, 10x4 inches. Bake 55 minutes.

Increase temperature to 350° and bake 10 to 15 minutes longer. Invert on funnel; let hang until cold. Frost with Orange Butter Icing. If desired, arrange mandarin orange segments around base of cake; garnish top of cake with a flower of orange segments and a maraschino cherry.

If using Self-Rising Flour, omit baking powder and salt.

Lemon Chiffon Cake: Follow recipe above except— omit orange peel. Add 2 teaspoons vanilla and 2 teaspoons grated lemon peel. Frost with Lemon Butter Icing (below).

Orange (or Lemon) Butter Icing

⅓ cup soft butter or margarine
3 cups confectioners' sugar
1½ tablespoons grated orange (or lemon) peel
About 3 tablespoons orange (or lemon) juice

Mix butter, sugar, peel and juice until smooth.

Dinner Deluxe

Broiled Steak and Lobster
Broiled Tomatoes   Dilled Zucchini
Noodles Romanoff with Poppy Seed   Tossed Endive Salad
Hard Rolls   Butter
Honey Bee Sundaes   Sugar Cookies
Coffee

When the occasion calls for splurging, when you've less time than money, or when the guest list includes someone that rates real V.I.P. treatment, nothing could be more delightful or surer to please than an offering of two pure-luxury dishes—steak and lobster. It's expensive, to be sure, but it's absolutely guaranteed to send your stock soaring with the company.

A broiler meal like this does call for the cook's undivided last-minute attention, but it doesn't require preparation during the day. A perfect solution for the girl who leaves the office at five o'clock.

To live up to the grandeur of the menu, set the table with your loveliest cloth, your prettiest china and crystal and any heirloom table accessories you may have. If you happen to own finger bowls, this is the time to bring them out. With lobster, especially, they're practical as well as elegant.

Serving suggestions: The vital consideration in this menu is that the broiler foods must be served very hot. To do this, warm plates and serve them from the kitchen, two at a time, with steak, lobster, noodles and vegetables. Salad may be tossed and served at the table.

BROILED STEAK AND LOBSTER

4 medium lobster tails, fresh or frozen
  (if frozen, thaw)
1 pound sirloin steak, 1 inch thick
½ teaspoon salt
¼ teaspoon pepper
2 firm ripe tomatoes, halved
Melted butter
Lemon Cups (below)

Set oven control at broil and/or 550°. Cut away thin undershell of lobster tails with kitchen scissors. Bend each tail backward toward shell to crack. (This prevents tails from curling while they broil.) Place lobster tails shell side up on broiler rack. Place steak on broiler rack. Broil 2 to 3 inches from source of heat 7 minutes; season steak with half the salt and pepper. Turn lobster tails and steak. Place tomato halves on broiler rack; brush lobster and tomatoes with melted butter. Broil 7 minutes longer. Season steak with remaining salt and pepper. To accompany the lobster, serve Lemon Cups. *4 servings.*

Lemon Cups

Halve 2 lemons and cut a sliver off ends so they will stand upright. Scoop out pulp; press out the juice and reserve. Melt ½ cup butter and stir in the lemon juice. Pour into lemon cups.

PLAN FOR PREPARATION

Day before: 1. *Wash and dry salad greens; tear into bite-size pieces. Break up cauliflower. Chill in plastic bag. (If desired, olives and artichoke hearts can be drained and refrigerated in small plastic containers.)* **2.** *Bake or purchase cookies.* **3.** *Spoon ice cream into sherbet dishes; cover with foil and freeze. Prepare sundae sauce.*

Day of party: 1. *Set table.* **2.** *Wash and cut tomatoes and zucchini. Prepare Lemon Cups.* **3.** *Pour water. Place rolls in napkin-lined basket; set on table. Prepare coffee.* **4.** *Broil steak and lobster.* **5.** *Cook noodles.* **6.** *Cook zucchini. Add tomatoes to broiler tray.* **7.** *Arrange plates; fill Lemon Cups.*

DILLED ZUCCHINI

Cut 2 medium zucchini squash (unpared) in half lengthwise. Simmer uncovered in 1 inch boiling water about 10 minutes or until just tender; drain. Season with 1 or 2 tablespoons butter and ½ teaspoon dill weed. *4 servings.*

NOODLES ROMANOFF WITH POPPY SEED

Prepare our noodles Romanoff as directed on package except—stir in 1 teaspoon poppy seed. *4 servings.*

TOSSED ENDIVE SALAD

1 small head lettuce
½ bunch endive
½ small head cauliflower
1 can (7 ounces) artichoke hearts,
drained and halved
⅓ cup sliced pitted ripe olives
Bottled clear French dressing

Into salad bowl, tear greens into bite-size pieces. Break cauliflower into small pieces. Add cauliflower, artichoke hearts and olives to bowl; toss with dressing. *4 servings.*

HONEY BEE SUNDAES

Mix ½ cup honey and ½ cup apricot brandy. Divide 1 pint chocolate chip ice cream among 4 sherbet glasses. Spoon honey-apricot sauce over ice cream; sprinkle about ¼ teaspoon uncooked coffee grounds over each sundae. *4 servings.*

SUGAR COOKIES

1½ cups confectioners' sugar
1 cup butter or margarine
1 egg
1 teaspoon vanilla
½ teaspoon almond extract
2½ cups Gold Medal Flour* (regular or Wondra)
1 teaspoon soda
1 teaspoon cream of tartar

Cream confectioners' sugar and butter. Mix in egg, vanilla and almond extract. Stir dry ingredients together; blend into creamed mixture. Refrigerate 2 to 3 hours. Heat oven to 375°. Divide dough in half and roll out on lightly floured cloth-covered board. Roll 3/16 inch thick. Cut into 2- or 2½-inch rounds or other desired shapes. Sprinkle with granulated sugar, if desired. Place on lightly greased baking sheet. Bake 7 to 8 minutes or until delicately golden. *Makes 5 dozen 2- to 2½-inch cookies.*

*If using Self-Rising Flour, omit soda and cream of tartar.

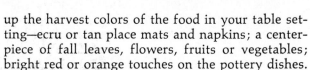

Harvest Feast

Pink Cucumber Float
Pork Platter Orangé   Smoky Green Beans
Lettuce Wedges with Blue Cheese Dressing
Parker House Rolls
Butterscotch Spice Cake   Coffee

Here's a dinner, handsome and hearty, that even an inexperienced hostess can undertake without qualms. The secret: pork chops, potatoes and onions cook together in one skillet, happily eliminating multiple preparation and pot-watching. The beans and salad are assembled in a matter of minutes; the rolls are from a package, and the dessert is an easy one-bowl loaf cake with a simple broiler frosting. This menu is perfect for the new bride or the girl on her own because the meat requires no carving. And it's good looking, too, especially if you pick up the harvest colors of the food in your table setting—ecru or tan place mats and napkins; a centerpiece of fall leaves, flowers, fruits or vegetables; bright red or orange touches on the pottery dishes.

Serving suggestions: Begin dinner in the living room with mugs of the cold, conversation-making soup to be sipped around the coffee table. Then move into the dining room where salad and rolls are already on the table; the host serves the main dish from a platter, and the beans can be passed. Coffee and cake wait in the kitchen for dessert time.

PLAN FOR PREPARATION

Day before: 1. *Bake cake.* **2.** *Prepare appetizer soup; cover and chill.* **3.** *Prepare salad dressing; cover and chill.* **4.** *Wash, dry and chill head lettuce.*

Day of party: 1. *Slice onions, sweet potatoes and oranges. Cook chops.* **2.** *Wrap rolls in foil.* **3.** *Set table.* **4.** *Cut cake (don't remove from pan until serving).* **5.** *Prepare coffee.* **6.** *Heat rolls.* **7.** *Cook beans.* **8.** *Cut lettuce wedges; place salads on table.* **9.** *Serve soup.* **10.** *Pour water.* **11.** *Just before serving, arrange meat platter; thicken sauce.*

Permanent Party Gear

A guest book is a wonderful way of making a permanent record of all your parties. Use a handsomely covered loose-leaf book; the signatures in it will bring back memories of fun at your house for years to come.

PINK CUCUMBER FLOAT

1 teaspoon Worcestershire sauce
½ teaspoon curry powder
1 can (10½ ounces) condensed tomato soup
2 cups buttermilk
1 medium cucumber, finely chopped
Cracked black pepper
6 cucumber slices

Blend Worcestershire sauce and curry powder; stir into tomato soup. Slowly add buttermilk, stirring until blended. Add chopped cucumber. Chill thoroughly. Sprinkle pepper over each serving; garnish with a cucumber slice. *6 servings.*

PORK PLATTER ORANGÉ

Delicious meal in one—pork chops, sweet potatoes and onion slices all simmer in an orange sauce.

6 pork chops, 1 inch thick
1½ teaspoons salt
¼ teaspoon pepper
1 onion, cut into 6 slices
⅓ cup brown sugar (packed)
½ cup water
1 teaspoon grated orange peel
⅓ cup orange juice
2 tablespoons lemon juice
½ teaspoon salt
2 pounds sweet potatoes or yams, pared and
cut into ½-inch slices
6 thin orange slices
1 tablespoon cornstarch
¼ cup cold water

Trim excess fat from chops; lightly grease heavy skillet with fat from one chop. Brown chops slowly, sprinkling with 1½ teaspoons salt and the pepper. Drain off any excess fat. Top each chop with an onion slice. Mix brown sugar, ½ cup water, the orange peel, orange juice, lemon juice and ½ teaspoon salt. Pour over chops. Cover and simmer 30 minutes. Lift chops and arrange sweet potato slices in sauce. Replace chops; top each onion slice with an orange slice. Cover; simmer 45 minutes, or until potatoes are tender and chops are done—no pink in center. Remove chops and sweet potatoes to a heated platter; keep warm. Blend cornstarch and ¼ cup water; stir into sauce in skillet. Cook, stirring constantly, until mixture thickens and boils. Boil and stir 1 minute. Pour over chops and sweet potatoes. Garnish with parsley, if desired. *6 servings.*

SMOKY GREEN BEANS

Prepare 2 packages (9 ounces each) frozen cut green beans as directed on package. Before serving, stir in ½ teaspoon smoky salt. Season with ¼ cup butter. *6 servings.*

LETTUCE WEDGES
WITH BLUE CHEESE DRESSING

1 package (4 ounces) blue cheese, crumbled
1 package (3 ounces) cream cheese, softened
½ cup mayonnaise or salad dressing
⅓ cup light cream
6 lettuce wedges

Mix blue cheese with cream cheese. Blend in mayonnaise and cream; beat until mixture is creamy. With knife, slash lettuce wedges crosswise, not cutting completely through. Spoon dressing over wedges. *6 servings.*

PARKER HOUSE ROLLS

Heat oven to 350°. Split and butter 1 package (12 ounces) Parker House rolls; wrap in aluminum foil. Heat 20 minutes. *6 to 8 servings.*

BUTTERSCOTCH SPICE CAKE

1½ cups Gold Medal Flour* (regular or Wondra)
1 cup brown sugar (packed)
½ cup granulated sugar
1 cup quick-cooking oats
1½ teaspoons soda
1 teaspoon cinnamon
½ teaspoon salt
½ teaspoon nutmeg
½ cup shortening
1 cup water
2 eggs (½ to ⅔ cup)
2 tablespoons dark molasses
Coconut Topping (below)

Heat oven to 350°. Grease and flour an oblong pan, 13x9x2 inches. Measure all ingredients except Coconut Topping into large mixer bowl. Blend 30 seconds low speed on mixer. Beat 3 minutes on medium speed, scraping bowl often. Pour into prepared pan. Bake 35 to 40 minutes, or until wooden pick inserted in center comes out clean. Let cool slightly. Carefully spread Coconut Topping over top of cake. Set oven control at broil and/or 550°. Broil 2 to 3 minutes until golden brown.

*Do not use Self-Rising Flour in this recipe.

Coconut Topping

Melt ¼ cup butter; stir together with ⅔ cup brown sugar (packed), ½ cup flaked coconut, ½ cup chopped pecans and 3 tablespoons light cream.

Diet Dinner in Disguise

Cheese Dip and Fruit Tray
Creole Haddock   Wild-White Casserole   Savory Beans
Salad of Three Greens   Crisp Toast Rounds
Iced Angel Torte   Coffee

If you're entertaining someone on a low-cholesterol or low-fat diet or even someone who is just mindful of calories, here's a dinner that fills all bills. Everyone gets the same thing, and there are none of those optional special sauces or seasonings for the other guests that always make the dieter feel deprived. Every dish is so delicious in itself and so pretty to look at that you'll probably repeat the menu even when no one is on a diet.

The fish topped with colorful chopped peppers and tomato would brighten any dinner table. The beans cooked in bouillon need little additional flavoring. The mixture of white and wild rice adds a gourmet touch at a reasonable price. And your guests won't believe the Iced Angel Torte is diet-minded. It can hold its own with the richest dessert! And the net cost of this meal to the dieter: Only 24 grams of fat (16 grams are polyunsaturated fatty acids) and 97 milligrams of cholesterol per serving—when this meal is prepared and served *exactly* as directed. And for the calorie conscious, you will find a calorie-per-portion count with each recipe.

Serving suggestions: Pass the conversation-making tray of appetizers in the living room and then steal off to the kitchen for last-minute attention to the dinner. Salad should be on the table when guests sit down. Pass the fish on a platter, the beans and rice in bowls. Present the handsome torte intact.

CHEESE DIP AND FRUIT TRAY

⅓ cup skim milk
1 teaspoon vinegar
1 cup dry cottage cheese (large curd)
¼ cup of our safflower oil
½ teaspoon salt
½ teaspoon garlic salt or 2 teaspoons chopped chives or 1 tablespoon dry onion soup mix, if desired
12 saltine crackers, 2x2 inches
1 large orange, pared and cut into cubes
1 large red apple, cut into wedges

Place milk, vinegar, cottage cheese, oil and seasonings in blender; blend 15 seconds. Scrape sides with rubber spatula. Blend about 1 minute longer or until smooth. Cover and refrigerate several hours or overnight.

To serve, mound cheese dip in a small bowl and place on tray with saltine crackers for dipping. Insert wooden picks in orange cubes and apple wedges; arrange on tray. *6 servings.* (195 calories and 10 grams fat for each serving, allowing about 2½ tablespoons dip per serving.)

PLAN FOR PREPARATION

Day before: 1. *Prepare lime ice and bake cake.* 2. *While cake is baking, prepare cheese dip.* 3. *Wash, dry and chill salad greens.* 4. *Prepare salad dressing.* 5. *Fill and frost cake; freeze.*

Day of party: 1. *Set table.* 2. *Spread toast rounds; cover and set aside.* 3. *Prepare sauce for fish; set aside.* 4. *Tear up salad greens; refrigerate.* 5. *Cook rice.* 6. *Prepare coffee.* 7. *Arrange appetizer tray and serve.* 8. *Pour water.* 9. *Cook beans.* 10. *Bake fish and toast rounds.* 11. *Toss salad.*

CREOLE HADDOCK

2 pounds fresh or frozen haddock fillets (thawed, if frozen)
1½ cups chopped fresh tomatoes
½ cup chopped green pepper
⅓ cup lemon juice
1 tablespoon of our safflower oil
2 teaspoons salt
2 teaspoons instant minced onion
1 teaspoon crushed basil leaves
¼ teaspoon coarsely ground black pepper
4 drops Tabasco

Heat oven to 500°. Place fillets in oblong baking dish, 13½x9x2 inches. Combine remaining ingredients; spoon mixture over fillets. Bake 5 to 8 minutes. Place fillets on warm platter; garnish with tomato wedges and green pepper rings, if desired. *6 servings.* (155 calories and 3 grams fat per serving.)

WILD-WHITE CASSEROLE

½ cup wild rice
2 cups boiling water
½ cup uncooked regular rice
1½ cups water
1 teaspoon salt

Wash wild rice by placing in wire strainer and running cold water through it. Lift rice with fingers to clean it thoroughly. Place cleaned wild rice in saucepan; pour 2 cups boiling water over it. Cover and let stand 20 minutes; drain. Combine partially cooked wild rice with remaining ingredients in 3-quart saucepan with a tightly fitted lid. Heat to boiling, stirring once or twice. Reduce heat to simmer. Cover and cook 14 minutes *without removing lid or stirring*. (All water should be absorbed.) Remove pan from heat. Fluff rice lightly with fork. Cover and let stand 5 to 10 minutes to steam dry. *6 servings*. (106 calories per serving; no fat.)

SAVORY BEANS

1 beef bouillon cube
½ cup boiling water
2 packages (10 ounces each) frozen whole
  green beans
⅛ teaspoon pepper

Dissolve bouillon cube in boiling water in saucepan. Add beans and heat to boiling. Cover; simmer 5 minutes or until tender. Season with pepper. *6 servings*. (25 calories per serving; no fat.)

SALAD OF THREE GREENS

1 head romaine
½ small bunch endive
½ small bag spinach (2 cups)
Clear Dressing (below)

Have greens washed, dried and well chilled. Using choicest parts, tear into bite-size pieces (do not cut). Discard stems. Just before serving, toss with Clear Dressing. *6 servings*. (102 calories and 9 grams fat per serving.)

Clear Dressing

¼ cup of our safflower oil
2 tablespoons vinegar
¼ teaspoon salt
⅛ teaspoon <u>each</u> dry mustard and paprika

Beat all ingredients with rotary beater or shake well in covered jar. Keep in covered jar in refrigerator. Just before serving, shake. *Makes about ⅓ cup*.

CRISP TOAST ROUNDS

Cut 12 slices French bread ¼ inch thick. Spread each slice with about ⅛ teaspoon soft-type margarine.* Place bread slices on baking sheet. Toast in 500° oven 4 minutes or until browned. *Makes 12 rounds*. (36 calories and 1 gram fat per slice.)

*A margarine high in safflower oil. (To check type of margarine, see ingredient listing on package label. Safflower oil should be listed first if it is the one present in the largest amount.)

ICED ANGEL TORTE

1 package (6 ounces) lime-flavored gelatin
1½ cups boiling water
1 cup sugar
¼ cup plus 2 tablespoons lemon juice
1½ cups buttermilk (type made with skim milk)
1½ cups skim milk
1 package of our white angel food cake mix

Dissolve gelatin in boiling water. Add sugar, lemon juice, buttermilk and milk; stir until sugar dissolves. Pour into oblong pan, 10x6x1½ inches; freeze several hours or until firm. Bake cake as directed on package. Invert and cool at least 2 hours.

When ready to assemble torte, remove lime gelatin mixture from freezer and let stand at room temperature about 15 minutes. Remove cake from pan and place wide side down on plate or board. Cut a slice from top of cake about 1 inch down. Lift off top and set aside. Cut down into the cake 1 inch from outer edge and 1 inch from hole, leaving a substantial "wall" of cake about 1 inch thick. Remove center of cake with a curved knife or spoon, leaving a base of cake 1 inch thick. Place cake on serving plate. Place lime gelatin mixture in large mixer bowl; break up and beat until smooth. Reserve part of the whipped lime mixture for frosting cake. Fill cake cavity with remaining lime mixture, gently pushing it into cavity to avoid air holes. Place top over filled cake; press down gently. Cover sides and top with spoonfuls of reserved lime mixture, swirling it lightly to resemble frosting. Freeze overnight. Remove from freezer about 10 minutes before serving for easier slicing. Garnish plate,. if desired, with twists of lime slices or flowers. *Makes sixteen 2-inch slices*. (209 calories and 1 gram fat per slice.)

French Formality

Vichyssoise
Fruited Chicken en Crème
Fluffy Rice   Green Beans Almondine
Bibb Lettuce Salad   Classic French Dressing
Brioches   Butter Curls (page 71)
La Bombe Rose   Bonbon Cookies
Demitasse

Some occasions seem to call for daintiness and delicacy: a table set with pastel linens, a centerpiece of spring flowers, lighted candles, gleaming silver and a menu to match. When the guest of honor is a woman—perhaps a bride-to-be or an out-of-town guest—the food you serve should be light and pretty.

French cuisine seems to lend itself to this, so we have used it as the basis of the menu. In spite of its fragile look, don't imagine that the men of the party won't enjoy this meal, too; we'll guarantee their enthusiasm for the creamy Vichyssoise, the refreshingly different chicken and hot brioches.

Serving suggestions: For this dinner the most formal service you can manage is appropriate. Set the table according to the plan diagrammed on page 12 . The first course and the salad should be in place when the guests sit down, the brioches and butter curls on butter plates. After the first course, remove the soup service; arrange the dinner plates individually in the kitchen, and bring them in two at a time. When the main course is finished, clear the table completely and *then* present La Bombe Rose, your dramatic dessert. Coffee may be served later in the living room.

PLAN FOR PREPARATION

Day before: 1. *Prepare and freeze bombe.* **2.** *Bake cookies.* **3.** *Prepare salad dressing.* **4.** *Prepare soup base; chill.* **5.** *Wash, dry and chill lettuce.*

Day of party: 1. *Set table.* **2.** *Bake chicken.* **3.** *Toast almonds for beans; set aside.* **4.** *Arrange salads; refrigerate.* **5.** *Cook rice.* **6.** *Decorate bombe; freeze.* **7.** *Bake rolls and cook beans.* **8.** *Pour water; set salads on table.* **9.** *Add cream to Vichyssoise and pour into bowls; set on table.* **10.** *Place rolls and butter curls on bread-and-butter plates.*

VICHYSSOISE

1 small or medium onion, grated
3 chicken bouillon cubes
1 cup water
¼ teaspoon salt
½ cup milk
1¼ cups of our mashed Potato Buds (dry)
1½ cups milk
1 cup light cream
Snipped chives or watercress

Combine onion, bouillon cubes, water and salt in large saucepan. Heat to boiling. Cover; simmer 10 minutes. Remove from heat. Add ½ cup milk. Stir in Potato Buds and whip with fork until fluffy. Gradually stir in 1½ cups milk; heat just to boiling. Cover and chill thoroughly. Just before serving stir in cream, beating vigorously with fork until well mixed. Spoon into small cups or bowls. Sprinkle with chives or watercress. *6 to 8 servings.*

FRUITED CHICKEN EN CRÈME

2 tablespoons butter or margarine
2 tablespoons salad oil
6 large chicken breast halves (2½ to 3 pounds)
1 can (10½ ounces) condensed cream of
   chicken soup
½ cup light cream
½ cup dry sherry
1 can (13½ ounces) pineapple tidbits, drained
½ cup sliced seedless green grapes
1 can (6 ounces) sliced mushrooms, drained

Heat oven to 350°. Heat butter and oil in baking dish, 13½x9x2 inches. Place chicken pieces skin side up in baking dish; bake 1 hour. Heat soup, cream and sherry in saucepan, stirring occasionally. Stir pineapple, grapes and mushrooms into soup mixture. Remove baking dish from oven; drain off fat. Pour soup-fruit mixture over chicken; cover baking dish with aluminum foil and bake 15 to 20 minutes longer. If desired, garnish with clusters of green grapes. *6 servings.*

FLUFFY RICE

2 cups water
1 cup uncooked regular rice
1 teaspoon salt

Oven Method: Heat water to boiling; combine with rice and salt in 1½-quart casserole or oblong baking dish, 10x6x1½ inches. Cover dish tightly with casserole lid or aluminum foil. (Lid or foil cover must be tight enough to prevent escape of steam.) Bake in 350° oven 25 to 30 minutes, or until liquid is absorbed and rice is tender. Fluff with fork.

Range-top Method: Combine water, rice and salt in 3-quart saucepan with a tightly fitted lid. Heat to boiling, stirring once or twice. Reduce heat to simmer. Cover and cook 14 minutes *without removing lid or stirring.* All water should be absorbed. For drier, fluffier rice, remove pan of cooked rice from heat. Fluff rice lightly with a fork and let stand in covered pan 5 to 10 minutes to steam dry. *4 to 6 servings.*

GREEN BEANS ALMONDINE

Prepare 2 packages (9 ounces each) frozen French-style green beans as directed on package. Cook ¼ cup slivered blanched almonds in ¼ cup butter until toasted and brown. Toss gently with green beans. *6 servings.*

BRIOCHES

Heat 2 packages (8 ounces each) frozen brioches as directed on package. *12 rolls.*

BIBB LETTUCE SALAD

Wash and dry 3 medium heads Bibb lettuce or 3 small heads Boston lettuce. Remove "heart" from each lettuce head. Place one "heart" on each of 3 salad plates; spread out leaves slightly. (Each "heart" will resemble a whole head of lettuce.) Place an outer section of leaves on each of 3 additional salad plates; push leaves together to resemble head of lettuce. Tuck radish slices between lettuce leaves. Serve with Classic French Dressing (below). *6 servings.*

Classic French Dressing

¼ cup olive oil (or half salad oil)
2 tablespoons wine or tarragon vinegar
¾ teaspoon salt
1 small clove garlic, crushed
⅛ to ¼ teaspoon freshly ground pepper
⅛ to ¼ teaspoon monosodium glutamate

Beat all ingredients with rotary beater or shake well in tightly covered jar. Keep in covered jar in refrigerator. Just before using, shake to blend.

LA BOMBE ROSE

½ gallon (2 quarts) vanilla ice cream
¼ cup rose water*
½ teaspoon nutmeg
Red food coloring
¼ cup finely chopped walnuts
¼ cup finely chopped maraschino cherries
1 cup whipping cream
1 tablespoon confectioners' sugar
Red food coloring
Crystallized violets or purple gumdrop flowers**

Reserve 1 cup ice cream; soften remainder and stir in rose water and nutmeg. Spoon softened ice cream into 2-quart metal bowl or mold; freeze just until partially set. Remove mold from freezer and with a spoon push ice cream to sides of bowl, forming a hollow in center about the size of large custard or coffee cup. Freeze until firm. Soften reserved ice cream; tint pink with few drops red food coloring. Stir nuts and cherries into tinted ice cream; spoon into hollow center of molded ice cream. Freeze several hours or until firm.

Shortly before serving time, whip cream with confectioners' sugar until stiff. Tint pink with few drops red food coloring. Turn mold onto chilled platter. Dip a cloth in hot water; wring out and place over top of mold *just* a few minutes. Lift off cloth and bowl. If ice cream has melted over surface, return mold to freezer for a brief time. Fill decorators' tube with pink whipped cream and decorate top of mold. Trim with crystallized violets or purple gumdrop flowers. *8 to 10 servings.*

Rose water is available at drugstores.
**With scissors, snip the wide part of small purple gumdrops into 6 sections—do not cut through. Carefully spread gumdrop "petals" apart and place sugared side up on bombe. Slice green gumdrops for leaves.*

BONBON COOKIES

Pastel and pretty. These little cookies look like bonbon candies.

½ cup soft butter or margarine
¾ cup confectioners' sugar
1 tablespoon vanilla
Food coloring, if desired
1½ cups Gold Medal Flour* (regular or Wondra)
⅛ teaspoon salt
Cherries, dates, nuts and chocolate pieces
Pastel Icing (below)

Heat oven to 350°. Blend butter, sugar, vanilla and few drops food coloring. Mix in flour and salt thoroughly with hands. (If dough is dry, mix in 1 to 2 tablespoons milk.) Mold about 1 tablespoon dough around cherry, date, nut or chocolate piece. Place cookies about 1 inch apart on ungreased baking sheet. Bake 12 to 15 minutes, or until set but not brown. Dip tops of cookies into Pastel Icing. If desired, decorate each with coconut, nuts, decorators' sugar, or chocolate pieces or shot. *Makes 20 to 25 cookies.*

Do not use Self-Rising Flour in this recipe.

Pastel Icing

Blend about 1½ tablespoons milk and 1 teaspoon vanilla into 1 cup confectioners' sugar until dipping consistency. If desired, stir in few drops food coloring to tint icing. (Divide icing before tinting if you wish to have various colors.)

Starring Beef Wellington

*Ruby Consommé   Daisy*s
Tenderloin of Beef Wellington
Potatoes Parmesan
Glazed Carrots   Green Peas and Onions
Spinach-Apple Toss
Chantilly Cake   Coffee*

Here is a menu that very clearly stars a spectacular entrée. Dramatic, delicious Beef Wellington demands all the cook's time and talent, so everything that goes with it is as super-simplified as planning and convenience foods can make it. A smart hostessing trick! The star turn is a superb beef tenderloin encased with mushroom filling and flaky pastry. If you want to gild the lily further, use pastry cutouts that match the season—daisy shapes for spring, holly leaves brushed with green food coloring for Christmas—to decorate the top of the tenderloin.

This stunning main dish is accompanied by canned and frozen vegetables chosen to ease the preparation and to color complement the meat. The quick-mix dessert is glamorously garnished and can be served flaming, if you like.

Serving suggestions: Pour consommé into cups or glasses and serve with snacks in the living room. Salads should be on the table when guests sit down. While the host carves and serves the meat, the hostess serves the vegetables. The handsome cake, ignited or not, should be cut and served at the table.

PLAN FOR PREPARATION

Day before: 1. *Bake cake.* **2.** *While cake is baking, prepare filling for Wellington; refrigerate.* **3.** *Prepare sauce for Wellington; refrigerate.* **4.** *Wash, dry and chill spinach for salad.* **5.** *Frost cake; refrigerate. Frost grapes, if desired.* **6.** *Prepare Ruby Consommé if serving chilled.*

Day of party: 1. *Bake Beef Wellington.* **2.** *Set table.* **3.** *Fry bacon for salad; mix salad dressing.* **4.** *Bake potatoes.* **5.** *Prepare coffee.* **6.** *Serve Ruby Consommé.* **7.** *Pour water.* **8.** *Cook carrots and peas.* **9.** *Toss salad and arrange on plates; set on table.*

Permanent Party Gear

Place-card holders of china or silver add a lovely touch to your table. You can use matching holders, or you can have a different one at each place. What an attractive and diplomatic way to seat a good listener next to a talker.

RUBY CONSOMMÉ

Combine 2 cans (10½ ounces each) beef consommé, 1 cup tomato juice and 1 cup water; heat through. Serve hot, or chill and serve over ice. *8 servings.*

TENDERLOIN OF BEEF WELLINGTON

3-pound beef tenderloin
2 tablespoons soft butter
1 teaspoon salt
½ teaspoon pepper
3 of our pie crust sticks
Mushroom Filling (below)
1 egg
1 tablespoon water
Brown Sauce (below)

Heat oven to 425°. Tie a heavy string at several points around tenderloin. Place on rack in shallow pan. Spread butter over top and sides of tenderloin; sprinkle with salt and pepper. Bake 20 minutes. Remove to cooling rack; let stand until cool, about 30 minutes. Remove string; pat tenderloin dry with paper towel. Prepare pie crust sticks as directed on inside wrapper for One-crust Pie except—use three times the designated amount of boiling water or cool milk. On aluminum foil, roll pastry into rectangle, 24x18 inches; cut to make edges even. Place tenderloin at edge of longer side of pastry. Spread Mushroom Filling over remaining surface of pastry, leaving a 1-inch margin on each side. Roll tenderloin and pastry; seal seam and ends securely, moistening with water if necessary. Roll out leftover pastry; cut out small designs—flowers, stars or other cutouts. Garnish top of pastry with cutouts. Mix egg and water; brush over top and sides of pastry.

Reduce oven to 400°. Carefully place pastry-wrapped tenderloin seam side down on baking sheet. (Use the foil and two spatulas to help transfer tenderloin.) Remove foil. Bake 30 minutes or until pastry is golden brown. Serve Brown Sauce over tenderloin. *8 servings.*

Mushroom Filling

In small skillet, cook and stir 1 pound fresh mushrooms, finely chopped, ½ cup chopped onion, ½ cup dry sherry, ¼ cup butter and ¼ cup snipped parsley until onion is tender and *all* liquid absorbed.

Brown Sauce

In saucepan combine 2 cups beef bouillon, ½ cup dry sherry, 3 tablespoons finely chopped onion, 3 tablespoons finely chopped carrot, 1 tablespoon finely chopped celery, 2 sprigs parsley, 1 bay leaf, crumbled, and ⅛ teaspoon crushed thyme leaves; simmer 30 minutes. Strain mixture through a fine sieve. Discard vegetable mixture. Stir in 3 tablespoons dry sherry; simmer 5 minutes longer. Stir in 2 tablespoons butter, a little at a time.

POTATOES PARMESAN

Drain 2 cans (1 pound each) small whole potatoes. Place in square baking dish, 9x9x2 inches. Toss potatoes with ½ cup melted butter; sprinkle with ¼ cup grated Parmesan cheese. Bake uncovered in 400° oven 30 minutes. Garnish with snipped parsley, if desired. *8 servings.*

GLAZED CARROTS

Prepare 2 packages (10 ounces each) frozen carrot nuggets in butter sauce as directed on package. Just before serving, sprinkle with ¼ cup brown sugar. *8 servings.*

GREEN PEAS AND ONIONS

Prepare 2 packages (10 ounces each) frozen green peas and onions in butter sauce as directed on package. *8 servings.*

SPINACH-APPLE TOSS

2 bags (10 ounces each) spinach
2 tart red apples, sliced
8 slices bacon, crisply fried and crumbled
⅔ cup salad dressing or mayonnaise
⅓ cup frozen orange juice concentrate (thawed)

Wash and dry spinach leaves; tear into bite-size pieces. Combine spinach, apples and bacon. Mix salad dressing and orange juice; pour over spinach-apple mixture and toss lightly. *8 servings.*

CHANTILLY CAKE

A sunshiny lemon cake with a luscious filling of green grapes and pistachio nuts. Serve dramatically garnished with ring of nuts and frosted grapes.

1 package of our lemon velvet cake mix
1 package of our lemon velvet frosting mix
2 cups whipping cream
½ cup chopped well-drained seedless green grapes (about 1 cup whole)
½ cup pistachio nuts

Bake cake in 9-inch layers as directed on package. In small mixer bowl, combine frosting mix and cream; chill. Whip chilled frosting mixture on medium speed until stiff. Remove 1 cup frosting mixture; fold in grapes and nuts. Spread between cooled cake layers. Spread remaining frosting on sides and top. Refrigerate at least 2 hours. If desired, garnish top of cake with a ring of chopped pistachio nuts; arrange frosted green grapes* around base of cake.

To frost grapes, wash and dry small bunches of grapes. Brush slightly beaten egg white over grapes. Dip in granulated sugar and dry on rack.

Flaming Chantilly Cake: Follow recipe above except —cut a lemon in half crosswise. (Store one half for later use.) Scoop out pulp; cut scallop edges. Press "lemon cup" into top of frosted cake. Just before serving, place several sugar cubes in cup; pour lemon extract over cubes. Ignite cubes and serve.

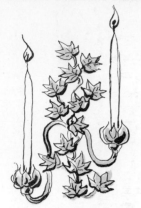

Regal Roast Dinner

Salt-sparked Tomato Juice
Crown Roast of Pork with Mushroom Stuffing
Buttered Brussels Sprouts   Tiny Cloved Onions
Relish Tray of Corn Relish, Crab Apples, Watermelon Pickles
Fan-Tan Rolls
Butter Brickle Silhouette Pie   Coffee

Succulent pork takes on brand-new glamor when it's served in the distinctive shape of a crown roast, piled high with a delicious mushroom stuffing. This eye-catching entrée is ideal for a good-sized crowd and, believe it or not, it's easy to prepare. But do give your meatman sufficient notice (at least one or two days) to cut and shape the crown for you. Causing more complimentary table talk are the onions, beautifully glazed with whole cloves inserted in each, and a tangy colorful relish tray.

We've included a recipe for corn relish in case you want to make your own, but you can just as happily buy it ready-made along with the crab apples and watermelon pickles.

Serving suggestions: Have tomato juice on the table when dinner is announced. The host will be pleasantly surprised to find it so easy to serve the stuffing and carve the crown. The other dishes may be passed. The pie should be cut in the kitchen and served on individual dessert plates.

PLAN FOR PREPARATION

Day before: 1. *Prepare stuffing; cover and refrigerate.* **2.** *Chill relishes.* **3.** *Bake pie shells.* **4.** *Prepare tomato juice mixture, if desired; chill.*

Day of party: 1. *Bake meringue in shells.* **2.** *While meringue bakes, salt glasses for tomato juice.* **3.** *Roast pork.* **4.** *Scoop ice cream for dessert, if desired.* **5.** *Set table.* **6.** *Prepare coffee.* **7.** *Cook onions.* **8.** *Heat rolls.* **9.** *Cook Brussels sprouts.* **10.** *Arrange relish tray; set on table.* **11.** *Pour water and tomato juice.*

CROWN ROAST OF PORK WITH MUSHROOM STUFFING

7½- to 8-pound pork crown roast (about 20 ribs)
2 teaspoons salt
1 teaspoon pepper
Mushroom Stuffing (right)

Heat oven to 325°. Sprinkle roast with salt and pepper. Place bone ends up in roasting pan; wrap bone ends with aluminum foil to prevent excessive browning. Place a small mixing bowl in crown to hold shape of roast. Insert meat thermometer so tip is in thick part of meat. Roast uncovered 3 to 4 hours, or until meat is tender. Thermometer should register 185°. An hour before meat is done, remove bowl and fill center of crown with Mushroom Stuffing; cover just the stuffing with aluminum foil during first 30 minutes. When done, place roast on large platter. Remove foil wrapping; place paper frills on bone ends. To carve, slice between ribs. *12 servings.*

SALT-SPARKED TOMATO JUICE

1 can (46 ounces) tomato juice
¼ cup lemon juice
2 teaspoons salt
1 teaspoon Worcestershire sauce
1 drop Tabasco
1 egg white, slightly beaten
Salt

Combine all ingredients except egg white and salt; chill. Before serving, brush rim of each glass with egg white; dip into salt. Fill glasses with chilled juice. *12 servings.*

Mushroom Stuffing

½ cup minced onion
⅔ cup butter
8 cups croutons
1 cup chopped celery
1 teaspoon salt
½ teaspoon pepper
1 teaspoon crushed thyme or marjoram leaves or
    ground sage
1 teaspoon poultry seasoning
1 can (6 ounces) sliced mushrooms, drained, or
    1 pound fresh mushrooms, washed, trimmed
    and sliced

Cook and stir onion in butter until tender. Stir in part of croutons; heat slowly, stirring to prevent excessive browning. Place in large bowl. Mix in remaining croutons and ingredients. Garnish top of stuffing, if desired.

How to Carve a Crown Roast

1. Carving a crown roast is simpler than it looks! First remove any garnish from center that might interfere. If the stuffing is the loose, fluffy type, spoon it into an auxiliary bowl. Compact stuffing may be sliced with the meat.

2. Slice down between the ribs, serving one or two chops at a time. For easier carving, the backbone should be removed by the meatman.

BUTTERED BRUSSELS SPROUTS

Prepare 3 packages (10 ounces each) frozen Brussels sprouts as directed on package. Season with ¼ cup butter. *12 servings.*

TINY CLOVED ONIONS

Whole cloves
3 cans (1 pound each) whole onions
½ cup butter or margarine
1 cup brown sugar (packed)

Insert cloves in ends of each onion. Cook onions (with liquid) 5 minutes over low heat; drain. Melt butter in skillet; add onions and stir gently to coat. Sprinkle with brown sugar. Cook, stirring often, until onions are golden brown and caramelized. *12 servings.*

CORN RELISH

½ cup sugar
½ teaspoon salt
½ teaspoon celery seed
¼ teaspoon mustard seed
½ cup vinegar
¼ teaspoon Tabasco
1 can (12 ounces) whole kernel corn
2 tablespoons chopped green pepper
1 tablespoon chopped pimiento
1 tablespoon instant minced onion

In small saucepan heat sugar, salt, celery seed, mustard seed, vinegar and Tabasco to boiling; boil 2 minutes. Remove from heat; stir in remaining ingredients. Cool and refrigerate in covered bowl. For better flavor let stand several days. *Makes 2 cups.*

FAN-TAN ROLLS

Wrap 12 baked fan-tan rolls in aluminum foil. Heat in 325° oven 20 minutes. *12 rolls.*

BUTTER BRICKLE SILHOUETTE PIE

Prepare two Silhouette Parfait Pies (page 130) except—substitute Butter Brickle ice cream for the vanilla.

Buckingham Dinner

Cream of Almond Soup
Roast Beef with Yorkshire Pudding
Horseradish Sauce   Asparagus with Olives
Spiced Fruit Plates
Raspberry Crown Royal
Tea   Coffee

If you want to do something very special for a man—celebrate his birthday or his promotion or simply entertain *his* friends—here's a surefire way to please him, and everyone else too. He'll never look more lordly than when the impressive rib roast is placed before him and he begins the masterful carving. (But just in case he's not a practiced carver, we've included an alternate rolled roast recipe. It's a bit costlier but easier to handle.) Actually a big roast, standing or rolled, isn't the extravagance it may seem. First, there's practically no margin for error; even the newest cook can be sure of success if she follows the roasting chart. And secondly, with a marvelous piece of meat, the go-alongs can be simple and inexpensive. Yorkshire Pudding, for example, is a conversation-maker that costs mere pennies, and the cream soup makes the gourmet most of a handful of almonds.

Serving suggestions: Soup may be served in cream soup bowls at the dining room table. Then—man's big moment—the roast is brought in and the host carves and serves it along with the Yorkshire Pudding. The asparagus and sauce are passed. After the main course the hostess takes over and serves dessert. Coffee may be served with dessert, or later in the living room.

PLAN FOR PREPARATION

Day before: 1. *Prepare dessert.* **2.** *Chill spiced peaches. Wash, dry and chill endive. Prepare cream cheese filling for salads, if desired.*

Day of party: 1. *Place meat in oven; roast.* **2.** *Set table.* **3.** *Arrange salads; refrigerate.* **4.** *Prepare Horseradish Sauce; refrigerate.* **5.** *Prepare soup; keep hot.* **6.** *Prepare Yorkshire Pudding; place in oven to bake.* **7.** *Prepare coffee.* **8.** *Cook asparagus.* **9.** *Pour water.*

CREAM OF ALMOND SOUP

1 tablespoon butter or margarine
1 tablespoon flour
¾ teaspoon salt
⅛ teaspoon pepper
1½ cups chicken broth or bouillon
½ cup finely chopped almonds, toasted
2 cups light cream
2 teaspoons grated lemon peel
Paprika

Melt butter over low heat. Blend in flour, salt and pepper. Cook over low heat, stirring until mixture is smooth and bubbly. Remove from heat. Add chicken broth and almonds. Boil 1 minute, stirring constantly. Stir in cream. Heat through but do not boil. Sprinkle with lemon peel and paprika. *8 appetizer-size servings.*

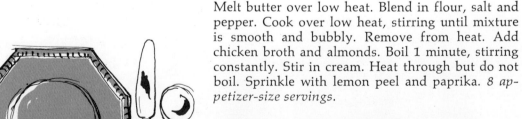

ROAST BEEF WITH YORKSHIRE PUDDING

Select a standing or rolled rib roast. For a company meal, choose one larger than necessary for adequate servings. To serve 8 generously (with some meat left over), we suggest an 8-pound standing rib roast or a 4- to 5-pound rolled roast. For easier carving, be sure to check that the meatman has separated the backbone from the ribs, so the backbone can be easily removed in the kitchen after roasting.

Heat oven to 325°. Wipe roast with damp cloth or paper towel, if desired; do not wash. Season meat with salt and pepper. Place a standing rib roast fat side up in shallow open pan (ribs form a natural rack). Place a rolled rib roast fat side up on rack in shallow roasting pan. Insert meat thermometer so the bulb is in the center of the thickest part of meat and the point does not rest in fat or on bone. Add no water and do not cover; do not baste or turn roast. Roast according to timetable (right), using thermometer reading as the final guide to correct doneness. (Roast will be easier to carve if allowed to "set" 15 to 20 minutes after removing from oven. Since meat continues to cook upon removal from oven, it should be removed when the thermometer reads 5 to 10° lower than the desired doneness.)

Fifteen minutes before roast is removed from oven, prepare Yorkshire Pudding (below). Heat square pan, 9x9x2 inches, in oven. Remove roast from oven; spoon off ½ cup of the hot drippings.

Increase oven temperature to 425°. Return roast to oven. Place hot drippings in heated square pan; pour in pudding batter. Bake 15 minutes. Remove roast and continue baking pudding another 20 minutes. This means that the roast and batter bake in the same oven 15 minutes, then the roast is removed to set for easier carving.

To serve, cut pudding into 9 squares. For au jus, spoon off excess fat from pan drippings (fat plus juices); quickly reheat juices and pour into a gravy boat. Serve juices spooned over meat and pudding, as desired.

YORKSHIRE PUDDING

It will puff high during baking, then collapse, leaving high crisp edges.

1 cup Gold Medal Flour* (regular or Wondra)
½ teaspoon salt
1 cup milk
2 eggs

If using Gold Medal regular flour, beat all ingredients with a rotary beater *just* until smooth. When using Wondra flour, stir ingredients together with a fork just until smooth. Bake as directed above.

*Do not use Self-Rising Flour in this recipe.

Timetable for Rib Roast		
	Approximate Cooking Time (Minutes per Pound)	Interior Temperature When Removed from Oven
Standing Rib Roast (6 to 8 pounds)		
Rare	23 to 25	140°
Medium	27 to 30	160°
Well done	32 to 35	170°
Rolled Rib Roast (5 to 7 pounds)		
Rare	32	140°
Medium	38	160°
Well done	48	170°

How to Carve Standing Rib Roast

1. Remove backbone in the kitchen after meat is roasted. If necessary, remove wedge-shaped slice from large end of roast so it will stand firmly on this end. Place meat with ribs at left of carver, rib ends toward him.

Insert fork between top ribs. Starting at right outside edge, carve a ¼-inch slice across "face" of roast to rib bone.

2. Cut along rib bone with tip of knife to release slice.

3. Slide knife back under slice and steady it with fork; lift slice to side of platter or auxiliary platter.

How to Carve Rolled Rib Roast

Stand a rolled rib roast on end, with the broader cut surface down and smaller end up. (Do not remove cords.) Insert fork into left side of meat and carve across "face" of meat.

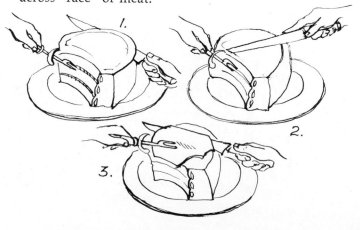

ASPARAGUS WITH OLIVES

Prepare 2 packages (10 ounces each) frozen asparagus spears as directed on package; drain. Toss gently with ¼ cup butter and ¼ cup sliced pitted ripe olives until butter melts. *8 servings.*

HORSERADISH SAUCE

Whip ½ cup whipping cream. Fold in 3 tablespoons well-drained horseradish and ½ teaspoon salt. *Makes 1 cup.*

SPICED FRUIT PLATES

2 packages (3 ounces each) cream cheese, softened
½ cup chopped celery
1 jar (1 pound 1 ounce) spiced peaches,
    drained and halved
Curly endive
4 oranges, pared and sectioned

Whip cream cheese until fluffy; stir in celery. Fill centers of peach halves with cream cheese mixture. Arrange curly endive on individual salad plates. Place filled peach half in center of each plate; surround with orange sections. If desired, top mound of cream cheese with celery slice. *8 servings.*

RASPBERRY CROWN ROYAL

3 packages (10 ounces each) frozen raspberries,
    partially thawed and broken apart
2 envelopes (2 tablespoons) unflavored gelatin
3 tablespoons granulated sugar
1 tablespoon lemon juice
5 egg whites
Dash salt
¼ cup granulated sugar
1 teaspoon unflavored gelatin
3 tablespoons water
3 cups whipping cream
1 tablespoon confectioners' sugar

Extend rim of 7½-cup soufflé dish 3 inches by taping band of double thickness aluminum foil around edge. Reserve a few whole raspberries for garnish, if desired. In saucepan combine remaining raspberries, 2 envelopes gelatin, 3 tablespoons granulated sugar and the lemon juice. Heat to boiling, stirring constantly, until gelatin dissolves. Remove from heat; chill until mixture mounds when dropped from spoon. Beat egg whites with salt until frothy; gradually beat in ¼ cup granulated sugar. Continue beating until stiff and glossy. Soften 1 teaspoon gelatin in the water; dissolve over boiling water. Beat cream, confectioners' sugar and dissolved gelatin until soft peaks form. Reserve 1 cup whipped cream mixture; cover and refrigerate. Fold egg whites and half of remaining whipped cream into raspberry mixture. Spoon raspberry mixture into soufflé dish until it is even with rim of dish. Alternate thin layers of remaining whipped cream and raspberry mixture, ending with raspberry mixture. Refrigerate overnight. Just before serving, run edge of knife around inside of foil band and remove band. Place reserved whipped cream in decorators' tube; decorate top of soufflé. Garnish with reserved raspberries, if desired. To serve, scoop up from bottom of soufflé so each person will receive both raspberry and cream portions. *10 to 12 servings.*

Chafing Dish Buffet

Stroganoff Superb
Oven-easy Rice   Buttered Green Beans
Tomatoes Vinaigrette   Crisp Celery Fans
Small Crusty Rolls
Bowl of Sherbet Balls   Russian Tea Cakes
Coffee

There's something particularly appetizing about a rich, creamy main dish like Beef Stroganoff bubbling in a chafing dish on a sideboard or buffet table. The chafing dish makes a simple yet elegant serving dish—and it's terrific for keeping your main dish hot for second-serving time. Because the meat is cut into bite-size pieces, this is a meal that can be eaten from a plate or tray on the lap—no need for knives or individual table space.

Serving suggestions: Everything except dessert should be on the buffet table at dinner call. Guests serve themselves to rice, stroganoff and beans and, if they like, they may make a separate salad course of the tomatoes. When the main course is finished and the dishes have been removed, bring in the sherbet balls arranged in an attractive glass serving bowl, along with individual sherbet glasses or bowls. Serve from the buffet with cookies and coffee.

⌢⌢⌢⌢⌢ PLAN FOR PREPARATION ⌢⌢⌢⌢⌢

Day before: 1. *Bake or purchase cookies. (Store in covered container.)* **2.** *Scoop sherbet balls; freeze.*

Day of party: 1. *Prepare Tomatoes Vinaigrette; cover and chill. Wash lettuce and prepare lettuce cups. Place on tray; cover and chill.* **2.** *Set table.* **3.** *Cut up and measure ingredients for stroganoff; set aside.* **4.** *Bake rice.* **5.** *Prepare coffee.* **6.** *Fill water glasses; place on tray for passing to seated guests later.* **7.** *Cook stroganoff.* **8.** *While stroganoff simmers, cook beans.* **9.** *Arrange tomato salads on serving platter.*

Permanent Party Gear

A chafing dish is a boon to the hostess. It's ideal for buffet service—for main dishes, sauces, hot hors d'oeuvres. But it's a special blessing for the pressed-for-time working girl who entertains with a main dish that she can prepare gracefully in the chafing dish in full view of her guests.

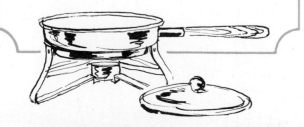

STROGANOFF SUPERB

2 pounds sirloin steak or beef tenderloin
1 pound fresh mushrooms, sliced
1 cup minced onion
¼ cup butter or margarine
2 cans (10½ ounces each) beef bouillon
¼ cup catsup
2 small cloves garlic, crushed
2 teaspoons salt
⅓ cup Gold Medal Flour (regular or Wondra)
2 cups dairy sour cream
Oven-easy Rice (page 54)

Cut meat into bite-size pieces. In skillet or blazer pan of chafing dish, cook and stir mushrooms and onion in butter until onion is tender; remove mushrooms and onion. In same skillet brown meat lightly on both sides. Set aside ¾ cup bouillon; add remaining bouillon, the catsup, garlic and salt to skillet; stir to mix. Cover and simmer 15 minutes. Blend reserved bouillon and the flour; stir into meat mixture. Add mushrooms and onion. Heat to boiling, stirring constantly; boil 1 minute. Stir in sour cream; heat. Serve over rice. *6 servings.*

OVEN-EASY RICE

3 cups boiling water
1½ cups uncooked regular rice
1½ teaspoons salt

Heat oven to 350°. Mix ingredients thoroughly in 1½-quart casserole or oblong baking dish, 11½x7½ x1½ inches. Cover dish tightly with casserole lid or aluminum foil. (Lid or foil cover must be tight enough to prevent escape of steam.) Bake 25 to 30 minutes, or until liquid is absorbed and rice is tender. Fluff and spoon into bowl to serve. *6 servings.*

BUTTERED GREEN BEANS

Prepare 2 packages (9 ounces each) frozen cut green beans as directed on package. Season with ¼ cup butter. *6 servings.*

TOMATOES VINAIGRETTE

12 thick tomato slices
1 cup olive oil
⅓ cup wine vinegar
2 teaspoons crushed oregano leaves
1 teaspoon salt
½ teaspoon pepper
½ teaspoon dry mustard
2 cloves garlic, crushed
6 lettuce cups
Minced green onion
Minced parsley

Arrange tomato slices in square baking dish, 8x8x2 inches. Combine oil, vinegar and next 5 seasonings; spoon over tomatoes. Cover. Chill 2 to 3 hours, spooning dressing over tomatoes occasionally. To serve, arrange tomato slices in lettuce cups and sprinkle with minced green onion and parsley. Drizzle each salad with small amount of the dressing. *6 servings.*

BOWL OF SHERBET BALLS

With small scoop make sherbet balls from 1 quart lime sherbet and 1 pint lemon sherbet. Place on baking sheet or waxed paper; freeze. At serving time, alternate colored sherbet balls in glass serving bowl. *6 servings.*

RUSSIAN TEA CAKES

1 cup soft butter or margarine
½ cup sifted confectioners' sugar
1 teaspoon vanilla
2¼ cups Gold Medal Flour* (regular or Wondra)
¼ teaspoon salt
¾ cup finely chopped nuts

Heat oven to 400°. Mix butter, sugar and vanilla thoroughly. Stir flour, salt and nuts together. With hands, work in flour mixture until dough holds together. Form dough into 1-inch balls. Place on ungreased baking sheet. Bake 10 to 12 minutes or until set but not brown. While warm, roll in confectioners' sugar. Cool. Roll in sugar again. *Makes about 4 dozen 1-inch cookies.*

Do not use Self-Rising Flour in this recipe.

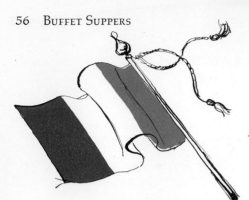

Old Italy Buffet

Baked Lasagne
Kabobed Antipasto Salad   Garlic Toast
Fruit Platter Pie   Espresso

If your friends are legion but your table space limited, here's a party tailor-made for you. You can serve as many people as you have chairs for, because this delicious colorful meal can be eaten from a plate or tray balanced on the lap. There's nothing to cut with a knife, nothing to run off a tipped plate. Furthermore, the eye-catching antipasto salad arranged like a bright bouquet is all the centerpiece your buffet table needs. And, hidden asset, nearly everything can be ready well before the guests arrive.

Be sure to set the stage for any party with a foreign theme. Use two flags—one American and, in this case, one Italian—crossed and attached to the outside of the front door. Or honor the national colors in your choice of tablecloth and napkins.

Serving suggestions: Have the entire meal on display when company comes in to the dining area. Place the lasagne at one end of the table so you can spoon it easily onto guests' plates, then let them help themselves to bread and the antipasto salad. On a separate table or tea cart set out dessert and coffee service. When the main course is finished, guests return their plates to the cart and pick up pie and espresso.

BAKED LASAGNE

1½ pounds ground beef
½ pound ground lean pork
1 cup chopped onion
1 clove garlic, crushed
1 can (1 pound 12 ounces) tomatoes
1 can (15 ounces) tomato sauce
1½ tablespoons parsley flakes
1½ tablespoons sugar
1 teaspoon salt
1 teaspoon crushed basil leaves
1 carton (2 pounds) creamed cottage cheese
   (large curd)
½ cup grated Parmesan cheese
1 tablespoon parsley flakes
1 teaspoon salt
1 teaspoon crushed oregano leaves
8 ounces lasagne noodles, cooked and well drained
¾ pound mozzarella cheese, shredded
½ cup grated Parmesan cheese

Cook ground beef, ground pork, onion and garlic in heavy Dutch oven or roaster until meat is browned and onion is tender. Drain off excess fat. Add tomatoes and break up with a fork. Stir in tomato sauce, 1½ tablespoons parsley flakes, the sugar, 1 teaspoon salt and the basil; simmer uncovered 1 hour, or until mixture is as thick as a good spaghetti sauce.

Heat oven to 350°. Mix cottage cheese, ½ cup Parmesan cheese, 1 tablespoon parsley flakes, 1 teaspoon salt and the oregano. In oblong baking dish, 13½x9x2 inches, layer half each of noodles, sauce, mozzarella cheese and cottage cheese mixture. Repeat; reserve enough sauce for a thin top layer. Spread sauce over top; sprinkle with ½ cup Parmesan cheese. Bake uncovered 45 to 55 minutes, or until cheese is bubbly in center. Let stand 15 minutes after removing from oven. To serve, cut into squares. *8 to 10 servings.*

KABOBED ANTIPASTO SALAD

Celery stalks (with leaves)
Green onions (with tops)
Cheddar cheese cubes
Sliced pepperoni
Sliced prosciutto
1 can (2 ounces) anchovies rolled with capers
Garlic Olives (below)
1 large eggplant
Crisp salad greens
4 hard-cooked eggs, sliced

Alternate all ingredients except eggplant, salad greens and egg slices on wooden skewers. (Holding celery at a diagonal angle, insert skewer through center.) Stand eggplant upright (it may be necessary to level off bottom); insert skewers in eggplant. For an attractive arrangement, rotate ends of celery so leaves fill any large vacant areas. Place on bed of salad greens. Arrange egg slices on greens. *10 servings.*

Garlic Olives

1 can (8 ounces) pitted ripe olives, drained
1 jar (7 ounces) green olives, drained
½ cup vinegar
½ cup olive oil
½ cup salad oil
1 small onion, sliced
1 clove garlic, sliced

Split olives slightly; place in jar with remaining ingredients. Cover tightly and shake. Refrigerate 2 or 3 hours or overnight.

PLAN FOR PREPARATION

Day before: 1. *Marinate olives for antipasto salad; hard cook eggs.* **2.** *Prepare lasagne, if desired; cover and refrigerate.* **3.** *Bake pie shell.* **4.** *Prepare sauce for pie.*

Day of party: 1. *Complete preparation of pie; refrigerate.* **2.** *Arrange antipasto salad; refrigerate.* **3.** *Set table and dessert cart.* **4.** *Bake lasagne.* **5.** *Prepare and heat toast.* **6.** *Prepare espresso.* **7.** *Remove lasagne from oven; let stand.*

GARLIC TOAST

Mix ½ cup soft butter, ¼ cup snipped parsley and ½ teaspoon garlic powder. Diagonally slice 1 loaf (1 pound) French bread into 1-inch slices. Spread cut surfaces with butter mixture. Reassemble loaf; place on baking sheet. Bake in 350° oven 30 minutes. *10 servings.*

FRUIT PLATTER PIE

2 of our pie crust sticks
Green grapes, orange, banana and peach slices, strawberry halves (drained, if necessary)
1 to 2 tablespoons sugar
Clear Orange Sauce (page 76)
Sweetened whipped cream

Heat oven to 475°. Prepare pastry as directed on inside wrapper except—roll into a 13- to 14-inch circle on lightly floured cloth-covered board. Roll dough around rolling pin and unroll on pizza pan. Pinch or pleat pastry; prick. Bake 8 to 10 minutes. Cool. Arrange fruit on pastry; sprinkle with sugar. Spoon Clear Orange Sauce over fruit. Cut into wedges; serve with whipped cream and additional sauce.

Ham Buffets Tailore

A truly smart hostess is one who knows the special delight (economy, too) of first-of-the-season foods. Always memorable are the early fresh strawberries and asparagus, the straight-from-the-garden green onions and leaf lettuce of spring. And just as warmly welcome, later in the year, are the first fresh squash, cauliflower and Brussels sprouts of fall.

The companion-piece menus here are both built around a beautiful big pre-sliced ham, one of the happiest choices a hostess can make. But there the resemblance ends. The autumn version, perfect for an after-the-football-game supper, lends itself to a casual presentation with bright-colored cloth, pottery dishes and a harvest centerpiece of fruits, vegetables or nuts. The springtime variation may be dressed up with white linen, fine china and spring flowers to do full honor to a wedding rehearsal dinner or an anniversary party.

Two Seasons

Serving suggestions: In both cases, although the guests serve themselves from a buffet, the meal requires table space for eating. Follow the buffet and table arrangements described on page 13.

〰〰〰 **PLAN FOR PREPARATION** 〰〰〰

Day before: 1. *Prepare dough for rolls; refrigerate.* **2.** *Bake pie crusts.* **3.** *Stud ham with cloves, if desired.* **4.** *Wash, dry and chill salad greens. Cut salad vegetables; cover and chill.* **5.** *Chill relish (jar of pickled cauliflower or watermelon pickles).* **6.** *If serving Spring Ham Buffet, prepare Chive Dressing; cover and refrigerate.*

Day of party: 1. *Fill pies and chill (early in day).* **2.** *Shape rolls, let rise and bake.* **3.** *Set table.* **4.** *Prepare ham glaze.* **5.** *Bake ham.* **6.** *Prepare and cook vegetables.* **7.** *Prepare coffee.* **8.** *Reheat rolls.* **9.** *Pour water.* **10.** *Toss salad.*

〰〰〰〰〰〰〰〰〰〰〰〰〰〰

Spring Ham Buffet

Horseradish-glazed Buffet Ham
Parsleyed New Potatoes   Buttered Fresh Asparagus
Garden-fresh Salad Bowl   Watermelon Pickles
Easy Refrigerator Rolls   Butter
Strawberry Glacé Cream Pies   Coffee

HORSERADISH-GLAZED BUFFET HAM

5½- to 6-pound fully cooked boneless ham, cut
  into ¼-inch slices and tied
1 cup brown sugar (packed)
⅓ cup horseradish
¼ cup lemon juice

Your meatman will cut ham into ¼-inch slices and
reassemble ham in its original form by tying slices
together with cord. Heat oven to 325°. If desired,
insert whole cloves in ham. Place ham on rack in
roasting pan; bake 1 to 1½ hours. Combine remaining ingredients in small saucepan. Heat to boiling.
To glaze ham, turn oven temperature to 400°; pour
brown sugar mixture over ham and return to oven
15 minutes. Baste ham occasionally with glaze. If
desired, garnish ham with orange-slice "daisies."
10 to 12 servings.

PARSLEYED NEW POTATOES

Lightly scrub 5 pounds new potatoes. Pare a band
around center of each potato, if desired. Boil about
30 minutes or until tender. Just before serving, season with ½ cup melted butter; sprinkle with 2 tablespoons snipped parsley. *12 servings.*

BUTTERED FRESH ASPARAGUS

Break off tough ends of 4 pounds fresh asparagus;
wash asparagus. Remove scales if sandy or tough.
Leave stalks whole; tie in bunches with string. Cook
upright in salted water in narrow deep pan 10 to 20
minutes or until tender. Drain; season with butter.
12 servings.

GARDEN-FRESH SALAD BOWL

1 bunch leaf lettuce
1 head romaine
1 bunch escarole
1 cup sliced radishes
6 green onions, cut into short strips
Chive Dressing (below)

Tear greens into bite-size pieces. Toss greens, radishes and onions with Chive Dressing. *12 servings.*

Chive Dressing

½ cup salad oil
¼ cup vinegar
2 tablespoons finely chopped chives
1 tablespoon finely chopped green pepper
1 teaspoon sugar
1 teaspoon dry mustard
¾ teaspoon salt
½ teaspoon monosodium glutamate
⅛ teaspoon red pepper

Shake all ingredients well in tightly covered jar.
Keep in covered jar in refrigerator. Just before serving, shake again to blend. *Makes 1 cup.*

EASY REFRIGERATOR ROLLS

No need to knead this dough! Bake half the rolls for one party; bake and freeze the remainder for another time. Or shape the other half of dough into a coffee cake for a family treat.

 2 packages active dry yeast
 2 cups warm water (105 to 115°)
 ½ cup sugar
 ¼ cup shortening
 1 egg
 2 teaspoons salt
 6½ to 7 cups Gold Medal Flour*
 (regular or Wondra)

In mixing bowl dissolve yeast in warm water. Add sugar, shortening, egg, salt and half the flour; beat until smooth. Mix in remaining flour with spoon or hand until dough is easy to handle. Place in greased bowl; turn once to bring greased side up. Cover loosely with plastic wrap or aluminum foil. Refrigerate at least 2 hours. When dough rises, punch it down occasionally. When fresh rolls are desired, remove dough from refrigerator; cut off amount needed and return remaining dough to refrigerator. Dough may be kept 3 to 4 days.

About 2 hours before baking, shape dough into desired rolls (below). Cover and let rise until double, 1½ to 2 hours. Heat oven to 400°. Bake rolls 12 to 15 minutes or until golden brown. *Makes 3 to 4 dozen rolls or 5 dozen butterhorns.*

*If using Self-Rising Flour, omit salt.

Cloverleaf Rolls: Form bits of dough into balls about 1 inch in diameter. Place 3 balls in each greased muffin cup. Brush with margarine or butter.

Quick Four-leaf Clover Rolls: Form pieces of dough into balls about 2 inches in diameter. Place each in greased muffin cup. With scissors, cut each ball of dough in half, then into quarters.

Butterhorns: Roll about ¼ of dough at a time into a 12-inch circle, ¼ inch thick. Spread with soft butter or margarine. Cut into 16 wedges. Beginning at rounded edge, roll up. Place point side down on greased baking sheet. Curve to form crescents.

Picnic Buns: Roll about ¼ of dough at a time into a 7½-inch square, about ½ inch thick. Cut into nine 2½-inch squares. Place on greased baking sheet.

STRAWBERRY GLACÉ CREAM PIES

 2 of our pie crust sticks
 ½ cup finely chopped almonds
 2 cups dairy sour cream
 2 cups milk
 2 packages (about 3½ ounces each) vanilla instant pudding
 2 pints fresh strawberries, sliced
 1 cup water
 1 cup sugar
 3 tablespoons cornstarch

Prepare two 9-inch Baked Pie Shells as directed on inside wrapper except—add almonds to crumbled mix.

Beat sour cream and milk with rotary beater until smooth. Blend in pudding (dry mix) until mixture is smooth and slightly thickened. Divide equally between cooled baked pie shells.

Combine 1 cup sliced strawberries and ½ cup of the water in small saucepan; simmer about 3 minutes. Stir together sugar and cornstarch; blend in remaining ½ cup water. Stir into hot strawberry mixture. Cook, stirring constantly, until mixture thickens and boils. Boil and stir 1 minute. Cool. Arrange remaining sliced berries equally over cream fillings. Pour cooled strawberry glacé over berries; chill until firm, at least 2 hours. *Makes 2 pies.*

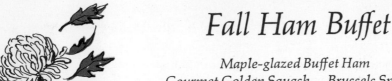

Fall Ham Buffet

Maple-glazed Buffet Ham
Gourmet Golden Squash   Brussels Sprouts
Iceberg Salad   Pickled Cauliflower
Easy Refrigerator Rolls (page 61)   Butter   Currant Jelly
Ambrosial Cream Pies   Coffee

MAPLE-GLAZED BUFFET HAM

Follow recipe for Horseradish-glazed Buffet Ham (page 60) except — omit brown sugar, horseradish and lemon juice. Pour Maple Glaze (below) over ham and bake as directed. If desired, garnish with Kieffer pears, spiced peaches and curly endive.

Maple Glaze

Combine ¾ cup brown sugar (packed), 1 cup dark corn syrup, 2 tablespoons prepared mustard and 1 tablespoon maple flavoring.

GOURMET GOLDEN SQUASH

12 cups cubed pared Hubbard squash
¼ cup butter or margarine
2 cups dairy sour cream
1 cup finely chopped onion
2 teaspoons salt
½ teaspoon pepper
½ cup milk

Place squash in saucepan with small amount boiling salted water. Cover; cook 15 minutes or until tender. Drain squash and add remaining ingredients; mash. Mound mixture into 2-quart casserole. Bake in 400° oven 20 to 30 minutes or until heated. *12 servings.*

BRUSSELS SPROUTS

Remove discolored leaves and stem ends from 4½ pounds fresh Brussels sprouts. Cook uncovered in enough boiling salted water to cover, 8 to 10 minutes or until tender. *12 servings.*

ICEBERG SALAD

1 bag spinach, torn into bite-size pieces (about 6 cups)
2 heads lettuce, torn into bite-size pieces (about 12 cups)
½ cup chopped green pepper
2 cups sliced fresh mushrooms
Bottled oil and vinegar dressing

Combine all ingredients except dressing in large bowl; cover and refrigerate. Just before serving, toss greens with dressing. *12 servings.*

AMBROSIAL CREAM PIES

2 of our pie crust sticks
2 cans (1 pound each) pitted dark sweet cherries, drained
2 cans (13 ounces each) pineapple chunks, drained
2 cans (11 ounces each) mandarin orange segments, drained
1 cup flaked coconut
1 cup dairy sour cream
1 cup whipping cream
⅔ cup brown sugar (packed)
Toasted slivered almonds

Prepare two 9-inch Baked Pie Shells as directed on inside wrapper. Combine fruit and coconut in bowl. In small mixer bowl, beat sour cream and whipping cream until thick. Fold in sugar. Pour 2 cups of the cream mixture over fruit and coconut. Dividing fruit mixture equally, pour into pie shells. Spread half of the remaining cream mixture over top of each pie. Chill at least 3 hours. Before serving, sprinkle pies with almonds. *Makes 2 pies.*

"Dutch Lunch" Buffet

Corned Beef and Caraway Cheese Platter
Cream Mustard
Honey-glazed Barbecued Ribs
Speedy Baked Beans   Buffet Slaw
Best Rye Bread   Swiss Loaf   Butter
Deviled Eggs and Sliced Tomatoes
Square Apple Pie   Cinnamon Ice Cream
Coffee

Outdoor appetites sharpened by an afternoon in the stadium or an evening skating party demand hearty, savory fare, and lots of it. This buffet is guaranteed to satisfy even the hungriest sports enthusiast. Furthermore, practically everything can be prepared ahead of time, enabling the hostess to join wholeheartedly in the outdoor portion of the party and still have supper on the buffet before the guests have finished thawing out. Keep in mind, too, that it's a meal men like any time, and with all the "do-aheads" it's an especially easy way to entertain for a stag party or when you have weekend company. The touches that make it special: two unusual homemade breads and an entirely different kind of pie à la mode.

Serving suggestions: Everything except dessert goes on the buffet at one time and each guest serves himself. When the main course is finished, clear the dishes and serve the warm apple pie and cinnamon ice cream from either the buffet or the kitchen.

PLAN FOR PREPARATION

Day before: 1. *Prepare and bake ribs. Cool; cover and refrigerate.* **2.** *Prepare and bake Rye Bread.* **3.** *Prepare dough for Swiss Loaf; cover and refrigerate.* **4.** *Flavor ice cream; freeze.*

Day of party: 1. *Bake Swiss Loaf.* **2.** *Prepare and bake apple pie.* **3.** *Arrange corned beef and cheese platter; cover and chill.* **4.** *Prepare deviled eggs; slice tomatoes. Cover and chill.* **5.** *Prepare Cream Mustard; cover and refrigerate.* **6.** *Combine ingredients for baked beans; cover and refrigerate.* **7.** *Shred cabbage and green peppers; cover tightly and refrigerate.* **8.** *Set table.*

Just before serving: 1. *Heat ribs and bake beans.* **2.** *Prepare coffee.* **3.** *Toss slaw salad.* **4.** *Arrange egg and tomato platter.* **5.** *Pour water.* **6.** *While serving, heat apple pie.*

CORNED BEEF AND CARAWAY CHEESE PLATTER

On large platter or serving plate lined with curly endive, arrange 1½ pounds sliced corned beef and ¾ pound sliced caraway cheese. *8 servings.*

CREAM MUSTARD

1 tablespoon prepared mustard
¼ teaspoon lemon juice
Dash salt
Dash pepper
½ cup whipping cream, whipped

Combine mustard, lemon juice, salt and pepper. Fold into whipped cream. Serve with corned beef. *Makes 1 cup.*

HONEY-GLAZED BARBECUED RIBS

4 pounds loin back ribs, cut into 1½-inch pieces
1 cup soy sauce
½ cup dry sherry
2 tablespoons honey
1 clove garlic, crushed
½ cup honey

Place ribs in plastic bag or shallow glass dish. Combine remaining ingredients except ½ cup honey; pour over meat. Fasten bag securely or cover dish with plastic wrap. Refrigerate 4 hours, turning ribs occasionally. Remove ribs from marinade; reserve marinade.

Heat oven to 325°. Place ribs in jelly roll pan, 15½x10½x1 inch; bake 1½ hours, basting occasionally with reserved marinade. Remove from oven; brush with ½ cup honey. If desired, chill overnight.

To heat ribs, wrap in aluminum foil and place in 350° oven 45 minutes. *8 servings.*

SPEEDY BAKED BEANS

6 slices bacon, diced
1 cup minced onion
3 cans (1 pound 3 ounces each) baked beans (with pork)
1½ teaspoons prepared mustard
⅓ cup chili sauce

Heat oven to 350°. Cook and stir bacon and onion until bacon is crisp. Stir in remaining ingredients; pour into 2-quart casserole. Bake uncovered 45 minutes, or until beans are heated through. *8 servings.*

BUFFET SLAW

12 cups shredded cabbage
2 green peppers, shredded (about 1¼ cups)
¼ cup sugar
2 teaspoons salt
1 teaspoon dry mustard
⅛ teaspoon pepper
⅔ cup vinegar
⅓ cup salad oil

Combine cabbage and green pepper in large mixing bowl. Stir together remaining ingredients. Pour mixture over cabbage and green pepper; toss to mix thoroughly. Place salad in bowl lined with cabbage leaves; garnish with green pepper strips, if desired. *8 servings.*

BEST RYE BREAD

2 packages active dry yeast
1½ cups warm water (105 to 115°)
¼ cup molasses
⅓ cup sugar
1 tablespoon salt
2 tablespoons shortening
3 to 4 tablespoons grated orange peel or
    1 teaspoon anise seed
2½ cups medium rye flour
2¼ to 2¾ cups Gold Medal Flour*
    (regular or Wondra)
Cornmeal

In mixing bowl dissolve yeast in warm water; stir in molasses, sugar, salt, shortening and orange peel. Mix in rye flour with a spoon until smooth. Stir in flour, mixing with hands until thoroughly blended. Turn out onto lightly floured board. Cover and let rest 10 to 15 minutes. Knead until smooth. Place in greased bowl; turn greased side up. Cover; let rise in warm place (85°) until double, about 1 hour. Punch dough down, round up, cover and let rise again until double, about 40 minutes.

Punch down; divide dough in half; shape into two round, slightly flattened loaves. Grease a baking sheet and sprinkle with cornmeal. Place loaves on opposite corners of baking sheet. Cover; let rise 1 hour. Heat oven to 375°. Bake 30 to 35 minutes. *Makes 2 loaves.*

*If using Self-Rising Flour, omit salt.

SWISS LOAF

1 package active dry yeast
¼ cup warm water (105 to 115°)
¼ cup lukewarm milk, scalded then cooled
1½ teaspoons sugar
1 teaspoon salt
½ cup soft butter or margarine
3 eggs
2¾ cups Gold Medal Flour* (regular or Wondra)
1 cup diced Swiss cheese (¼-inch cubes)

Dissolve yeast in warm water. Add milk, sugar, salt, butter, eggs and half the flour. Beat 10 minutes on mixer. Add remaining flour; blend in with spoon until smooth. Cover with cloth and let rise in warm place (85°) until double, 1 to 2 hours. (If kitchen is cool, place dough on a rack over a bowl of hot water and cover completely with a towel.) Punch down; cover and refrigerate overnight.

Punch down; form flat ball. Knead in cheese until well distributed. Form round ball; place in greased 8-inch pie pan. Let rise until double, 1 to 2 hours. Heat oven to 375°. Bake 30 minutes. *Makes 1 loaf.*

If using Self-Rising Flour, omit salt.

DEVILED EGGS AND SLICED TOMATOES

8 hard-cooked eggs, cut in half and yolks removed
¼ cup mayonnaise or salad dressing
1½ teaspoons horseradish
2 teaspoons Worcestershire sauce
1½ teaspoons lemon juice
½ teaspoon salt
Dash pepper
Paprika
Sliced tomatoes

Mash yolks thoroughly with fork. Blend in remaining ingredients except paprika and tomatoes. Fill egg-white halves with yolk mixture; sprinkle with paprika. Arrange in center of platter; surround with tomato slices. *8 servings.*

SQUARE APPLE PIE

Heat oven to 425°. Prepare pastry for Two-crust Pie as directed on inside wrapper of one package of our pie crust sticks. Divide pastry in half. Roll each into a rectangle, 12x10 inches. Place 1 rectangle on baking sheet; spread 1 can (1 pound 5 ounces) apple pie filling over pastry to within 1 inch of edge. Cover wth second rectangle which has slits cut in it; seal edges and flute. Bake 20 to 25 minutes or until golden brown.

Just before serving, place pie in 350° oven; *turn control off.* Heat 15 minutes or until heated through. Serve with Cinnamon Ice Cream (below). *8 servings.*

CINNAMON ICE CREAM

Soften 1 quart vanilla ice cream; stir in 2 teaspoons cinnamon. Freeze until firm. *8 servings.*

Permanent Party Gear

A tea cart can be used in the traditional way —for serving tea or coffee and dessert in the living room. Or it can act as an extension of the buffet table—the ideal spot for beverage service or dessert. Rolled up alongside the hostess at a dinner table, a tea cart aids immeasurably as a serving table.

Company Favorites for Dinner Parties

ARTICHOKES

For each serving, remove any discolored leaves and the small leaves at the base of artichoke; trim stem even with base of artichoke. Cutting straight across, slice 1 inch off top; discard top. Snip off points of the remaining leaves with scissors. Rinse artichoke under cold water. To prevent leaves from spreading during cooking, tie string around artichoke and from top to bottom to hold leaves in place. Invert cleaned artichoke in bowl containing 1 tablespoon lemon juice for each quart of water. (This prevents edges from discoloring.)

Artichokes should be cooked in large kettle so they have sufficient space. For 4 medium artichokes, heat 6 quarts water, ¼ cup salad oil, 2 tablespoons lemon juice, 1 clove garlic, quartered, and 1 teaspoon salt to boiling. Add artichokes; heat to boiling. Reduce heat; simmer uncovered 30 to 40 minutes, rotating occasionally, or until leaves pull out easily and bottom is tender when pierced with a knife. Remove artichokes carefully from water; place upside down to drain.

To serve as a chilled first course: Cool artichokes; cover and refrigerate at least 4 hours. Remove string. Cut out choke, if desired: Open each artichoke like a flower to reach the interior; pull out tender center cone of leaves; scrape off exposed choke with spoon. (Choke is fuzzy growth covering artichoke heart.) Replace cone of leaves, if desired.

Place each artichoke in center of a luncheon plate or special artichoke plate. Accompany with a small cup of hollandaise sauce (right) or melted lemon butter. If choke has been removed, the cavity may be filled with the sauce.

To serve as a hot vegetable preceding meal: Remove string but do not remove choke. Place artichoke upright on plate. Accompany each with a small cup of hollandaise sauce (right) or melted lemon butter.

MOCK HOLLANDAISE SAUCE

1 package (3 ounces) cream cheese, softened
2 egg yolks
2 tablespoons lemon juice
Salt

Place cream cheese in small saucepan. Stir egg yolks, one at a time, into cream cheese; beat well. Blend in lemon juice and salt. Stir vigorously over low heat until mixture thickens. *Makes ⅔ cup.*

BLENDER HOLLANDAISE

3 egg yolks
1 tablespoon lemon juice
½ teaspoon salt
2 drops Tabasco
½ cup butter, melted

Mix all ingredients except butter in blender. Remove cover; pour in butter while mixing slowly in blender. *Makes ⅔ cup.*

THE ARTICHOKE ART

To eat artichokes, pluck leaves one at a time. Dip base of leaf into a sauce or lemon butter. Turn leaf meaty side down and draw between teeth, scraping off meaty portion. Place leaf on plate next to artichoke.

When all outer leaves have been removed, a center cone of small light-colored leaves covering the fuzzy center choke will be exposed—unless the choke has been removed before serving. Pull or cut off cone of leaves. Slice off fuzzy choke with knife and fork; discard. Cut the remaining "heart," the prize section, into bite-size pieces; dip into sauce.

CORNISH HENS WITH ORANGE-RAISIN SAUCE

4 Rock Cornish game hens (1 to 1¼ pounds each)
Salt
Melted butter
1 cup wild rice
1 can (14 ounces) chicken broth
½ teaspoon salt
⅔ cup raisins
⅔ cup orange juice
¼ cup butter or margarine
¼ cup Gold Medal Flour (regular or Wondra)
1 teaspoon salt
¼ teaspoon paprika
⅛ teaspoon pepper
2 cups milk

Thaw hens, if frozen. Heat oven to 350°. Wash hens and pat dry. Rub cavities with salt. Place hens breast side up on rack in shallow baking pan; brush with melted butter. Do not add water and do not cover. Bake 50 minutes, brushing often with melted butter. Increase oven temperature to 400°; bake hens 10 minutes longer or until brown. Meanwhile, wash rice thoroughly; drain well.

In large saucepan, measure broth and add water to measure 3 cups liquid. Add rice and ½ teaspoon salt. Heat to boiling, stirring once or twice. Reduce heat; cover and simmer until liquid is absorbed and rice is tender, about 45 minutes. Combine raisins and orange juice in small pan; heat to boiling. Reduce heat and simmer 5 minutes. Set aside. Melt ¼ cup butter in small saucepan. Remove from heat; blend in flour, 1 teaspoon salt, the paprika and pepper. Cook over low heat, stirring until mixture is smooth and bubbly. Remove from heat; stir in milk. Heat to boiling, stirring constantly. Boil 1 minute. Stir in raisin-orange juice mixture. Place hens on rice; pour some of the sauce over hens. Serve remaining sauce separately. *4 servings*

SHRIMP COCKTAIL

1 cup chili sauce
1 to 2 tablespoons horseradish
1 tablespoon lemon juice
½ teaspoon Worcestershire sauce
¼ teaspoon salt
Dash pepper
36 cooked medium shrimp, chilled

Combine all ingredients except shrimp; chill sauce thoroughly. To serve as individual appetizers, mix shrimp with sauce and serve in lettuce-lined sherbet glasses. For a party snack, fill a large bowl with crushed ice and center with a dish of sauce; arrange shrimp over ice. Serve with wooden picks for dipping shrimp into sauce. *6 servings.*

JELLIED WATERCRESS SOUP

Gently stir together 2 cans (10½ ounces each) consommé, ¼ cup finely chopped watercress and 1 tablespoon finely chopped pimiento-stuffed olives. Cover and chill about 6 hours, or until mixture reaches soft-gel stage. Gently spoon into bowls; serve immediately. *6 servings.*

BAKED HAM WITH ORANGE GLAZE

Allow ⅓ pound uncooked boneless ham, ½ to ¾ pound bone-in uncooked ham, ¼ pound cooked boneless ham and ⅓ to ½ pound bone-in cooked ham per person.

Heat oven to 325°. Place ham fat side up on rack in shallow pan; insert meat thermometer in center of the thickest muscle so point does not rest in fat or on bone. Bake as directed in timetable (below). Thirty minutes before ham is done, remove from oven. Pour off drippings from pan. Remove any skin from ham. Score ham, cutting uniform diamond shapes ¼ inch deep in fat. If desired, insert whole clove in each diamond. Pour half of Orange Glaze (below) over ham. Bake ham 30 minutes longer, basting occasionally with remaining glaze. Remove to warm platter; let ham stand 15 to 20 minutes for easier carving.

Orange Glaze

1 can (6 ounces) frozen orange juice concentrate, thawed
¼ cup brown sugar (packed)
¼ teaspoon cloves
¼ teaspoon cinnamon

Combine all ingredients. *Makes about 1 cup—enough to glaze a 4½- to 5-pound ham.*

How to Carve Whole Ham

1. Place ham on platter with shank end to carver's right. Remove two or three thin slices from the thin side of ham which contains knee cap. (Thin side of ham will face host if the ham is a left leg; it will face away from him if ham is a right leg.) Turn ham to rest on cut surface.

2. Cut perpendicular slices down to leg bone.*

3. Release slices by cutting along leg bone as shown.

*Or lift off the complete section of meat above bone; remove to platter or board and slice.

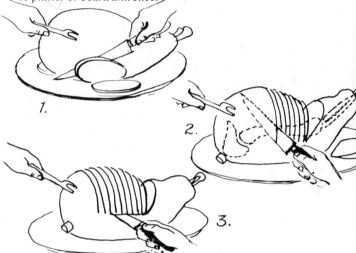

Timetable for Baked Ham				
	Approximate Weight (Pounds)	Oven Temperature	Interior Temperature When Removed from Oven	Approximate Cooking Time (Minutes per Pound)
Fully Cooked Type				
Whole ham	10 to 14	325°	130°	15
Half	5 to 7	325°	130°	18 to 24
Cook-before-eating Type				
Whole ham	10 to 14	325°	160°	18 to 20
Half	5 to 7	325°	160°	22 to 25
Shank or butt portion	3 to 4	325°	160°	35 to 40
Picnic Shoulder	5 to 8	325°	170°	35
Shoulder Roll	2 to 3	325°	170°	35 to 40

SCHWEIZERSCHNITZEL

A European classic of veal steak, boiled ham and Swiss cheese.

  4 slices boiled ham
  4 slices Swiss cheese
  1 pound veal steak, cut into 4 pieces and pounded
    very thin
  2 tablespoons flour
  ½ teaspoon salt
  ¼ teaspoon pepper
  ¼ teaspoon allspice
  1 egg, beaten
  ½ cup dry bread crumbs
  2 tablespoons shortening
  ½ cup dry white wine
  Poppy Seed Noodles (below)

Place 1 slice *each* of boiled ham and Swiss cheese on each piece of veal steak. Roll up carefully, beginning at narrow end; secure rolls with wooden picks. Mix flour and seasonings; dust veal with seasoned flour. Dip floured rolls into beaten egg; coat with bread crumbs. Brown in hot shortening. Pour wine over meat. Cover and simmer 55 minutes; uncover, simmer 5 minutes longer. Serve on hot Poppy Seed Noodles; pour liquid and melted cheese from skillet over meat and noodles. *4 servings.*

POPPY SEED NOODLES

Cook and drain 4 cups noodles as directed on package. Melt 1 tablespoon butter or margarine in small skillet; cook and stir ½ cup slivered blanched almonds in butter until almonds are lightly browned. Stir in 1 tablespoon poppy seed. Add almond mixture to hot cooked noodles; toss gently.

LEG OF LAMB DELUXE

Lamb roast filled with a ground meat stuffing that's marvelously flavored with touches of oregano, garlic and orange marmalade. To serve when you want to be "one up" on a gourmet guest! Pictured below.

  1 partially boned leg of lamb, about 5½ pounds
  ½ pound ground veal
  ½ pound ground cooked ham
  ½ cup fine dry bread crumbs
  ½ pound fresh mushrooms, finely chopped
  1 egg
  1 teaspoon salt
  ½ teaspoon oregano
  ¼ teaspoon pepper
  1 small clove garlic, crushed
  1 tablespoon Worcestershire sauce
  1 tablespoon orange marmalade

Ask the meatman to bone a leg of lamb, leaving about 3 inches of shank bone in place so roast will retain its characteristic shape.

Heat oven to 325°. Mix ground meats, bread crumbs and remaining ingredients. Pack tightly into lamb leg. Secure opening with skewers and string or cover lamb leg with aluminum foil and tie with string. Place fat side up on rack in shallow pan. Bake 30 to 35 minutes per pound. Let lamb stand about 10 minutes before carving. *12 to 14 servings.*

Garnish Greats

Choose garnishes from this basket bouquet to brighten your company meals. Let them add color to meat and fish platters, salads, even desserts.

1. Daisies: Cut pared small turnip or rutabaga into thin slices; cut out circles with scalloped or round cutter. Cut V-shaped notches around plain rounds to form petals. For centers attach thin carrot shapes to circles with wooden pick or dab of cream cheese.

2. Citrus Blossoms: Cut thin slice from stem end of large lemon or lime. Holding cut side down, make slanted gashes in staggered fashion around sides of fruit. Cut short gash across top. Cut slices from a smaller lemon or lime; halve. Insert half-slices, peel side out, in gashes, using the larger ones at base of flower.

3. Lemon Roses: Cut thin slice from stem end of lemon to form base. Starting just above base, cut around lemon without removing knife to form spiral of peel. Curl peel onto base to resemble rose. Lime Roses may also be made.

4. Painted Turnips: Cut deep wedge-shaped gashes in staggered fashion around pared turnip to form petals. With small brush, paint edges with diluted red or green food coloring. Cover until serving time.

5. Radish Rosettes: Cut stem and root ends from large radish. Make gashes and insert radish half-slices as for Citrus Blossoms (above). Chill in iced water.

6. Tomato Tulips: Score five lines through skin of cherry tomato, cutting at regular intervals from stem end halfway down sides. Carefully peel back skin to form petals. Remove stem; tuck in sprig of parsley.

7. Carrot Cutups: Thinly slice pared carrot crosswise. Notch around edge to form petals; add vegetable or parsley centers as desired.

8. Party Beetspurs: Drain a jar of tiny whole pickled beets, reserving beet juice; halve beets. Cut thin slice from rounded end of each half to form base. Flavor softened cream cheese with horseradish; tint with beet juice. Using decorators' tube, pipe cheese onto flat side of beet.

9. Spiked Radishes: Wash untrimmed radishes; cut off stem ends; leave roots. Cut a thin slice from two opposite sides of each. Mix softened cream cheese with milk. Using decorators' tube, pipe cheese onto a cut side.

10. Lilies of the Cucumber: Cut 3-inch piece from end of cucumber; notch out to form five petals at cut end of piece. Hollow out small amount of seed section. With knife, separate green peel from pulp on petals. Chill in water. Place olive slice in center of lily.

Party Ways with Butter

Butter Pats: You may buy pre-sliced butter or cut your own pats with wire butter cutter or a knife. If using knife, fold strip of waxed paper or butter wrapper over knife; cut ¼-pound bar firm butter into pats. Center each with sprig of parsley. Refrigerate.

Butter Balls: Scald a pair of wooden butter paddles in boiling water 30 seconds; chill in iced water. Cut ¼-pound bar firm butter into 1-inch squares. Cut each square in half; stand each half upright on paddle. Smack butter between paddles. Holding bottom paddle still, rotate top paddle to form ball. If butter clings to paddles, dip them again into hot water; then into iced water. Drop finished balls into iced water. Cover and refrigerate. Dip paddles into iced water before making each ball.

Butter Curls: Let butter curler stand in hot water at least 10 minutes. Pull curler firmly across surface of ¼-pound bar firm butter. (Butter should not be too cold or curls will break.) Drop curls into iced water; cover and refrigerate. Dip curler into hot water before making each curl.

After-Dinner Coffees

BELGIAN COFFEE

Topped with a fluff of whipped-cream meringue that bobs along right to the bottom of the drink.

1 egg white
⅓ cup sugar
¼ cup whipping cream, whipped
4 cups boiling water
2 tablespoons plus 2 teaspoons instant coffee

Beat egg white until frothy. Gradually beat in sugar; continue beating until stiff and glossy. Fold meringue into whipped cream. Pour boiling water over coffee; stir until coffee is dissolved. Place 2 tablespoons meringue mixture into each demitasse or other small cup; fill with coffee. *10 servings.*

FROSTY MOCHA

In small mixer bowl, beat until smooth 2½ cups chilled strong coffee, 1 pint softened vanilla ice cream, ¼ cup chocolate syrup and ½ teaspoon aromatic bitters. Pour into small ice-frosted glasses. *8 servings.*

SPICED COFFEE

2 cups water
1 tablespoon brown sugar
2 cinnamon sticks
¼-inch strip orange peel
¼ teaspoon whole allspice
1 tablespoon instant coffee

Combine all ingredients except coffee in saucepan; heat to boiling. Strain mixture; pour liquid over coffee and stir until coffee is dissolved. Serve in demitasse or other small cups. *4 servings.*

INTERNATIONAL COFFEE

Mix ⅓ cup instant cocoa mix and ¼ cup instant coffee in a serving pot. Pour in 4 cups boiling water; stir. Serve steaming hot and top with sweetened whipped cream. Serve in demitasse or other small cups. *8 servings.*

MOCHA ESPRESSO

To each cup of hot milk, stir in 1 tablespoon instant cocoa mix and 2 teaspoons instant espresso coffee. Serve in demitasse or other small cup. If desired, sprinkle with cinnamon.

Bright Little Brunches and Lunches

A party at midday offers a change of pace from evening entertaining, and a brunch or lunch has charms quite different from those of a dinner party.

Brunch, as the name implies, is a combination of breakfast and lunch and may be served any time between ten or ten-thirty and one o'clock. A weekday brunch may precede a committee meeting or any feminine business, even shopping, but probably the most popular brunches are co-ed affairs served late on Sunday morning.

Borrow an idea from fine restaurants and offer each guest a cup of coffee the minute he arrives. Serve English-style from a sideboard and let everyone help himself from chafing dishes or platters on a hot tray. If you like, you can provide some lazy after-eating entertainment.

Buy three or four Sunday papers and set them out for browsing. Have a giant jigsaw puzzle ready for assembling. Encourage your guests to do as they please. Some may want to listen to records, some may favor a walk, still others may prefer to work on the crossword puzzle.

A weekday lunch is a nice way to fete a bride or mother-to-be, a gracious gesture on behalf of a neighbor's houseguest or a pleasant prelude to an afternoon of bridge.

Keep the menu light but make the most of it with the little flourishes so dear to the female heart. Rose the radishes, curl the butter, bring out the fingerbowls and float a real flower petal or drop a Japanese water flower in each one. Provide table favors—a single carnation or a nosegay at each place.

Be a little adventurous. Most women love trying something new. Serve an exotic Oriental tea, add a garnish of lemon or lime roses to the main course or sprinkle a few candied violets on the dessert.

Casserole Brunch

Sparkling Red Rouser
Continental Cheese Bake
Half-moon Salads   Bacon Curls
Quick Blueberry Coffee Cake with Lemon Sauce
Coffee

Here's a conventional breakfast fare—juice, fruit, bacon, eggs and coffee cake—with each dish so ingeniously embellished and presented that it becomes an unusual year-around party meal. (Only seasonal adjustments: when melon isn't at its sweetest, substitute avocado, fresh pineapple, green grapes or crisp apple slices in the fruit salad.) The tomato juice turns into a zippy appetizer when it's mixed with a sparkling fruit beverage. The egg casserole is rich with cheese and bits of mushroom, crusted with caraway rye bread. The bacon in crispy curls

makes a delightful garnish. And the coffee cake becomes a full-scale dessert with the addition of a sweet-tart lemon sauce.

Serving suggestions: Have the tomato juice cocktail on the table when guests sit down. After the glasses have been removed, bring in luncheon plates with casserole, bacon and fruit salad arranged on each plate. Dessert may be served in saucedishes or on cake plates—also from the kitchen. Or, if you'd rather, offer the whole meal as an easy serve-yourself buffet.

PLAN FOR PREPARATION

Day before: 1. *Chill can of tomato sauce and the carbonated beverage.* **2.** *Prepare casserole; cover and refrigerate.* **3.** *Bake coffee cake. After cooling, wrap in aluminum foil.* **4.** *Prepare Lemon Sauce; cover and refrigerate.*

Day of party: 1. *Set table.* **2.** *Bake casserole.* **3.** *Pour water.* **4.** *Prepare coffee.* **5.** *Arrange salads on luncheon plates.* **6.** *Prepare appetizer drink.* **7.** *Broil bacon.* **8.** *Reheat Lemon Sauce.* **9.** *While brunch is being served, reheat coffee cake.*

SPARKLING RED ROUSER

At serving time, pour 1 can (8 ounces) tomato sauce and 2 bottles (7 ounces each) carbonated lemon-lime beverage into pitcher; mix gently. Serve over ice. *6 servings.*

CONTINENTAL CHEESE BAKE

1 cup sliced onion
1 tablespoon butter or margarine
8 hard-cooked eggs, sliced
2 cups shredded process Swiss cheese (8 ounces)
1 can (10½ ounces) condensed cream of
    mushroom soup
¾ cup milk
1 teaspoon prepared mustard
½ teaspoon seasoned salt
¼ teaspoon dill weed
¼ teaspoon pepper
6 slices caraway rye bread, buttered and cut into
    4 triangles

Heat oven to 350°. Cook and stir onion in butter until onion is tender. Spread mixture in baking dish, 11½x7½x1½ inches. Top with egg slices; sprinkle with cheese. Beat remaining ingredients except bread in bowl with rotary beater. Pour soup mixture over cheese*; overlap bread slices on top of casserole. Bake 30 to 35 minutes or until heated through.

Set oven control at broil and/or 550°. Place casserole 5 inches from source of heat; broil 1 minute, or until bread is toasted. *6 servings.*

*Do-ahead Note: To make casserole in advance, prepare casserole as directed above except—do not top with bread slices or bake. Refrigerate several hours or overnight. At baking time, place bread slices over top and bake 40 to 45 minutes.

HALF-MOON SALADS

Cut half of a large honeydew melon into 12 slices; trim off rind. Pare and section 3 oranges. On 6 luncheon plates, arrange melon slices and orange sections on beds of lettuce. Garnish with parsley. *6 servings.*

BACON CURLS

Set oven control at broil and/or 550°. Cut 18 slices bacon in half; roll each and secure with wooden pick. Broil 4 to 5 inches from source of heat 2 minutes. Turn; broil 2 minutes longer, or until bacon is crisp. *Makes 36 bacon curls.*

QUICK BLUEBERRY COFFEE CAKE WITH LEMON SAUCE

Heat oven to 400°. Prepare 1 package of our wild blueberry muffin mix as directed on package except —add 2 tablespoons sugar when adding dry mix and pour batter into greased square pan, 8x8x2 inches. Bake 20 to 22 minutes. Serve warm with hot Lemon Sauce (below). Top with whipped cream, if desired. *6 servings.*

Do-ahead Note: Blueberry Coffee Cake may be prepared day before serving. Cool and cover with foil. Just before serving, heat cake (with foil cover) in 350° oven 15 minutes.

Lemon Sauce

⅓ cup sugar
1 tablespoon cornstarch
1 teaspoon grated lemon peel
1 cup water
3 tablespoons butter or margarine
3 tablespoons lemon juice

Mix the sugar, cornstarch and lemon peel. Stir in water. Cook, stirring constantly, until mixture thickens and boils. Boil and stir 1 minute. Remove from heat; stir in butter and lemon juice.

Brunch Parisienne

Fruit Plate Carrousel
Puffy Omelet with Cheese Sauce
Frizzled Ham Slices   Sautéed Mushrooms
Brioches or French Puffs   Butter Balls (page 71)
Café au Lait

Off to a spectacular start is this French-accented brunch that greets guests with a revolving "centerpiece" first course. It's a brilliantly colorful carrousel of the nicest fruits of any season arranged on a lazy Susan (or an Oriental curry tray, if you have one). A pineapple tower occupies the center; surrounding it are the other fruits, alternating with sauces for dipping. We guarantee that the brunchers will occupy themselves happily with this long enough for you to finish preparing the main course.

Serving suggestions: When the appetizer excitement has subsided, bring in the big showy omelet, mushrooms and ham on a platter; pass bread and cheese sauce.

FRUIT PLATE CARROUSEL

For this fruit plate arrangement, you will need a lazy Susan or tiny bowls arranged on a pedestal plate. Place Pineapple Tower (below) in center. Select as many fruits and sauces from those listed here as you have compartments or bowls on your lazy Susan or tray; arrange fruits and sauces alternately in bowls around tray so guests can help themselves to one of each as the tray turns.

Pineapple Tower

With a paring knife or potato parer, cut a cone-shaped wedge around "eye" or groups of two "eyes," spacing cuts evenly around entire pineapple. Cut off any core from wedged piece. Insert a plastic or wooden pick in each wedge; plug into pineapple. To eat, guests pull out wedges and dip in confectioners' sugar or sour cream.

Fruit Suggestions

Choose luscious in-season fruits; be sure to serve them well chilled.

Whole strawberries with stems
Fresh or canned sliced peaches mixed with cut-up
    crystallized ginger
Orange cartwheel slices sprinkled with blueberries
Clusters of grapes
Melon balls
Grapefruit sections
Lemon-dipped banana slices
Lemon-dipped apple slices

SAUCE SUGGESTIONS

Sour Cream Sauce

Mix 1 cup dairy sour cream with 2 tablespoons dark brown sugar; spoon into bowl and sprinkle with small amount brown sugar.

Clear Orange Sauce

1 cup sugar
2 tablespoons cornstarch
¼ teaspoon salt
¾ cup water
1 cup orange juice
¼ cup lemon juice
½ teaspoon each grated orange and lemon peel

In small saucepan stir together sugar, cornstarch and salt. Blend in water, orange juice and lemon juice. Cook, stirring constantly, until mixture thickens and boils. Boil and stir 1 minute. Stir in orange and lemon peel. Serve hot or chilled. *Makes 2¼ cups.*

Raspberry Sauce

1 tablespoon sugar
1½ teaspoons cornstarch
2 tablespoons orange juice
1 package (10 ounces) frozen raspberries, partially
    thawed
1 teaspoon grated orange peel

In small saucepan stir together sugar and cornstarch. Blend in orange juice. Stir in raspberries. Cook, stirring constantly, until mixture thickens and boils. Boil and stir 1 minute. Stir in orange peel. Chill. *Makes 1 cup.*

Day before: 1. *Prepare and chill sauces.* **2.** *Wash, cover tightly and chill fruit.* **3.** *Wash, trim and slice mushrooms.* **4.** *Prepare Brioche dough (if Brioches are to be served).*

Day of party: 1. *Set table.* **2.** *Shape dough for Brioches, proof and bake. Or bake French Puffs. Keep rolls warm.* **3.** *Prepare coffee.* **4.** *Arrange fruit tray.* **5.** *Pour water.* **6.** *Prepare cheese sauce, omelet; frizzle ham and sauté mushrooms.*

PUFFY OMELET

8 eggs, separated
½ cup milk or light cream
¼ teaspoon <u>each</u> salt and pepper
¼ cup butter or shortening
Cheese Sauce (below)

Beat egg whites until stiff but not dry. Beat egg yolks until thick and lemon colored; beat in milk and seasonings. Fold into egg whites. Heat butter moderately hot in heavy 12-inch skillet.

Heat oven to 350°. Pour omelet mixture into skillet, leveling surface. Cook over low heat about 10 minutes, or until omelet is puffy and light brown on bottom (lift omelet at edge to judge color). Place skillet in oven. Bake 10 to 15 minutes until light brown on top and no imprint remains when touched lightly. With spatula make cut halfway through omelet at right angle to handle and slightly above center. Place spatula under part of omelet nearest handle, tip skillet to nearly vertical position and carefully fold upper half over lower half. Roll omelet top side down onto hot platter. Spoon hot Cheese Sauce over omelet and serve at once. Pass remaining sauce. *6 to 8 servings.*

Cheese Sauce

¼ cup butter or margarine
¼ cup Gold Medal Flour (regular or Wondra)
½ teaspoon salt
¼ teaspoon pepper
2 teaspoons dry mustard
2 cups milk
1 teaspoon Worcestershire sauce
2 cups shredded process American cheese
  (8 ounces)

Melt butter over low heat in heavy saucepan. Stir in flour and seasonings. Cook over low heat, stirring until mixture is smooth and bubbly. Remove from heat. Stir in milk. Heat to boiling, stirring constantly. Boil 1 minute. Stir in Worcestershire sauce and cheese. Cook and stir over low heat until cheese is melted. *Makes 2½ cups.*

FRIZZLED HAM SLICES

Melt 2 tablespoons butter in skillet. Frizzle 8 slices boiled ham 1 minute on each side. Remove from skillet; roll ham and secure with wooden picks, if desired. *6 to 8 servings.*

SAUTÉED MUSHROOMS

Wash, trim and slice ½ pound fresh mushrooms. Cook and stir mushrooms in ¼ cup butter 5 to 7 minutes or until tender. Season with ½ teaspoon salt and ¼ teaspoon pepper. *6 to 8 servings.*

BRIOCHES

As French as a sidewalk café or a corner flower stand. (This dough is the refrigerated kind, which lets you do half the preparation ahead of time.)

> 1 package active dry yeast
> ¾ cup warm water (105 to 115°)
> ½ cup sugar
> ½ teaspoon salt
> 3 eggs
> 1 egg yolk
> ½ cup soft butter or margarine
> 3½ cups Gold Medal Flour* (regular or Wondra)
> 1 egg white, slightly beaten
> 1 tablespoon sugar

In mixer bowl dissolve yeast in water. Add ½ cup sugar, the salt, eggs, egg yolk, butter and half the flour. Beat 10 minutes medium speed on mixer or by hand. Scrape sides and bottom of bowl frequently. Blend in remaining flour with spoon. Scrape batter from sides of bowl. Cover and let rise in warm place (85°) until double, about 1 hour. Stir down batter by beating 25 strokes. Cover tightly and store in refrigerator overnight.

Stir down batter; divide in half. Place one half on lightly floured board. (Refrigerate other half.) Shape a roll about 8 inches long. Cut into 16 slices. Shape 12 slices into balls; place in greased medium muffin cups. (Work quickly with floured hands as dough is soft.) Flatten each ball; press indentation in center. Cut each of the remaining 4 slices into 3 parts. Form smaller balls and place in indentations. Shape second half of dough as first. Let rise in warm place until double, about 40 minutes. Mix egg white and 1 tablespoon sugar; brush over tops of rolls.

Heat oven to 375°. Bake 15 to 20 minutes. *Makes 24 rolls.*

If using Self-Rising Flour, omit salt.

FRENCH PUFFS

> ⅓ cup shortening
> ½ cup sugar
> 1 egg
> 1½ cups Gold Medal Flour* (regular or Wondra)
>   or Softasilk Cake Flour
> 1½ teaspoons baking powder
> ½ teaspoon salt
> ¼ teaspoon nutmeg
> ½ cup milk
> ½ cup sugar
> 1 teaspoon cinnamon
> ½ cup butter or margarine, melted

Heat oven to 350°. Grease 12 medium muffin cups. Cream shortening, ½ cup sugar and the egg. Stir together flour, baking powder, salt and nutmeg; add alternately with milk to creamed mixture. Fill muffin cups ⅔ full. Bake 20 to 25 minutes. Mix ½ cup sugar and the cinnamon. Immediately after baking, roll muffins in melted butter, then in cinnamon-sugar mixture. Serve hot. *Makes 12 puffs.*

If using Self-Rising Flour, omit baking powder and salt.

CAFÉ AU LAIT

Simultaneously pour 3 cups hot strong coffee from one pot and 3 cups hot milk from another into cups. *6 to 8 servings.*

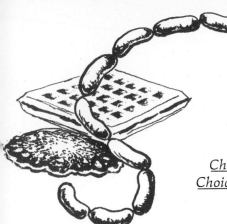

Pancake Party

Chilled Fruit Juice
Choice of one or more: Hawaiian Pancakes,
Washington Pancakes, Fruit-patch Delight,
Woodsman's Special
Choice of one: Pigs on Blankets or Denver Pancakes
Choice of one: Toasted Pecan Waffles with Honey Butter
or Mock Belgian Waffles
Baked Bacon Platter   Coffee   Milk

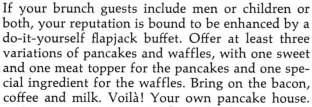

If your brunch guests include men or children or both, your reputation is bound to be enhanced by a do-it-yourself flapjack buffet. Offer at least three variations of pancakes and waffles, with one sweet and one meat topper for the pancakes and one special ingredient for the waffles. Bring on the bacon, coffee and milk. Voilà! Your own pancake house.

Serving suggestions: To keep this happy operation orderly, serve juice in the living room. Then place the griddle and a bowl of pancake batter at one end of the buffet. Arrange the coffee urn and cups at the opposite end. In the center of the table, group the "fixings" that belong together side by side—sour cream and cherries for the Washington Pancakes in one place; butter, sausages and maple syrup for Pigs on Blankets in another. It's a good idea to set up a small card table for waffle making —be sure to use a different electric outlet. Let the host be short-order chef at the pancake griddle while you preside over the waffle maker.

PLAN FOR PREPARATION

Day before: 1. *Prepare waffle batter; cover and refrigerate.* **2.** *Prepare butters and syrups; cover and refrigerate.*

Day of party: 1. *Set table.* **2.** *Reheat sauces; prepare other ingredients as needed for selected pancake and waffle variations.* **3.** *Prepare coffee.* **4.** *Bake bacon.* **5.** *Stir down waffle batter.* **6.** *Set out batters, syrups, butters and other ingredients.* **7.** *Serve fruit juice; begin baking pancakes and waffles.*

Permanent Party Gear

An electric hot tray that keeps food hot without further cooking it will find a job to do at any buffet or cocktail party. What an easy way to keep your main dish ready for second servings. And it would really come in handy for this Pancake Buffet to keep the sauces at just the right temperature.

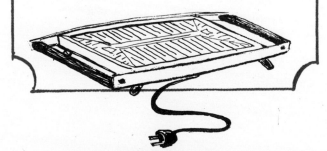

PANCAKES

Combine 4 cups Bisquick, 2 eggs and 3⅓ cups milk; beat with rotary beater until smooth. Grease griddle, if necessary. (When few drops water sprinkled on griddle sizzle, temperature is right for baking.) Pour batter from pitcher or large measuring cup. Turn pancakes when bubbles appear and before they break. For thinner pancakes, add more milk; for thicker pancakes, add more Bisquick. *Makes about 6 dozen 3-inch pancakes. (Enough for 8 servings of 8 or 9 pancakes each.)*

HAWAIIAN PANCAKES

Set out a bowl of Aloha Cream Topper (below), a pitcher of Pineapple Syrup (below) and a bowl of chopped macadamia nuts. Guests top a small stack of pancakes with desired amount of topper, syrup and chopped nuts.

Aloha Cream Topper

Drain 1 can (8¾ ounces) crushed pineapple, reserving the syrup. Stir the pineapple into 1 cup dairy sour cream. *Makes about 1⅓ cups.*

Pineapple Syrup

Combine reserved pineapple syrup and ¼ cup maple syrup; heat to boiling. *Makes about ¾ cup.*

WASHINGTON PANCAKES

Set out a small bowl of dairy sour cream. Pour contents of 1 can (1 pound 5 ounces) cherry pie filling into another bowl. Guests spread each pancake of a small stack with sour cream and top with a spoonful of cherry filling.

FRUIT-PATCH DELIGHT

Set out a bowl of sweetened fresh raspberries and a pitcher of Orange Sauce (below). Guests pour sauce over small stack of pancakes and spoon on raspberries.

Orange Sauce

Combine ⅓ cup butter or margarine, 2 tablespoons sugar and ⅓ cup orange juice; heat to boiling, stirring constantly. *Makes about ½ cup.*

WOODSMAN'S SPECIAL

Drain 1 can (14 ounces) blueberries, reserving the syrup. Place drained blueberries in a bowl; set out a pitcher of Blueberry Syrup (below) and a bowl of Orange Butter (below). Guests spread each pancake of a small stack with Orange Butter and top with blueberries and Blueberry Syrup.

Blueberry Syrup

Combine the reserved blueberry syrup and ½ cup maple syrup; heat to boiling. *Makes about 1¼ cups.*

Orange Butter

In small mixer bowl, whip 1 cup soft butter with 2 teaspoons grated orange peel until fluffy.

DENVER PANCAKES

Set out a bowl of Denver Filling (below), a small dish of Mustard Butter (below) and a pitcher of warm maple syrup. Guests spread pancakes with Mustard Butter and assemble, sandwich style, with the filling. Pour maple syrup over pancakes.

Denver Filling

Cook and stir ½ cup minced onion and ½ cup minced green pepper in 2 tablespoons butter or margarine until onion is tender. Stir in 1 cup diced ham; heat through. Serve warm. *Makes about 1½ cups.*

Mustard Butter

In small mixer bowl, whip 1 cup soft butter with 2 tablespoons prepared mustard.

PIGS ON BLANKETS

Set out a platter of cooked pork sausage links, a bowl of soft butter and a pitcher of warm maple syrup. Guests spread each of a small stack of pancakes with soft butter and top with sausage links and maple syrup.

WAFFLE BATTER

1 package active dry yeast
¼ cup warm water (105 to 115°)
1¾ cups lukewarm milk, scalded then cooled
2 tablespoons sugar
1 teaspoon salt
3 eggs
¼ cup soft butter or margarine
2 cups Gold Medal Flour* (regular or Wondra)

In mixing bowl dissolve yeast in warm water. Add milk, sugar and salt. Beat in remaining ingredients with rotary beater. Cover; let rise in warm place (85°) about 1½ hours. (If kitchen is cool, place dough on a rack over a bowl of hot water and cover completely with a towel.) Stir down; cover and refrigerate overnight or until ready to use. Bake as directed.

**If using Self-Rising Flour, omit salt.*

TOASTED PECAN WAFFLES

Stir down Waffle Batter (above). For each waffle, sprinkle ¼ cup chopped pecans on heated waffle grids. Close iron and heat until pecans are golden brown, about 3 minutes. Lift top of iron and pour on batter. Bake until waffles are done—check manufacturer's directions for timing. Serve with Honey Butter (below) and warm maple syrup. *Makes eight 7-inch waffles.*

Honey Butter

In small mixer bowl, whip ½ cup soft butter with ½ cup honey until fluffy.

MOCK BELGIAN WAFFLES

Whip 1 cup whipping cream with 2 tablespoons confectioners' sugar. Fold in 1 cup halved fresh strawberries or 1 package (16 ounces) frozen sliced strawberries, thawed and drained.

Stir down Waffle Batter (left). Pour batter onto hot waffle grids. Bake until waffles are done—check manufacturer's directions for timing. Divide each baked waffle into sections; fill 2 waffle sections with cream-strawberry mixture and sprinkle sifted confectioners' sugar over top of each "waffle sandwich." *Makes 16.*

BAKED BACON PLATTER

Heat oven to 400°. Allowing 2 slices per person, separate sliced bacon and arrange on rack in broiler pan. Allowing 1 or 2 slices per person, arrange sliced Canadian bacon on a rack in pan. (Do not overlap slices.) Bake until brown, about 10 minutes. Do not turn.

Club Luncheon

Golden Shrimp Puff
Fresh Fruit Salad with Limeade Dressing
Toasted Snack Rye
Chocolate-Mint Parfaits   Salted Nuts   Tea

When it's your turn to entertain the club, committee or reading group, here's a menu that's light and colorful and surprisingly speedy, especially designed to make you look well organized. The shrimp casserole goes into the oven well before guests arrive; almost everything else is ready even earlier. One trip to the kitchen to pop the bread into the oven is all the last-minute attention this meal requires.

Serving suggestions: For this easy-to-serve meal, guests may be seated at the dining room table or individual card tables. Arrange the entire main course on individual luncheon plates in the kitchen and bring in—two at a time. Let guests help themselves to the salad dressing. When the casserole course is finished and the table cleared, bring in the delicate, tangy parfaits on a tray.

PLAN FOR PREPARATION

Day before: 1. *Prepare parfaits, if desired; freeze.* **2.** *Wash grapes, apples and blueberries. Place in plastic bags; chill.* **3.** *Wash lettuce and prepare lettuce cups. Place on tray or baking sheet; cover and chill.* **4.** *Prepare dressing for salads. Place in covered jar; refrigerate.*

Day of party: 1. *Set table.* **2.** *Prepare and bake casserole.* **3.** *Butter rye bread; place on baking sheet and cover with plastic wrap; set aside.* **4.** *Place salted nuts in serving dish or in individual nut cups; set aside.* **5.** *Arrange fruit in lettuce cups; refrigerate until serving time.* **6.** *Toast snack rye.* **7.** *Prepare tea; pour water.*

GOLDEN SHRIMP PUFF

10 slices white bread
6 eggs
3 cups milk
2 tablespoons minced parsley
¾ teaspoon dry mustard
½ teaspoon salt
2 cups shredded process sharp American cheese (8 ounces)
2 cups cleaned cooked or canned shrimp

Heat oven to 325°. Remove crusts from bread; cut slices into cubes. Beat eggs, milk and seasonings. Stir in bread cubes, cheese and shrimp. Pour into oblong baking dish, 11½x7½x1½ inches. Bake uncovered 1 hour, or until center is set. Serve immediately. *8 servings.*

FRESH FRUIT SALAD WITH LIMEADE DRESSING

2 medium unpared apples, quartered and cut into ¼-inch slices
1 pound seedless green grapes
2 oranges, pared and sliced
8 lettuce cups
½ cup fresh or frozen blueberries
Limeade Dressing (below)

Arrange apple slices, grapes and orange slices in lettuce cups; sprinkle with blueberries. (If you wish to make salads ahead of time, dip apple slices into Limeade Dressing. Refrigerate salads.) Pour Limeade Dressing over fruit cups. *8 servings.*

Limeade Dressing

With rotary beater mix ⅓ cup frozen limeade concentrate (thawed), ⅓ cup honey and ⅓ cup salad oil.

TOASTED SNACK RYE

Spread 16 slices snack rye bread with butter; place on baking sheet. Heat in 325° oven 10 to 12 minutes or until crusty. *16 slices.*

CHOCOLATE-MINT PARFAITS

In small saucepan cook and stir ¼ cup mint-flavored apple jelly and 2 tablespoons water until mixture is smooth. Cool slightly. Whip ½ cup whipping cream until stiff; stir in jelly mixture. Using 3 pints chocolate ice cream, alternate layers of ice cream and jelly mixture in 8 parfait glasses. Freeze until firm. *8 servings.*

Permanent Party Gear

Entertaining means coffee—and lots of it. If you're having a party for eight, it's a good idea to plug in two electric coffee makers (the 10-cup size) so you'll be ready for seconds—even if it means borrowing one from your neighbor. For a bigger party, a large electric percolator urn may be a better answer. You can make up to 30 cups of coffee in some of these urns.

Mixed Foursome Lunch

Party Lamb Chops
Hot Minted Fruits   Tomato Aspic Molds
Crescent Rolls   Butter
Lemon Chiffon Pie   Assorted Nuts
Coffee

A noon-hour party with another couple can be a very pleasant change of pace from the typical ladies-only luncheons. It might be a meal before the tennis or golf matches, or a reunion with old friends who are driving through town. In any case, when the guest list includes men the menu should be on the slightly hearty side, preferably featuring a man's idea of a real meat. Every part of this menu is a conversation point: the cheese-and-onion-topped chops, the hot fruits, crisp celery in flavorful aspic and a time-honored chiffon pie.

Serving suggestions: Have the molded salads on the table when lunch is announced; serve a chop, a ramekin of fruit and a roll on each plate. Or, you can arrange a platter with the chops and surround them with the ramekins. The rolls can be passed.

∽∽∽∽∽∽∽ PLAN FOR PREPARATION ∽∽∽∽∽∽∽

Day before: 1. *Bake pie shell and fill.* **2.** *Mold salads.* **3.** *Bake rolls and wrap in foil, if desired.*

Day of party: 1. *Set table.* **2.** *Arrange salads; refrigerate.* **3.** *Prepare chops and minted fruits.* **4.** *Prepare coffee.* **5.** *Garnish pie with whipped cream, if desired.*

PARTY LAMB CHOPS

4 Saratoga or loin lamb chops, 1 inch thick
4 thin onion slices
4 slices process Swiss cheese

Set oven control at broil and/or 550°. Broil lamb chops 4 to 5 inches from source of heat 7 to 8 minutes. Turn; place onion and cheese slice on each chop and broil 7 to 8 minutes longer. *4 servings.*

HOT MINTED FRUITS

⅓ cup mint-flavored apple jelly
1 tablespoon butter or margarine
1 tablespoon lemon juice
1 can (1 pound) pear halves, drained
 and quartered
1 can (13½ ounces) pineapple chunks, drained

In small saucepan cook and stir jelly, butter and lemon juice until jelly is melted. Stir in pears and pineapple; heat through. Serve hot in small individual dishes. *4 servings.*

TOMATO ASPIC MOLDS

1 package (3 ounces) lemon-flavored
 gelatin
1¼ cups boiling water
1 can (8 ounces) tomato sauce
1½ tablespoons vinegar
½ teaspoon salt
Dash each Tabasco, cayenne pepper and
 ground cloves
2 cups diced celery
Crisp salad greens
Mayonnaise or salad dressing

Dissolve gelatin in water. Stir in tomato sauce, vinegar and seasonings. Chill until partially set; fold in celery. Pour into 6 individual molds; chill until firm. Unmold on salad greens; garnish with ripe olives, if desired. Pass mayonnaise. *6 servings.*

CRESCENT ROLLS

2 packages active dry yeast
¾ cup warm water (105 to 115°)
½ cup sugar
1 teaspoon salt
2 eggs
½ cup shortening (part butter)
4 cups Gold Medal Flour* (regular or Wondra)
Soft butter or margarine

In large mixing bowl, dissolve yeast in warm water. Stir sugar, salt, eggs, shortening and half the flour into yeast. Add remaining flour; mix until smooth. Scrape dough from sides of bowl; cover with cloth. Let rise in warm place (85°) until double, about 1½ hours. Divide dough in half; roll each part into a 12-inch circle, ¼ inch thick. Spread with soft butter. Cut each circle into 16 wedges. Roll up each wedge, beginning at rounded edge. Place point side down on greased baking sheet. Curve to form crescents. Cover; let rise until double, 1 hour.

Heat oven to 400°. Bake 12 to 15 minutes or until a rich golden brown. Brush with soft butter. *Makes 32 crescents.*

*If using Self-Rising Flour, omit salt.

Note: Leftover rolls may be wrapped and frozen for later use.

LEMON CHIFFON PIE

9-inch Baked Pie Shell (page 129)
4 egg yolks, slightly beaten
½ cup sugar
1 envelope (1 tablespoon) unflavored gelatin
⅔ cup water
⅓ cup lemon juice
1 tablespoon grated lemon peel
4 egg whites
½ teaspoon cream of tartar
½ cup sugar

Prepare Baked Pie Shell. In saucepan blend egg yolks, ½ cup sugar, the gelatin, water and lemon juice. Cook over medium heat, stirring constantly, just until mixture comes to boiling. Stir in lemon peel. Place pan in cold water; cool until mixture mounds slightly when dropped from spoon. Beat egg whites with cream of tartar until frothy. Gradually beat in ½ cup sugar. Continue beating until stiff and glossy. Do not underbeat. Fold in lemon mixture. Pile into cooled pie shell. Chill several hours or until set. Serve with whipped cream, if desired.

Note: Refrigerate leftover pie immediately.

Two-table Bridge Luncheon

Paradise Chicken Salad in Pineapple Boats
Popovers   Butter
Lemon Velvet Cream Cake (page 124)
Coffee

Make the exotic main dish of this meal your point of departure for a bit of South Seas decor. Use Gauguin color combinations like pink and orange for cloths and napkins. And since the card tables will be doubling as dining tables, create a small centerpiece for each. Perhaps a few shiny green leaves arranged luau fashion or a delicate single flower floating in a seashell.

Serving suggestions: For drama, have the pineapple boats on a large platter on the buffet table, and at serving time bring in the hot popovers in a napkin-lined basket. Later the cake may be cut at the buffet and the coffee served from there. Forego the buffet service if you wish. Your salad luncheon will be just as impressive with plate service, a little basket of popovers on each table.

PARADISE CHICKEN SALAD IN PINEAPPLE BOATS

2 fresh pineapples
2½ cups cubed cooked chicken or turkey
¾ cup diced celery
¾ cup mayonnaise or salad dressing
2 tablespoons chopped chutney
1 teaspoon curry powder
1 medium banana, sliced
⅓ cup salted peanuts
½ cup flaked coconut
1 can (11 ounces) mandarin orange segments, chilled and drained

Select firm pineapples with fresh green leaves. To prepare pineapple boats, first remove any brown leaves from the top. With a sharp large knife, cut pineapple in half lengthwise through the green top. Then cut each in half again, making 4 pieces, each with part of the green top. Remove fruit from pineapple by cutting along curved edge with a grapefruit knife. Cut away the eyes and fibrous core. Cut fruit into chunks for salad. Drain pineapple shells (upside down) and the fruit on paper towels.

Combine pineapple, chicken and celery in large bowl. In a small bowl, mix mayonnaise, chutney and curry powder. Cover each bowl and refrigerate. Just before serving, drain any juice from fruit-chicken mixture. Add banana and peanuts; toss lightly with mayonnaise mixture. Fill pineapple boats. Sprinkle each with coconut and garnish with mandarin orange segments. *8 servings.*

PLAN FOR PREPARATION

Day before: 1. *Bake, cool and frost cake; refrigerate.* **2.** *Cook chicken for salad.*

Day of party: 1. *Prepare salad ingredients; chill.* **2.** *Set up card tables.* **3.** *Prepare and bake Popovers.* **4.** *Prepare coffee.* **5.** *Pour water.* **6.** *Combine salad ingredients; fill pineapple boats with salad.*

POPOVERS

4 eggs, slightly beaten
2 cups milk
2 cups Gold Medal Wondra*
1 teaspoon salt

Heat oven to 450°. Grease 12 deep custard cups or 16 muffin cups. Measure all ingredients into mixing bowl. Stir with fork just until smooth. Do not overbeat. Fill custard cups half full, muffin cups ¾ full. Bake 25 minutes; *lower temperature to 350°* and bake 15 to 20 minutes longer or until deep golden brown. Remove from cups immediately and serve hot. *Makes 12 to 16 popovers.*

*If using Gold Medal Flour (regular), beat all ingredients with rotary beater just until smooth. Do not use Self-Rising Flour in this recipe.

Teas and Receptions

Although most of us lead casual lives today, certain occasions seem to call for a rather formal, fairly large daytime party. At such times a tea or reception is the perfect solution.

The tea is one party that remains steeped in tradition. Its hours are pre-scribed "from three to five" or "from four to six" as they have always been. Guests may arrive any time after the starting hour, but they are expected to leave promptly at five, or at six. The table is set, as it was in our grand-mothers' day, with an assortment of dainty sandwiches, cookies, petits fours and candies. Even the most casual hostess eschews such convenient-at-other-times shortcuts as tea bags or instant coffee and presents a menu of old-fashioned elegance. The coffee service stands at the end of the table nearest the door, the tea service at the other. Generally, close friends of the hostess are asked to pour and each cup is served and handed directly to the guest by a pourer.

Because of its unchanging traditions, this kind of party provides an ideal climate for mixing guests of all ages. It offers an atmosphere in which older people feel particularly at home and a lovely study in manners for teenagers.

Much less formal, but still traditional, is the intimate tea for a few friends. At such a get-together just tea (no coffee) is served to a group of five or six, who are usually gathered around the living-room coffee table. The food con-sists of a few delicate sandwiches or cookies; the hostess pours. This is also the perfect time for the true tea-lover to offer her guests the more exotic brands of tea.

Reception Tea

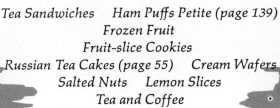

Tea Sandwiches   Ham Puffs Petite (page 139)
Frozen Fruit
Fruit-slice Cookies
Russian Tea Cakes (page 55)   Cream Wafers
Salted Nuts   Lemon Slices
Tea and Coffee

TEA SANDWICHES

Choose interesting breads...

For variety, try rye, whole wheat, raisin, date, nut, fig or Boston brown bread.

For color, use two kinds of bread in one sandwich.
For attractiveness, use fresh sandwich bread for rolled sandwiches, day-old for open sandwiches.

Select appetizing fillings...

For eye appeal, use fillings of various pastel colors.
For taste interest, season fillings to accent the mild flavors of the bread and teatime cookies. Choose a filling to complement the type of bread and to give sandwiches a different appearance as well as flavor.

Prepare sandwiches properly...

To prevent soaking, spread a thin layer of soft butter or margarine over bread, covering all edges and corners. Cream butter before using; do not melt it.
To spread fillings easily, use moist but not wet ones.

Store sandwiches correctly...

To keep fresh, store in a large shallow pan. Place a damp towel on bottom, allowing edges to hang over sides. Cover towel with waxed paper. Stack the sandwiches with waxed paper over each layer. Fold edges of towel snugly over the layered sandwiches.
To freeze sandwiches, box in layers with waxed paper separating each layer. Wrap box with moisture-vapor-proof paper; label; date. (Or use a plastic box or other moisture-vapor-proof container for storage.) Rolled and ribbon sandwiches may be wrapped uncut and then sliced after defrosting. Thaw in original wrapping 1 to 2 hours. (If not used immediately, store in refrigerator.) Sandwiches may be stored in the freezer up to 3 weeks. Do not refreeze.

Do not freeze jelly, mayonnaise, salad dressing, hard-cooked egg whites, lettuce, celery, tomatoes or carrots.

Tea Sandwich Chart

	Sandwich Loaf	Pullman Loaf
Approximate length of loaf	12½ inches	15½ inches
Number of crosswise slices	23 (½-inch slices)	32 (½-inch slices)
Number of lengthwise slices	6 (½-inch slices)	6 (½-inch slices)
Amount of filling needed	For crosswise slice: 2 tablespoons	For crosswise slice: 2 tablespoons
	For lengthwise slice: ⅓ cup	For lengthwise slice: ½ cup

PINWHEELS

Remove entire crust from unsliced pullman loaf bread. Cut loaf lengthwise into ¼-inch slices. Spread one side of each long slice with 2 tablespoons soft butter or margarine and ½ cup of a colorful sandwich spread. Cut each slice in half crosswise. Beginning at short side, roll up tightly as for jelly roll. Secure with wooden picks. Wrap and chill; slice ½ inch thick. *One roll makes 6 sandwiches.*

CUCUMBER SANDWICHES

Cut sandwich bread slices into rounds; lightly cover each with soft butter (about ¼ teaspoon) or 1 teaspoon whipped cream cheese.* Fill each 2 rounds with a thin cucumber slice. *3 rounds (2 inches) per slice.*

OPEN-FACE DAINTIES

Crimson Hearts

Cut sandwich bread slices into heart shapes with cookie cutter; lightly cover each with soft butter (about ¼ teaspoon). Spread each heart with 1 teaspoon red jam or jelly. If desired, place whipped cream cheese* in decorators' tube and outline edge of heart. *2 hearts (2½ x 2¼ inches) per slice.*

Deviled Diamonds

Cut sandwich bread slices into diamond shapes with cookie cutter; lightly cover each with soft butter (about ¼ teaspoon). Moisten canned deviled ham or chicken spread with mayonnaise; spread over buttered diamonds. Garnish with sliced pimiento-stuffed olives. *2 diamonds (3½ x 2¼ inches) per slice.*

Cheese Cutups

Cut sandwich bread slices into rounds or squares. Spread each with 1 teaspoon whipped cream cheese —plain, chive or pimiento.* Sprinkle with chopped nuts or garnish each with a single nut. *3 rounds (2 inches) or 4 squares (2 inches) per slice.*

Shrimp-Cucumber Rounds

Cut sandwich bread slices into rounds. Spread each with 1 teaspoon whipped cream cheese.* Top each with a thin cucumber slice, a dab of cream cheese and a cooked small shrimp. *3 rounds (2 inches) per slice.*

Or use regular cream cheese moistened with milk.

RIBBON SANDWICHES

Trim crusts from 1 white and 1 whole-wheat unsliced pullman loaf bread. Cut each loaf lengthwise into 6 slices. For each ribbon loaf, spread each of 2 slices white and 1 slice whole-wheat bread with ½ cup of your choice of sandwich spreads (below). Assemble loaf, alternating white and whole-wheat slices. Top with an unspread whole-wheat slice. Wrap and chill. Cut loaves into slices, about ½ inch thick. Cut each slice in half. *Makes 3 ribbon loaves— about 180 sandwiches.*

SANDWICH SPREADS

Golden Spread

2 cups shredded Cheddar cheese (8 ounces)
1 package (3 ounces) cream cheese, softened
¼ cup mayonnaise or salad dressing
½ teaspoon Worcestershire sauce
⅛ teaspoon onion salt
⅛ teaspoon garlic salt
⅛ teaspoon celery salt

Mix all ingredients thoroughly. *Makes 1½ cups.*

Chicken-Olive Spread

3 cups minced cooked chicken or turkey
½ cup finely chopped celery
¼ cup chopped green olives
½ teaspoon salt
¾ cup mayonnaise or salad dressing

Mix all ingredients thoroughly. *Makes 2⅔ cups.*

Hawaiian Filling

2 cups ground cooked ham
1 can (8¾ ounces) crushed pineapple, drained
½ cup finely chopped celery
½ cup dairy sour cream
¼ teaspoon paprika
⅛ teaspoon <u>each</u> salt, pepper and cloves

Mix all ingredients. *Makes 2⅔ cups.*

Shrimp Spread

Drain and rinse 3 cans (4½ ounces each) broken shrimp; mix with ⅓ cup finely chopped celery, 1 tablespoon lemon juice, 1 tablespoon minced onion and ½ cup mayonnaise or salad dressing. *Makes 3 cups.*

FRUIT-SLICE COOKIES

Cookies shaped like slices of fruit and tinted with the colors of citrus. For lovely tea service, arrange rows of lemon, lime and orange on a silver tray. (When it's a summertime tea party, serve one of each with a tall glass of iced tea.)

    ¾ cup shortening (part butter or margarine)
    1 cup sugar
    2 eggs
    ½ teaspoon lemon extract or 1 teaspoon vanilla
    2½ cups Gold Medal Flour* (regular or Wondra)
    1 teaspoon baking powder
    1 teaspoon salt
    20 drops yellow food coloring
    1½ teaspoons grated lemon peel
    5 drops green food coloring
    1½ teaspoons grated lime peel
    5 drops red food coloring
    1½ teaspoons grated orange peel
    1 egg white
    1 teaspoon water
    Yellow, green and orange decorators' sugar
    Icing (below)

Mix shortening, sugar, eggs and flavoring thoroughly. Stir together flour, baking powder and salt; blend into shortening mixture.

Divide dough into thirds. To one third add 10 drops yellow food coloring and the lemon peel. To another third add green food coloring and lime peel. To remaining dough add 10 drops yellow food coloring, the red food coloring and orange peel. Work in coloring and peel with hands. Wrap colored doughs separately in waxed paper; chill at least 1 hour.

Heat oven to 400°. Roll dough ⅛ inch thick on lightly floured board; cut into 2-inch circles and cut each circle in half. Place on ungreased baking sheet. Bake 6 to 8 minutes. Cool. Mix egg white and water; dip rounded edge of each cookie into egg white mixture, then into yellow, green or orange** decorators' sugar. Let dry. Place Icing in decorators' tube; make thin line of icing ¼ inch from outside sugared edge of cookies. *Makes about 14 dozen.*

Icing

Mix 2 cups sifted confectioners' sugar, ½ teaspoon salt and about 2 tablespoons water until smooth.

*Do not use Self-Rising Flour in this recipe.

**If orange decorators' sugar is not available, mix equal parts of red and yellow sugars.

FROZEN FRUIT

Cut fresh fruits (apples, oranges, seedless green grapes, bananas or melon) into bite-size pieces to make 2 cups of fruit. Insert plastic pick in each piece. Melt 1 package (6 ounces) semisweet chocolate pieces and ¼ cup butter in small pan over hot water. Dip fruits into chocolate; place on lightly buttered waxed paper. Freeze fruits until solid, about 3 hours. *Makes 2½ to 3 dozen candies.*

CREAM WAFERS

    1 cup soft butter
    ⅓ cup whipping cream
    2 cups Gold Medal Flour (regular or Wondra)
    Sugar
    Filling (below)

Mix butter, cream and flour thoroughly. Chill. Heat oven to 375°. Divide dough into thirds. (Keep remainder in refrigerator until ready to roll.) Roll one third of dough ⅛ inch thick on floured cloth-covered board. Cut with 1½-inch round cutter. Place rounds on waxed paper that is heavily covered with sugar. Turn each round with spatula so both sides are coated with sugar. Place on ungreased baking sheet; prick each about 4 times with fork. Bake 7 to 9 minutes. Cool; put 2 cookies together with Filling. *Makes about 5 dozen double cookies.*

Filling

Blend ¼ cup soft butter with ¾ cup confectioners' sugar, 1 egg yolk and 1 teaspoon vanilla. Tint pink or light green with food coloring, if desired.

Frozen Fruit

Fruit-slice Cookies

Ham Puffs Petite

Cream Wafers

Russian Tea Cakes

Tea Sandwiches

Small Afternoon Tea

Cucumber Sandwiches (page 89)   Petal Tartlets
Hot Fruited Tea
Crystallized Ginger   Salted Nuts

PETAL TARTLETS

Sparkling "flowers" to brighten your tea tray.

½ cup shortening (part butter or margarine)
½ cup sugar
1 egg
¾ teaspoon vanilla
1½ cups Gold Medal Flour* (regular or Wondra)
½ teaspoon salt
¼ teaspoon soda
Strawberry, cherry or apricot preserves

Mix shortening, sugar, egg and vanilla. Stir flour, salt and soda together; blend into shortening mixture. Mix thoroughly with hands. Refrigerate dough several hours or overnight.

Heat oven to 400°. Roll dough ⅛ inch thick on lightly floured cloth-covered board. Cut with 3-inch round scalloped cutter. Ease rounds into muffin cups. Fill each with ½ tablespoon preserves. Bake about 12 minutes. Cool a few minutes before removing from muffin cups. Set each tartlet on a washed green leaf, if desired. *Makes about 18 tartlets.*

If using Self-Rising Flour, omit salt and reduce soda to ⅛ teaspoon.

HOT FRUITED TEA

5 cups boiling water
5 tea bags or 5 teaspoons tea
10 whole cloves
¼ teaspoon cinnamon
½ cup sugar
¼ cup lemon juice
⅓ cup orange juice
3 unpeeled orange slices, cut in half

Pour boiling water over tea, cloves and cinnamon. Cover and let steep 5 minutes. Strain tea; stir in sugar and fruit juices. Heat to just below boiling. Serve hot with orange slice in each cup. *6 servings.*

Weddings and Anniversaries—Times for Tradition

A wedding in the family usually generates a number of parties, all with delightfully happy overtones. From the announcement of an engagement to the celebration of a golden wedding anniversary, the mood of such occasions is one of tradition and sentiment, with flowers and white candles as table decorations, and often with some age-old customs adding to the spirit of the party. And it's no wonder that these memorable times seem even more meaningful when celebrated in one's own home or in the home of a good friend.

The Engagement Party

Breaking the news of a wedding-to-come is the privilege of the bride's parents. So if there's to be an engagement party, they are the ones to give it.

The announcement may be made at a luncheon if only ladies are to be present. The Club Luncheon (page 82) offers an ideal menu for such an occasion—but substitute the more appropriate Heart Meringues (page 144) for the dessert. If the announcement is to be made at a dinner party, the French Formality dinner (page 40) would be perfect. If the engaged couple have a great many friends, announcing the happy event at a tea or cocktail party is a good way to let everyone know the news at once.

The announcement itself can be made in any one of a dozen ways. Traditionally the bride-to-be's father waits until all the guests have assembled and then proposes a toast to his daughter and her fiance. However, the Twin Hearts Cake (page 144) topped by the couple's initials. may be all the announcement necessary. To let the rest of the world know about the engagement, a news release is timed to appear in the edition of the local newspaper following the party.

Showers

A bridal shower gives the bride's friends a chance to share in the festivities. (Showers should never be given by the mother or sisters of either the bride or groom.) A shower may be a girls-only party—perhaps a kitchen or personal or linen shower. If you want to give a shower built around a meal, it may be a brunch or luncheon—perhaps the Brunch Parisienne (page 76) or Two-table Bridge Luncheon (page 86), substituting a heart-shaped cake (page 144) for the dessert. A small afternoon tea, such as the one on page 92, also provides a lovely setting for a bridal shower. In an informal vein, it might be a morning coffee party (see pages 112-121), a dessert and coffee party (see pages 122-131) or a barbecue supper (see pages 100-104). The shower may be a co-ed party, with gifts appropriate for both the bride and groom—a picnic shower, paper shower or games shower. Often the gifts themselves serve as the table decoration, traditionally piled in and around an open parasol or a watering can. The opening of the presents provides all the entertainment necessary.

The Rehearsal Dinner

Sometimes called the bridal dinner, the party that follows or precedes the wedding rehearsal is usually given by the groom's parents. It always includes all the members of the wedding party (including husbands or wives of married attendants), both sets of parents and the clergyman and his wife. Beyond that the host may include as few or as many friends of both families as he wishes. Following an afternoon rehearsal, the menu should be a full-scale meal—possibly one of the Ham Buffets (pages 58-62). If the rehearsal is in the early evening, a somewhat lighter meal like our Midnight Snack Supper (page 140) may be served. In either case, this is an occasion usually marked by several toasts from the bridal party and, if there is space, by dancing.

The Wedding Reception

On the great day itself, the bride's parents are hosts at the party that follows the ceremony. If the wedding takes place before one o'clock in the afternoon, the meal that follows is called a breakfast although it is often quite a substantial luncheon menu. An afternoon or evening wedding is usually followed by what amounts to a tea—like the tea on page 88, with the addition of a wedding cake and a punch or champagne for toasting the bridal couple, or the reception on page 94. The table, set with handsome china, silver and crystal, should be decorated with flowers, or the cake may serve as the centerpiece.

Anniversaries

Informal anniversary celebrations—small dinner parties, cocktail parties, dessert parties—are usually the most popular. But it is fun to highlight these occasions with the traditional table decorations and gifts—paper for the first anniversary, wood for the fifth, tin for the tenth and so on.

A milestone such as the twenty-fifth or fiftieth anniversary calls for extra-special attention. Any celebration reminiscent of the long-past wedding reception would be appropriate, including perhaps the Twin Hearts Cake (page 144) or Double-ring Wedding Cake (page 97) or even the Tiered Wedding Cake (page 95) topped with the figures "25" or "50."

Wedding Reception

Tiered Wedding Cake   Groom's Cake
Ice-cream Molds
Salted Nuts   Mints
Coffee   June Punch

TIERED WEDDING CAKE

You will need:

**7 packages of our white cake mix
6 packages of our fluffy white frosting mix
4 pounds confectioners' sugar, sifted**

Bake cakes the day before they are to be assembled, or bake even earlier and freeze them.

Heat oven to 350°. Bake cake in round layer pans, 9x1½ inches, as directed on package. Cool. Repeat with 5 additional cake mixes. Trim rounded tops to make layers level.

Grease and flour two 3-pound shortening cans (about 4¾ inches in diameter). Prepare remaining package of cake mix as directed except—pour 2 cups batter into each can. Bake in 350° oven 40 to 45 minutes. (Use remaining batter to bake about 6 cupcakes as directed on package; use as desired.) Remove layers from cans. Cool and trim off rounded top crusts.

Prepare Wedding Cake Icing (right) as needed, *one recipe at a time.* You will need about 6 recipes to assemble and decorate cake.

Assemble cake on tray or serving plate. You will need 9 layers for the bottom tier, 3 layers for each section of cloverleaf. For each cake of the cloverleaf, use 1 recipe Wedding Cake Icing. Stack 3 layers with ⅓ cup of the icing between. Spread remaining frosting over sides and top of cake. (Diagram A)

Prepare 1 recipe Wedding Cake Icing, adding 1 to 2 cups sifted confectioners' sugar to make a decorating frosting stiff enough to hold its shape. Place frosting in decorators' tube; flute around bottom and top edge of each frosted cake.

Arrange the 3 cakes together to form a cloverleaf, leaving a small space in center for a support. (Diagram B) Place a glass or aluminum foil-covered container of the same height as the frosted cakes in center of cloverleaf.

Cover an 8-inch cardboard circle with aluminum foil. Stack the remaining 3 layers on foil circle, filling and frosting with 1 recipe Wedding Cake Icing. Place cake with circle on support. (Diagram B)

Cover a 4-inch cardboard circle with aluminum foil; stack the 2 small layers on foil circle, filling and frosting with 1 recipe Wedding Cake Icing. Place on top of center cake. With remaining decorating frosting in decorators' tube, flute around bottom and top edge of the top two cakes. Decorate cakes with scallops and flowers as desired.

After frosting sets (30 minutes to 1 hour), cover entire cake with plastic wrap, draping long pieces gently over cake. *Makes 100 servings.*

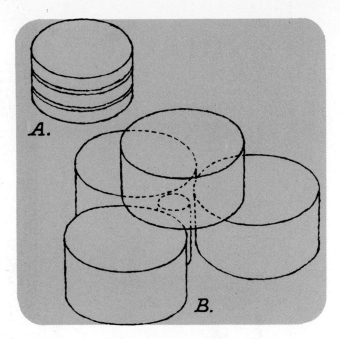

Wedding Cake Icing

In small mixer bowl, prepare 1 package frosting mix as directed. Transfer to large bowl and mix in 2 cups sifted confectioners' sugar, 1 cup at a time.

To Cut Wedding Cake...

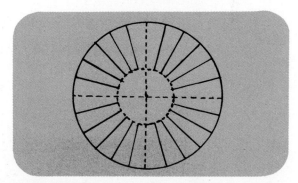

As the small top tier is often to be frozen for the couple's first anniversary, set aside the top tier and begin cutting from the second tier. For uniform servings, first cut the cake in a circle that is a little more than halfway to the center (see dotted lines above). Then cut the outer circle into quarters and serve 6 wedges from each quarter. Four wider wedges are then cut from the inner circle. When tier of cake is completely served, remove cardboard from top of next tier and cut in the same manner.

GROOM'S CAKE AT THE RECEPTION

Traditionally this is the cake to dream on. A dark rich fruitcake, it is often left unfrosted and cut into small pieces to be packed in special tiny boxes or wrapped in aluminum or colored foil and tied with ribbon. The boxes or beribboned packets are then arranged on a lovely tray and placed near the door so departing guests can take the cake home to tuck under their pillows.

Sometimes the groom's cake is iced and used as the top tier of the wedding cake, later to be wrapped and frozen until the first anniversary.

Certainly such a specialty cake is not a necessary, or even expected, item for a wedding reception. However, many brides do enjoy this added grace note, and thoughtful is a friend or relative if she chooses to bake and box groom's cake as a gift to the busy bride.

GROOM'S CAKE

1 cup shortening
2 cups brown sugar (packed)
4 eggs (1 cup)
½ cup dark jelly
½ cup fruit juice
3 cups Gold Medal Flour* (regular or Wondra)
1 teaspoon baking powder
1 teaspoon salt
1 teaspoon each cinnamon and mace
½ teaspoon each nutmeg and allspice
¼ teaspoon cloves
1½ pounds raisins
½ pound currants
½ pound citron, cut up
½ pound nuts, coarsely chopped

Heat oven to 275°. Line two loaf pans, 9x5x3 inches, with aluminum foil or heavy wrapping paper; grease. Cream shortening and brown sugar until fluffy. Beat in eggs. Beat jelly with a fork; stir in fruit juice; set aside. Stir together flour, baking powder, salt and spices. Blend into creamed mixture alternately with jelly-juice mixture. Stir in fruits and nuts. Fill prepared pans almost full. Bake 2½ to 3 hours (cover with paper the last hour), or until wooden pick inserted in center comes out clean. Cool. Wrap in plastic wrap or aluminum foil; refrigerate. Cut cake into ½-inch slices; cut each slice into 1¼-inch squares. *Makes about 192 1¼-inch squares.*

*If using Self-Rising Flour, omit baking powder and salt.

JUNE PUNCH

3 quarts water
2 cups sugar
2 cans (5½ ounces each) frozen lemon juice concentrate
1 quart apple juice
2 quarts cranberry cocktail
1 pint orange juice
1 pint strong black tea

Heat water and sugar to boiling, stirring constantly until sugar dissolves. Stir in remaining ingredients. Chill. *60 servings (½-cup size).*

Anniversary Buffet

Fresh Fruit Tray
Nut Bread Sandwiches
Twin Hearts Cake (page 144) or Double-ring Wedding Cake
Ice-cream Roses
Bonbons   Salted Nuts
Coffee   Tea   Golden Punch

NUT BREAD

For dainty tea treats, cut thin slices to sandwich together with softened cream cheese.

½ cup sugar
1 egg
1¼ cups milk
3 cups Bisquick
1½ cups chopped nuts

Heat oven to 350°. Grease a loaf pan, 9x5x3 inches. Mix sugar, egg, milk and Bisquick. Beat vigorously 30 seconds. Batter may still be slightly lumpy. Stir in nuts. Pour into prepared pan. Bake 45 to 50 minutes, or until a wooden pick inserted in center comes out clean. (Crack in top is typical.) Cool before slicing. *Makes 1 loaf.*

DOUBLE-RING WEDDING CAKE

Heat oven to 350°. Grease and flour a 10½-inch ring mold. Prepare 1 package of our white cake mix as directed except—pour batter into prepared mold. Bake 35 to 40 minutes. Cool slightly; remove from pan. Repeat, using another package of cake mix.

On a large plate or tray, place cakes side by side, edges touching. Prepare White Frosting (below); reserve 1½ cups for decorating. Frost cake with remaining frosting. Fold enough sifted confectioners' sugar (about 1 cup) into reserved frosting to make it stiff enough to hold its shape. With frosting in decorators' tube, flute around bottom and top edge of rings or make other designs as desired. Place wedding bells or flowers with streamers at center of double ring. *25 to 30 servings.*

White Frosting

Prepare 2 packages of our fluffy white frosting mix as directed on package except—mix in large mixer bowl and use 1 cup boiling water. Beat 5 to 7 minutes or until soft peaks form. Add 1 teaspoon almond extract. Adding 1 cup sifted confectioners' sugar at a time, blend in 4 cups at low speed on mixer.

ICE-CREAM ROSES

With an ice-cream scoop, make firm solid balls from choice of ice cream or sherbet; place each ball in green paper baking cup and freeze firm. To form a rose, make short crisscross cuts with tip of spoon in center of each ice-cream ball. Working around center cuts to edge of ball, cut slashes at irregular intervals with side-front tip of spoon, pushing gently outward in each cut to form petals. Freeze. At serving time, tuck in one or two green leaves, if desired.

GOLDEN PUNCH

2 cups lemon juice, chilled
2 cups orange juice, chilled
2 cups sugar
2 cups cold water
4 quarts ginger ale, chilled

Combine fruit juices, sugar and water in a large punch bowl. Stir until sugar dissolves. Just before serving, pour ginger ale down side of bowl; stir gently. Float Iced Fruit Garland (below) in bowl, if desired. Garnish with mint leaves. *Makes about 40 servings (½-cup size).*

Iced Fruit Garland

In a ring mold, arrange alternating slices of lemon and orange with washed unhulled strawberries. Add just enough water* to partially cover fruit. (Too much water will float the fruit.) Freeze. When frozen, add water to fill mold ¾ full. Freeze. Unmold and float fruit side up in punch bowl.

For a clear ice ring, boil the water and cool before using.

Coffee and Tea for a Crowd

FOR GOOD COFFEE...

• Always start with a coffee maker that is thoroughly clean.

• Never brew coffee at less than ¾ of the coffee maker's capacity. If a small quantity is all that's needed, select a smaller coffee maker.

• Freshness is vital to a good cup of coffee. Use fresh coffee and freshly drawn cold water.

• Serve hot steaming coffee as soon as possible after brewing. If necessary to let coffee stand any length of time, hold at serving temperature over very low heat on an asbestos pad. Keep coffee hot but do not boil it.

Coffee Chart		
Average 5½-ounce servings	Measure of Coffee	Amount of Water
20 (for 12 persons)	2 cups	1 gallon
40 (for 25 persons)	4 cups	2 gallons

To brew coffee in a saucepot:

Measure "regular" grind coffee into a clean cloth sack; fill only half full to allow for expansion of coffee and free circulation of water. (Before using sack, soak and rinse thoroughly.) Tie sack, allowing enough cord for fastening to pot handle.

In a clean large saucepot, heat measured amount of fresh cold water to a full rolling boil. Reduce heat to hold just below boiling. Fasten sack to pot handle; submerge in the water. Keep saucepot over low heat. Brew 6 to 8 minutes, pushing sack up and down frequently to get proper extraction. When coffee is ready, remove sack, permitting all extract to drain into saucepot.

To brew coffee in an automatic coffee maker:

Follow manufacturer's directions for selecting grind of coffee, brewing coffee and holding at serving temperature.

FOR BRISK TEA...

• Use a spotlessly clean teapot made of glass, china or earthenware. Rinse the teapot with boiling water and drain.

• Bring freshly drawn cold water to a full rolling boil, then use immediately.

• Taste to judge the strength of tea; don't assume strength by the color. Some weak teas produce a dark brew, some strong teas brew to a light tone.

For only a few servings, make tea in teapot:

Measure tea into teapot, using 1 teaspoon loose tea or 1 tea bag for each cup of tea needed. Pour boiling water over tea and let steep 3 to 5 minutes to develop full flavor. Strain tea leaves or remove tea bags. To use instant tea, follow directions on jar.

For 50 portions of tea, prepare a concentrate:

Place 16 family-size tea bags or ¼ pound (1½ cups) loose tea in a large container. Pour 2½ quarts boiling water over tea; steep 5 minutes. Remove tea bags or strain tea leaves. Using 1 part concentrate to 3 parts boiling water, mix and serve as needed.

Casual Get-togethers, Outdoors and In

*In addition to dress-up parties, there are all sorts of gay informal get-to-
gethers that seem particularly suited to certain seasons, occasions or groups
of friends.*

*A backyard cookout is a pleasant way to take advantage of summer and
gives you a chance to ask guests to bring their children. A spur-of-the-moment invitation to take potluck has the special charm of spontaneity. Ten
a.m. coffee is a wonderfully easy way to catch up on girl talk, while an invitation to come over for dessert and coffee means an early evening for com-
muting husbands. And a party built around snacks and drinks is perhaps
the most popular and relaxed way to entertain today.*

*But whether it's dinner, coffee, cocktails or midnight supper, and no matter
how spontaneous the invitation or how simple the refreshments, a good
hostess will manage to provide that little extra—a special sauce, an unusual
nibbler or a dramatic dessert—which makes the event really a party.*

Especially for Patio Parties

Undoubtedly the most popular kind of party for warm weather entertaining is the one served right in your own backyard. Whether you call it "barbecue supper," "cookout" or "patio party," and whether you serve gourmet chickens impressively prepared on a revolving spit or a thick steak simply tossed onto a charcoal grill, the keynote of the occasion is informality. Guests and host alike may dress in shorts, slacks or simple sports clothes.

More often than not the man of the house turns chef and takes over the meat while you serve the salad or relishes crisp from the refrigerator—and later, a delicious dessert that you prepared ahead of time. Paper plates and napkins are the order of the day, and everyone pitches in with the serving, passing and, perhaps, with the cleaning up.

Sometime during the meal someone is bound to remark that food always tastes twice as good when you eat it outdoors—because it does.

Malibu Barbecue

California Artichoke Plate
Coconut Ham Slice   Sweet Potato Grill
Garden Relishes on Ice   Patio Rolls
Mocha Squares   Coffee

Outdoor dining can be as elegant and festive as any company occasion—maybe more so, when you start with a hearty menu embellished with gourmet touches. Here the thick ham slice, drenched with a marvelous sweet-sour sauce of coconut syrup and orange segments, is accompanied by butter-grilled sweet potato slices. The fresh, cool relish tray of bright-colored raw vegetables arranged over a mound of crushed ice is pretty enough to double as the table centerpiece. For added effect, light your patio table with hurricane lamps and use an attractive pale green cloth or place mats and perhaps flowered napkins.

Serving suggestions: Let the head of the household mastermind the grilling operation while you chat with the guests and pass the artichoke hearts and dip. When the main course is finished, clear the table; serve the dessert and coffee from the kitchen.

CALIFORNIA ARTICHOKE PLATE

Prepare 2 packages (9 ounces each) frozen artichoke hearts as directed on package except—add 2 lemon slices to the cooking water; drain and chill. Serve artichokes on wooden picks with Onion Dip (below). *6 servings.*

Onion Dip

Mix ⅓ cup dairy sour cream, ⅓ cup mayonnaise or salad dressing and 1 tablespoon dry onion soup mix. Chill. *Makes ⅔ cup.*

Permanent Party Gear

A tote basket with special compartments for glasses, cups and silver cuts down on to-ing and fro-ing from the house.

COCONUT HAM SLICE

1 center ham slice, 1½ inches thick
1 jar (8 ounces) coconut syrup
1 can (11 ounces) mandarin orange segments, drained (reserve syrup)
¼ teaspoon allspice
1 tablespoon cornstarch
1 tablespoon vinegar
½ cup raisins
¼ cup flaked coconut

Score fat around edge of ham. Combine ⅓ cup coconut syrup with 2 teaspoons mandarin orange syrup and the allspice. Place ham on double thickness heavy-duty aluminum foil on grill 4 inches from medium coals. Grill 15 minutes on each side, basting frequently with coconut syrup mixture. Add enough cold water to remaining mandarin orange syrup to make 1 cup liquid in saucepan. Stir in cornstarch with remaining coconut syrup. Cook, stirring constantly, until mixture thickens and boils. Boil and stir 1 minute. Stir in vinegar, mandarin orange segments, raisins and coconut; serve hot over ham. *6 servings.*

Do-ahead Note: The accompaniment sauce may be made in advance and reheated covered in an aluminum foil pan about 15 minutes on side of grill.

SWEET POTATO GRILL

Pare 2 pounds sweet potatoes and cut on the diagonal into ½-inch slices. Parboil 10 minutes. Melt ½ cup butter or margarine; stir in 1 teaspoon salt. Grill potato slices 4 inches from medium coals 10 minutes on each side, basting frequently with butter mixture. *6 servings.*

GARDEN RELISHES ON ICE

Arrange fresh mushroom and cucumber slices, green pepper rings, green onions and cherry tomatoes on crushed ice.

PATIO ROLLS

Split 12 baked club rolls in half lengthwise. Spread cut surfaces with butter. Reassemble rolls; seal securely in heavy-duty aluminum foil. Grill 4 inches from medium coals 10 to 12 minutes, turning once. *12 rolls.*

MOCHA SQUARES

Bake Fudgy Brownies as directed on 1 package (1 pound) of our fudge brownie mix; cool. Cut into squares; top each with small scoop coffee ice cream. Pour Chocolate Sauce (below) over ice cream. *9 servings.*

Chocolate Sauce

In top of double boiler combine 1 package of our dark chocolate fudge flavor frosting mix, 3 tablespoons soft butter or margarine and 2 tablespoons light corn syrup. Gradually stir in ½ cup milk. Heat over rapidly boiling water 5 minutes, stirring occasionally. Remove from heat; stir in 2 tablespoons dark rum. Cool. Serve warm or slightly chilled. *Makes 1 pint.*

Company Favorites for Patio Parties

GRILLED "TARTARE STEAK" APPETIZERS

These steak "bites" were inspired by the classic raw steak tartare.

> ½ pound ground sirloin
> 1 egg
> 1 green onion, finely chopped
> ½ teaspoon salt
> 2 dashes Tabasco
> Soft butter or margarine
> 5 slices bread

Mix meat, egg, onion, salt and Tabasco thoroughly. Butter one side of each bread slice. Spread unbuttered side of bread with meat mixture. Carefully spread additional butter on meat mixture. Place bread side down on grill 2 inches from medium coals. Grill 1½ minutes, or until bread is toasted. Turn and grill 1½ minutes longer. With kitchen shears, cut each bread slice into 9 bite-size pieces. *45 appetizers.*

PIRATE STEAK

Steak with a great sauce—for men who like a bold, intriguing flavor!

> 1 can (12 ounces) beer
> ½ cup chili sauce
> ¼ cup salad oil
> 2 tablespoons soy sauce
> 1 tablespoon Dijon-style mustard
> ½ teaspoon Tabasco
> ⅛ teaspoon liquid smoke
> 1 medium onion, coarsely chopped
> 2 cloves garlic, crushed
> 3-pound sirloin steak, 1½ to 2 inches thick
> 1 teaspoon salt
> ½ teaspoon pepper

Mix all ingredients except steak, salt and pepper; simmer for 30 minutes. Brush the steak with the sauce. Grill steak 4 inches from medium-hot coals 15 minutes on each side; baste frequently with sauce. Season with salt and pepper after turning and after removing from grill. Serve with remaining sauce. *8 servings.*

GRILLED STEAK WITH SESAME BUTTER

Allow 1 pound of any bone-in steak for each person. For a boneless steak, allow ⅓ to ¾ pound for each person.

Trim excess fat from sirloin, porterhouse, club or T-bone steaks, 1 to 2 inches thick; slash edges at 2-inch intervals to prevent curling. Grill steaks 3 inches from hot coals suggested time (see chart below). Always handle steak with tongs (fork releases juices). Season steak with salt and pepper after turning and after removing from grill. Test doneness by making a knife slit alongside bone. To serve, spread Sesame Butter (below) over steaks.

Sesame Butter

Beat ¼ cup soft butter, 1 teaspoon Worcestershire sauce and ½ teaspoon garlic salt until fluffy. Stir in 1 tablespoon toasted sesame seed. *About ¼ cup—enough for 4 steaks.*

Grilling Time for Each Side			
	1 inch thick	1½ inches thick	2 inches thick
	Minutes	Minutes	Minutes
Rare	4 to 5	7 to 8	12 to 13
Medium	7 to 8	10 to 12	15 to 17
Well Done	10 to 11	14 to 15	22 to 25

TWIRLIN' TURKEY

Great for crowd-size servings. Pictured right.

**8- to 10-pound turkey
2 to 2½ tablespoons salt
Pepper
½ cup butter or margarine, melted**

Wash turkey; pat dry with paper towels. Rub cavities with salt; sprinkle with pepper. Fasten neck skin to back with skewer. Flatten wings over breast; tie with string to hold wings securely. Insert spit rod in neck skin parallel to backbone; bring it out just above tail. Secure breast and tail areas with holding forks. Check balance by rotating in palms of hands. Tie tail to rod; cross legs and tie to tail. Arrange medium-hot coals at back of firebox; place foil drip pan under spit area. Insert meat thermometer into heavy part of breast. Brush turkey with melted butter. Cook turkey on rotisserie about 3 hours, or until leg bone moves easily. (Meat thermometer should register 185°.) Add coals, if necessary, to maintain heat. *10 to 14 servings.*

CHICKEN ROUND 'N ROUND

Served plain or stuffed, it's party-perfect!

2 broiler-fryer chickens, about 3 pounds each
4 teaspoons salt
Pepper
⅓ cup butter or margarine, melted

Wash chickens and pat dry with paper towels. Rub cavity of each with 2 teaspoons salt and dash pepper. Fasten neck skin to back with skewer. Flatten wings over breast; tie with string to hold wings securely. Tie drumsticks securely to tail. Insert spit rod lengthwise through center of birds from tail toward front. Secure each with holding forks. Check balance by rotating in palms of hands. Arrange medium-hot coals at back of firebox; place foil drip pan under spit area. Cook chickens on rotisserie 2½ hours or until leg bone moves easily, brushing frequently with butter last 30 minutes of cooking time. (Meat thermometer should register 190°.) Add coals, if necessary, to maintain heat. *4 to 6 servings.*

Chicken with Pâté Dressing: Prepare Chicken Round 'n Round (above) except—before mounting chickens, rub the cavity of each with only ½ teaspoon salt. Fill cavities of chickens with mixture of 3 cups cooked rice, 8 ounces liverwurst, cubed, ¼ cup butter or margarine, melted, 2 tablespoons parsley flakes, ½ teaspoon salt and ½ teaspoon ground thyme. Brush chickens with ¼ cup salad oil; sprinkle with 2 teaspoons paprika. Cook as above except—do not brush with butter.

Note: If you have extra dressing, heat on grill in covered aluminum foil pan about 20 minutes.

SUMMERTIME HAMBURGERS

2 tablespoons instant minced onion
2 tablespoons water
1 pound ground beef
1 egg
¼ cup catsup
⅓ cup fine dry bread crumbs
2 tablespoons finely chopped mustard pickle
1 tablespoon Worcestershire sauce
1 teaspoon salt
¼ teaspoon pepper
Toasted hamburger buns

Mix all ingredients except toasted hamburger buns. Shape into 6 patties; chill thoroughly. Grill 4 inches from hot coals 6 minutes on each side. Serve in toasted hamburger buns. *6 servings.*

SWEET-GLAZED SPARERIBS

3 to 4 pounds loin back ribs
1 cup soy sauce
½ cup sherry or pineapple juice
2 tablespoons honey
1 clove garlic, crushed
½ cup honey

Place ribs in plastic bag or shallow glass dish. Combine remaining ingredients except ½ cup honey; pour over meat. Fasten bag securely or cover dish with plastic wrap. Refrigerate overnight, turning ribs occasionally. Remove ribs from marinade; reserve marinade. Lace ribs on spit rod; secure with holding forks. Check balance by rotating in palms of hands. Arrange medium coals at back of firebox; place foil drip pan under spit area. Cook ribs on rotisserie 1½ to 2 hours or until tender, basting frequently with reserved marinade. Add coals, if necessary, to maintain even heat. Brush ribs with the ½ cup honey during last half hour of cooking time. *4 servings.*

SWORDFISH SUPREME

Delicate swordfish with a creamy avocado sauce. Serve the sauce with any type of fish—or as a fluffy chip dip.

4 swordfish steaks (6 to 8 ounces each),
1 inch thick
1 teaspoon salt
¼ teaspoon pepper
¼ cup butter or margarine, melted
1 tablespoon lemon juice
1 teaspoon crushed chervil leaves
Avocado Sauce (below)
Lemon wedges

Sprinkle fish with salt and pepper. Combine butter, lemon juice and chervil. Place steaks on lightly greased grill 4 inches from medium coals. Grill 10 minutes on each side, brushing frequently with butter mixture. Serve steaks with Avocado Sauce and lemon wedges. *4 servings.*

Avocado Sauce

1 small ripe avocado, peeled and pitted
⅓ cup dairy sour cream
1 teaspoon lemon juice
¼ teaspoon salt
Few drops Tabasco

Mix all ingredients in blender or beat with rotary beater until smooth.

Spur-of-the-Moment Dinners

There's nothing more delightful than an impromptu party—and few hostessing performances are more impressive than being able to turn out a delicious meal with no advance warning. But spontaneous as your invitation to "come and take potluck with us" may be, it does call for some previous preparation.

First, your cupboard shelves must be stocked with such keepables as a few cans of different kinds of soup, some canned meat, chicken or seafood, the mix-makings of biscuits or muffins, noodles or potatoes and a dessert—and hopefully a supply of herbs, seasonings and garnishes to make them special. Your freezer, too, should offer an equally bountiful array of off-the-cuff dinner starters.

Secondly, even a spur-of-the-moment meal deserves a rehearsal. So don't wait for company to put your potluck dinners to the test. Serve an emergency menu to the family once or twice to get the feel and the timing of it. Then you'll be confident of a star performance before a larger audience.

Quick from the Cupboard Shelf

Spiced Soup
Pork and Peanuts   Buttered Green Beans
Hot Blueberry Muffins   Artichoke Toss with Onion Rings
Choco-Crème Parfaits   Coffee

In an hour or less you can have this meal on the table —and no one will ever guess that it all came out of the boxes and cans of a well-stocked cupboard.

Be sure to prepare the parfaits first; they have to chill. The hearty main dish and the muffins bake together in the oven while you heat the soup and beans and assemble the salad.

Serving suggestions: Prelude dinner at the table with mugs of the appetizer soup served in the living room. Individual plates of salad should be in place when dinner is announced. Then let the host take charge of serving. You take over, of course, when it comes to clearing the table and serving the dessert and coffee.

SPICED SOUP

1 can (11¼ ounces) condensed green pea soup
2 soup cans milk
¼ teaspoon nutmeg
Sliced pitted ripe olives

Combine soup, milk and nutmeg in saucepan with rotary beater; heat through, stirring occasionally. Pour into mugs; garnish with olives. *4 servings.*

PORK AND PEANUTS

2 cans (12 ounces each) pork luncheon meat
1 can (1 pound 1 ounce) vacuum-packed
    whole sweet potatoes, drained
½ cup dark corn syrup
½ cup crunchy peanut butter
¼ cup orange juice
1 tablespoon butter or margarine, melted
1 jar (1 pound 12 ounces) spiced crab apples,
    drained

Heat oven to 375°. Remove luncheon meat from cans; cut each loaf into 4 slices; place in square baking dish, 9x9x2 inches. Arrange sweet potatoes on top. Mix corn syrup and peanut butter; stir in orange juice and butter. Pour over meat and potatoes. Top with crab apples. Bake 25 to 30 minutes. *4 servings.*

BUTTERED GREEN BEANS

Empty 1 can (15½ ounces) small whole green beans into saucepan; heat through. Drain beans and season with 2 tablespoons butter. *4 servings.*

HOT BLUEBERRY MUFFINS

Prepare muffins as directed on 1 package of our wild blueberry muffin mix except—bake in 375° oven 20 to 25 minutes. *Makes 12 muffins.*

ARTICHOKE TOSS WITH ONION RINGS

1 head lettuce, torn into bite-size pieces
1 can (7 ounces) artichoke hearts, drained
    and quartered
Classic French Dressing (page 42)
1 can (3½ ounces) French fried onion rings

Just before serving, toss lettuce and artichoke hearts with Classic French Dressing. Garnish with onion rings. *4 servings.*

CHOCO-CRÈME PARFAITS

Prepare 1 package (3¾ ounces) vanilla whipped dessert mix as directed on package. In each of 4 parfait glasses, alternate layers of whipped dessert mix and about 2 tablespoons chocolate fudge sauce. Chill at least 1 hour. *4 servings.*

Quick from the Cupboard Dinner
∼∼∼∼∼ PLAN FOR PREPARATION ∼∼∼∼∼

1. *Prepare parfaits; chill.* **2.** *Wash, dry and chill lettuce; quarter and chill artichoke hearts.* **3.** *Prepare salad dressing.* **4. Prepare and bake main dish.* **5.** *Prepare and bake muffins.* **6. Set table.* **7.** *Prepare coffee.* **8.** *Heat green beans.* **9.** *Heat appetizer soup; serve.* **10.** *Pour water.* **11.** *Toss salad; place on individual salad plates; set on table.*

Fast from the Freezer Dinner
∼∼∼∼∼ PLAN FOR PREPARATION ∼∼∼∼∼

1. *Quick-chill can of pineapple in freezer.* **2.** *Remove rolls and melon balls from freezer; thaw according to recipe directions.* **3.** *Prepare herb butter for salmon.* **4.** *Prepare salad dressing, if not using bottled dressing.* **5.** *Prepare dip; serve.* **6.** *Prepare and bake salmon and potatoes.* **7.** *Set table.* **8.** *Prepare coffee.* **9.** *Cook green beans.* **10.** *Prepare salads; place on table.* **11.** *Pour water.* **12.** *Heat rolls while serving plates.*

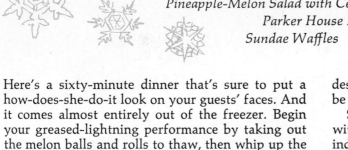

Fast from the Freezer

Chips and Garden Dip
Herbed Salmon Steaks   Potato Balls
Buttered Italian Green Beans
Pineapple-Melon Salad with Celery French Dressing
Parker House Rolls
Sundae Waffles   Coffee

Here's a sixty-minute dinner that's sure to put a how-does-she-do-it look on your guests' faces. And it comes almost entirely out of the freezer. Begin your greased-lightning performance by taking out the melon balls and rolls to thaw, then whip up the dip. Bake salmon steaks and potatoes (unthawed) together, staggering the pans in the oven so the heat can circulate freely. In a spare moment, prepare for dessert by setting out the toaster (for waffles) and dessert plates on a kitchen counter. The rolls can be heated while you arrange the dinner plates.

Serving suggestions: Keep your guests happy with chips and dip while you set the table. Place individual salad plates on the table; serve dinner, two plates at a time, from the kitchen. The rolls, of course, may be passed in a basket. For dessert, toast the waffles and serve them, sundaed, on individual dessert plates.

GARDEN DIP

In small mixer bowl, combine 1 cup dairy sour cream, ¼ cup shredded Parmesan cheese and 1 envelope (2⅛ ounces) dry garden vegetable soup mix; beat on high speed until fluffy. *Makes about 1¼ cups.*

HERBED SALMON STEAKS

3 packages (12 ounces each) frozen salmon steaks
¼ cup lemon juice
2 tablespoons butter or margarine, melted
2 teaspoons crushed marjoram leaves
2 teaspoons onion salt
½ teaspoon seasoned pepper
Paprika
Lemon wedges
Snipped parsley

Heat oven to 450°. Grease an oblong baking dish, 13½x9x2 inches; place frozen salmon steaks in pan. Stir together lemon juice, butter, marjoram, onion salt and seasoned pepper; brush both sides of steaks with mixture. Bake 35 minutes, or until fish flakes easily with a fork. (Do not turn steaks.) Sprinkle steaks with paprika; serve garnished with lemon wedges and parsley. *6 servings.*

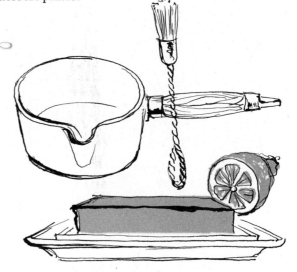

POTATO BALLS

Spread 1½ packages (1 pound each) frozen shredded potato balls in jelly roll pan, 15½x10½x1 inch. Heat in 450° oven 20 minutes or until crisp and hot, stirring once. *6 servings.*

Note: Remaining potato balls may be tightly wrapped and stored in freezer for later use.

BUTTERED ITALIAN GREEN BEANS

Prepare 2 packages (9 ounces each) frozen Italian green beans as directed on package. (Do not overcook.) Drain; season with butter. *6 servings.*

PINEAPPLE-MELON SALAD WITH CELERY FRENCH DRESSING

1 package (16 ounces) frozen melon balls
Crisp salad greens
1 can (1 pound 4½ ounces) pineapple slices, chilled and drained
Celery French Dressing* (below)

Immerse package of melon balls in bowl of hot water about 45 minutes to thaw. Remove melon balls from package and drain. Arrange salad greens on 6 small plates. Place a pineapple slice on each; top with melon balls. Spoon Celery French Dressing over fruit. *6 servings.*

Bottled clear French dressing may be used. Add 1 teaspoon celery seed to ½ cup dressing.

Celery French Dressing

1 tablespoon sugar
1 teaspoon salt
1 teaspoon paprika
1 teaspoon dry mustard
1 teaspoon celery seed
¼ teaspoon pepper
¼ cup vinegar or lemon juice
¾ cup salad oil
Few drops onion juice or 1 clove garlic, crushed

Shake all ingredients in covered jar. Just before using, shake again to mix. *Makes about 1 cup.*

PARKER HOUSE ROLLS

Remove 1 package (7½ ounces) frozen Parker House rolls from freezer 45 to 60 minutes before using. Allow rolls to defrost with cover on. Remove cover from package; cover with aluminum foil. Heat in 450° oven 5 minutes. *12 rolls.*

SUNDAE WAFFLES

1 package (5 ounces) frozen waffles
1 pint vanilla ice cream
Warm maple syrup or favorite chocolate sauce
Chopped walnuts

Toast waffles as directed on package; place on serving plates. Top each with scoop of ice cream. Pour syrup or sauce over ice cream and waffle; sprinkle with nuts. *6 servings.*

Company Favorites for Spur-of-the-Moment Dinners

HURRY-SCURRY MACARONI

2 packages of our macaroni and Cheddar
1⅓ cups coarsely diced celery
½ cup sliced pimiento-stuffed olives
1 cup water
1 cup mayonnaise or dairy sour cream
2 cans (6½ ounces each) tuna, drained

Heat oven to 350°. Prepare macaroni as directed on package for range-top method except—after draining, stir in celery and sliced olives. Pour into 3-quart casserole. In small saucepan mix water and cheese sauce mix. Cook over medium heat, stirring constantly, until thick and smooth. Stir in mayonnaise. Mix sauce with macaroni mixture; carefully fold in tuna. Cover and bake 20 to 25 minutes. *8 servings.*

COQ AU BROCCOLI

1 package of our noodles Romanoff
1 can (10½ ounces) condensed cream of mushroom soup
2 cans (5 ounces each) boned chicken, drained
1 package (10 ounces) frozen chopped broccoli, thawed and well drained
½ cup pitted ripe olives, cut into wedges
¼ cup dry sherry

Heat oven to 350°. Prepare noodles Romanoff as directed on package except—increase milk to ¾ cup. Stir in remaining ingredients; pour into 2-quart casserole. Cover and bake 25 to 30 minutes, or until broccoli is tender. *4 to 6 servings.*

NO-FUSS STROGANOFF

On the table in 25 minutes.

½ cup minced onion
2 tablespoons butter or margarine
1 pound ground beef
2 tablespoons flour
1 teaspoon salt
¼ teaspoon pepper
1 can (6 ounces) sliced mushrooms, drained
1 can (10½ ounces) condensed cream of
   chicken soup
1 package of our noodles Romanoff
1 cup milk
2 tablespoons minced parsley

Cook and stir onion in butter until onion is tender. Add meat; cook until browned. Stir in flour, salt, pepper and mushrooms. Cook 5 minutes, stirring occasionally. Stir in soup; simmer uncovered 10 minutes. Cook noodles as directed on package. Mix milk and packet of sour cream-cheese sauce mix into meat mixture; heat through. To serve, spoon meat sauce over noodles; sprinkle with minced parsley. *4 to 6 servings.*

SEAFOOD THERMIDOR

It's easy—it's elegant—worthy of a fancy chafing dish and your loveliest table setting. Remember this recipe even when you're not in a hurry.

1 can (4 ounces) sliced mushrooms
1 tablespoon butter or margarine
2 cans (10 ounces each) frozen cream of
   shrimp soup
1 can (7½ ounces) crabmeat, drained and
   cartilage removed
2 cans (4½ ounces each) shrimp, drained
1 can (5 ounces) lobster, drained
½ cup milk
¼ teaspoon dry mustard
¼ teaspoon paprika
Dash cayenne pepper
2 or 3 tablespoons dry sherry
Toast points

In saucepan cook and stir mushrooms (with liquid) in butter until heated through. Add remaining ingredients except sherry and toast points. Heat to boiling, stirring constantly. Stir in sherry. Serve over toast points. *6 servings.*

HURRY HURRY HAM

What could be easier? Practically all you need is a sharp can opener!

In large skillet, heat until bubbly 1 can (1 pound 5 ounces) cherry pie filling and 1 to 2 teaspoons cut-up crystallized ginger, stirring frequently. Cut 1½-pound canned ham in half lengthwise; place in skillet. Spoon pie filling mixture over ham. Cover; simmer gently 30 minutes, basting occasionally. To serve, spoon cherry sauce over ham. *4 or 5 servings.*

BRIEF BEEF GOURMET

Unexpected guests just arrived? Don't fret! This company version of creamed dried beef is ready in a jiffy.

2 tablespoons butter or margarine
8 ounces dried beef, shredded
2 cans (10½ ounces each) condensed cream
   of mushroom soup
½ cup white wine
1 cup shredded process American cheese
   (4 ounces)
2 tablespoons chopped pimiento
¼ cup snipped parsley
Toast points

Melt butter in saucepan; add beef and cook until edges curl. Mix soup and wine; stir into beef mixture. Cook, stirring constantly, until creamy. Stir in cheese, pimiento and parsley. Reduce heat; cook and stir until cheese is melted. Spoon over toast points. *8 servings.*

BLUE CHEESE-POTATO SCALLOP

2 packages of our scalloped potatoes
¼ cup butter or margarine
¼ cup crumbled blue cheese
4 cups boiling water
1⅓ cups milk

Heat oven to 400°. Empty potatoes into 3-quart casserole. Sprinkle with packets of seasoned sauce mix. Stir in remaining ingredients. Bake uncovered 30 to 35 minutes. *8 servings.*

FRUIT EN CRÈME

So easy and so delicious! Pictured below.

2 cups sliced seedless green grapes*
1 can (13½ ounces) pineapple tidbits, drained
⅓ cup dairy sour cream
¼ cup brown sugar (packed)

Combine grapes and pineapple tidbits. Blend sour cream and brown sugar (reserving 1 tablespoon brown sugar); toss with grape-pineapple mixture. Chill. At serving time, sprinkle with reserved brown sugar. Serve immediately. *4 servings.*

One can (1 pound) seedless green grapes, chilled and drained, may be substituted for fresh grapes. Serve immediately after tossing with sour cream.

CHOCOLATE VELVET PUDDING

In small mixer bowl, blend 1 package (about 4½ ounces) chocolate instant pudding and 1 cup milk on low speed. Add 2 cups whipping cream; beat on medium speed until soft peaks form, about 2 minutes. Pour into individual serving dishes; chill 15 to 20 minutes or until set. Garnish with whipped cream or chocolate curls, if desired. *6 to 8 servings.*

NO-TIME-TO-THINK TORTE

Cut a 12-ounce pound cake crosswise into 4 or 6 layers. Sprinkle each layer with 1 tablespoon dry sherry. Spread 2 or 3 layers with apricot preserves. Using ½ can* of our chocolate flavor satin ready-to-spread frosting, spread frosting on remaining layers; reassemble cake, alternating layers, and frost sides and top.

Cover and store remaining frosting in refrigerator and use to frost cupcakes or cookies.

"CHERRY CANE" PARFAITS

Here's proof that even when you're hurrying, there's no need for dessert doldrums.

Beat 1 cup dairy sour cream and 1 cup milk with rotary beater until smooth. Blend in 1 package (about 3½ ounces) vanilla instant pudding; beat until mixture is smooth and slightly thickened. Alternate layers of pudding with 1 can (1 pound 5 ounces) cherry pie filling in parfait glasses; chill 15 to 20 minutes or until set. *6 servings.*

The Morning Coffee Break

Is a study group due to meet at your house next? Has an old friend returned on a brief visit to town with a heavy schedule of luncheon and dinner dates, or a college-age cousin booked herself practically solid for a short vacation? Or would you just like a pleasant interruption in your workaday schedule? Whatever the occasion, have a midmorning gathering—anytime from 10 a.m. to noon—with one or two kinds of coffee cake, muffins or rolls and plenty of coffee.

The Germans call this kind of party a "kaffeeklatsch"; the British, "elevenses." Whatever you call it, it's a delightful way of mixing business with pleasure or sandwiching an extra little party into busy days.

SWEET DOUGH

1 package active dry yeast
¼ cup warm water (105 to 115°)
¼ cup lukewarm milk, scalded then cooled
¼ cup sugar
½ teaspoon salt
1 egg
¼ cup shortening
2¼ to 2½ cups Gold Medal Flour*
    (regular or Wondra)

*If using Self-Rising Flour, omit salt.

In mixing bowl dissolve yeast in warm water. Stir in milk, sugar, salt, egg, shortening and half the flour. Mix with spoon until smooth. Add enough remaining flour to handle easily; mix with hand or spoon. Turn onto lightly floured board; knead until smooth and elastic, about 5 minutes. Round up in greased bowl; turn once to bring greased side up. Cover; let rise in warm place (85°) until double, about 1½ hours. To test for rising, stick 2 fingers in dough. If holes remain but top stays smooth, dough is ready. Punch down. Divide dough for desired rolls or coffee cakes. Shape, let rise and bake as directed for individual recipe.

CHEESE DIAMONDS

Rich, tender fold-overs with a marvelous cream cheese filling. Pictured below, at left.

Sweet Dough (above)
1 package (8 ounces) cream cheese, softened
¼ cup sugar
3 tablespoons flour
1 egg yolk
½ teaspoon grated lemon peel
1 tablespoon lemon juice
½ cup favorite jam
Chopped nuts

Prepare dough. For filling, beat cream cheese and sugar until light and fluffy. Stir in flour, egg yolk, lemon peel and juice. Roll dough on lightly floured board into 15-inch square; cut into twenty-five 3-inch squares. Place on greased baking sheet. Place 1 tablespoon cheese mixture in center of each square. Bring two diagonally opposite corners to center of each square. Overlap corners slightly; pinch together. Cover; let rise until double, about 30 minutes.

Heat oven to 375°. Bake 12 minutes. Heat jam until melted. Brush lightly over hot rolls; sprinkle with nuts. *Makes 25 rolls.*

FRUIT ROLLS

Fruit-filled buns. Similar to traditional Bohemian kolaches. Pictured below, at right.

Sweet Dough (above)
½ pound (1 cup) prunes
4 ounces (¾ cup) dried apricots
¼ teaspoon allspice
½ cup sugar
1 tablespoon grated lemon peel
1 tablespoon lemon juice
Melted butter or margarine
Confectioners' sugar

Prepare dough. For filling, simmer prunes and apricots in enough water to cover, 30 minutes or until tender. Drain; chop fruit fine and stir in allspice, sugar, lemon peel and juice. Divide dough into 24 pieces. Shape each piece into round ball. Place 2 inches apart on greased baking sheet. With fingers of both hands, make a depression in each by pushing outward toward edge, leaving ½-inch ridge around outside. Fill with 1 tablespoon prune-apricot filling. Let rise about 30 minutes.

Heat oven to 375°. Bake 15 to 18 minutes. Brush with melted butter or margarine; dust lightly with confectioners' sugar. *Makes 24 rolls.*

CINNAMON ROLLS

Sweet Dough (page 113)
2 tablespoons soft butter or margarine
¼ cup sugar
2 teaspoons cinnamon
Creamy White Glaze (page 115)

Roll dough on lightly floured board into rectangle, 15x9 inches. Spread with butter and sprinkle with mixture of sugar and cinnamon. Beginning at long side, roll up tightly as for jelly roll. Seal well by pinching edges of roll together. Stretch roll slightly to make even. Cut into 15 slices; place slices a little apart in greased oblong pan, 13x9x2 inches, or in 15 greased muffin cups. Cover; let rise until double, about 45 minutes.

Heat oven to 375°. Bake 25 to 30 minutes. While warm, frost with Creamy White Glaze. *Makes 15 rolls.*

Butterscotch Rolls: Follow recipe for Cinnamon Rolls (above) except—coat bottom of baking pan with mixture of ½ cup butter or margarine, melted, ½ cup brown sugar (packed) and ½ cup pecan halves. Place rolls in pan. Bake. Immediately turn upside down on tray; let pan stay over rolls a minute so butterscotch mixture will run down over rolls. *(Pictured below, at left.)*

Frosted Orange Rolls: Follow recipe for Cinnamon Rolls (above) except—substituting half the Creamy Orange Frosting (below) for the butter and sugar-cinnamon mixture, spread frosting over rectangle of dough. After baking, remove rolls from pan and frost with remaining frosting.

Creamy Orange Frosting

Mix 3 tablespoons soft butter or margarine, 1 tablespoon grated orange peel, 2 tablespoons orange juice and 1½ cups confectioners' sugar until smooth.

SUGAR CRISPS

Pictured below, in center.

Sweet Dough (page 113)
Melted butter or margarine
1 cup sugar
1 cup finely chopped pecans

Roll dough on lightly floured board into rectangle, 18x9 inches. Brush with melted butter. Mix sugar and pecans; sprinkle dough with half the mixture. Beginning at long side, roll up as for jelly roll; cut into 1-inch slices. Roll and flatten each piece of dough into 4-inch circle, using remaining sugar-nut mixture to dust board. Place circles on greased baking sheet. Cover; let rise until double, about 30 minutes.

Heat oven to 375°. Bake 10 minutes. *Makes 18 rolls.*

SWEDISH TEA RING

Pictured below, at right.

Sweet Dough (page 113)
2 tablespoons soft butter or margarine
½ cup brown sugar (packed)
2 teaspoons cinnamon
½ cup raisins
Creamy White Glaze (page 115)

Roll dough on lightly floured board into rectangle, 15x9 inches; spread with butter. Stir together sugar, cinnamon and raisins; sprinkle over dough. Beginning at long side, roll up tightly as for jelly roll. Seal well by pinching edges of roll together. Stretch roll slightly to make even. Place sealed edge down in ring on lightly greased baking sheet. Pinch ends together. With scissors, make cuts ⅔ of the way through ring at 1-inch intervals. Turn each section on its side. Let rise until double, about 45 minutes.

Heat oven to 375°. Bake 25 to 30 minutes. While warm, frost with Creamy White Glaze and, if desired, decorate with nuts and cherries. *Makes 1 ring.*

BALLOON BUNS

1 package active dry yeast
¼ cup warm water (105 to 115°)
¾ cup lukewarm milk, scalded then cooled
¼ cup sugar
1 teaspoon salt
1 egg
¼ cup shortening
3½ to 3¾ cups Gold Medal Flour*
   (regular or Wondra)
24 large marshmallows
1 tablespoon cinnamon
1 cup sugar
½ cup butter or margarine, melted

In mixing bowl dissolve yeast in warm water. Add milk, ¼ cup sugar, the salt, egg, shortening and half the flour; mix with spoon until smooth. Add enough remaining flour to handle easily; mix with hand. Turn onto lightly floured board; knead until smooth and elastic, about 5 minutes. Round up in greased bowl; bring greased side up. Cover; let rise in warm place (85°) until double, about 2 hours. (The dough will retain a finger impression when touched.) Punch down; divide dough in half. Roll each half to ¼-inch thickness. Cut nine 3½-inch circles from each half. Mix cinnamon and sugar. Dip each marshmallow in melted butter and then in cinnamon-sugar mixture. Wrap a dough circle around a marshmallow, pinching tightly at the bottom. Dip roll in melted butter and then cinnamon-sugar mixture. Place in greased medium muffin cups, pinched side down. Let rise until light, about 30 minutes.

Heat oven to 375°. Bake 25 to 30 minutes. Serve warm. *Makes 18 buns.*

If using Self-Rising Flour, omit salt.

CHOCOLATE-CINNAMON ROLLS

How exciting! A panful of rich chocolate rolls drizzled with white icing.

1 package active dry yeast
¾ cup warm water (105 to 115°)
¼ cup shortening
1 teaspoon salt
¼ cup sugar
1 egg
⅓ cup cocoa
2¼ cups Gold Medal Flour* (regular or Wondra)
3 tablespoons sugar
1½ teaspoons cinnamon
1 tablespoon soft butter or margarine
Creamy White Glaze (below)

In mixer bowl dissolve yeast in warm water. Add shortening, salt, ¼ cup sugar, the egg, cocoa and 1 cup of the flour. Beat 2 minutes medium speed on mixer or 300 vigorous strokes by hand. Scrape sides and bottom of bowl frequently. Blend in remaining flour with spoon until smooth. Scrape batter from sides of bowl. Cover with cloth and let rise in warm place (85°) until double, about 1 hour. Stir down batter by beating 25 strokes. Turn onto well-floured cloth-covered board (dough will be soft). Roll into rectangle, 12x9 inches. Mix 3 tablespoons sugar and the cinnamon. Spread dough gently with soft butter and sprinkle with cinnamon-sugar mixture. Beginning at long side, roll up as for a jelly roll. Pinch edge into roll. Cut into 12 pieces. Place in greased square pan, 9x9x2 inches. Let rise in warm place (85°) until double, about 40 minutes.

Heat oven to 375°. Bake 25 minutes. Remove from pan; frost rolls immediately with Creamy White Glaze. Sprinkle with chopped nuts, if desired. Serve warm. *Makes 12 rolls.*

If using Self-Rising Flour, omit salt.

CREAMY WHITE GLAZE

Mix 1 tablespoon water or milk *or* 1½ tablespoons light cream into 1 cup confectioners' sugar and ½ teaspoon vanilla until of spreading consistency.

SOUR-CREAM YEAST DOUGH

2 cups dairy sour cream
2 packages active dry yeast
½ cup warm water (105 to 115°)
¼ cup soft butter or margarine
⅓ cup sugar
2 teaspoons salt
2 eggs
About 6 cups Gold Medal Flour* (regular or Wondra)

*If using Self-Rising Flour, omit salt.

Heat sour cream over low heat just until lukewarm. In large mixing bowl, dissolve yeast in warm water. Add warm sour cream, butter, sugar, salt, eggs and 2 cups of the flour; beat until smooth. Stir in remaining flour until dough cleans sides of bowl. Knead dough on well-floured board until smooth, about 10 minutes. Place in greased bowl; turn once to bring greased side up. Cover; let rise in warm place (85°) until double, about 1 hour. To test for rising, stick 2 fingers in dough. If holes remain but top stays smooth, dough is ready. Punch down. Finish as directed in individual recipe.

ALMOND CROWN

Three layers of pinwheel slices form this crown-shaped yeast bread. Pictured at left.

Sour-cream Yeast Dough (above)
2 cans (4½ to 5 ounces each) blanched almonds
1 egg
1 cup sugar
2 teaspoons almond extract
Melted butter or margarine

Prepare dough as directed except—reserve 2 tablespoons sour cream for filling.

Heat oven to 350°. Place oven rack in lowest position. Grease well a 9-inch springform pan. (Or use round layer pan, 9x1½ inches, with aluminum foil collar to extend height of sides. Make 3-inch collar from 4 thicknesses of foil; fasten ends and slip onto layer pan. Grease pan and collar well.)

Cut dough into thirds. Roll each third into a rectangle, 12x10 inches. For filling, grind almonds and mix with egg, sugar, almond extract and reserved sour cream. Spread each rectangle with ⅓ of filling. Beginning at long side, roll up as for jelly roll. Cut each roll into 12 slices. Place 12 slices in prepared pan. Arrange remaining slices in 2 layers on top of the 12 in pan. Bake 70 minutes. Brush surface with melted butter. Cool 20 minutes before removing sides of pan. If desired, drizzle Creamy White Glaze (page 115) over top. *Makes 1 coffee cake.*

GOOD MORNING COFFEE CAKE

Oranges and blueberries baked in a cake—lovely to serve, delicious to eat. Pictured at left.

Heat oven to 400°. Grease square pan, 8x8x2 inches. Prepare muffin batter as directed on our wild blueberry muffin mix package except—pour into prepared pan. Drain 1 can (11 ounces) mandarin orange segments; arrange drained segments over batter. Sprinkle with Streusel Mixture (below). Bake 25 to 30 minutes. Cut into squares. *6 to 9 servings.*

Streusel Mixture

Mix ¼ cup brown sugar (packed), 3 tablespoons flour, ¼ teaspoon cinnamon and 2 tablespoons firm butter with fingers or fork until crumbly.

COFFEE CAKE EXCEPTIONALE

This moist, tender quick bread has all the richness built right in. You won't even want to spread it with butter!

    ¾ cup soft butter or margarine
    1½ cups sugar
    3 eggs
    1½ teaspoons vanilla
    3 cups Gold Medal Flour* (regular or Wondra)
    1½ teaspoons baking powder
    1½ teaspoons soda
    ¼ teaspoon salt
    1½ cups dairy sour cream
    Cinnamon-Nut Filling (below)

Heat oven to 350°. Grease a tube pan, 10x4 inches, or two loaf pans, 9x5x3 inches. Cream butter and sugar thoroughly; beat in eggs and vanilla. Stir flour, baking powder, soda and salt together; mix into creamed mixture alternately with the sour cream. For tube pan spread ⅓ of batter (about 2 cups) into pan. Sprinkle with ⅓ of filling (about 6 tablespoons). Repeat twice. For loaf pan spread ¼ of batter (about 1½ cups) into each pan. Sprinkle each with ¼ of filling (about 5 tablespoons). Repeat. Bake 50 to 60 minutes. Cool slightly in pan(s) before removing. *Makes 1 round coffee cake or 2 loaves.*

Cinnamon-Nut Filling

Stir together ½ cup brown sugar (packed), ½ cup chopped nuts and 1½ teaspoons cinnamon.

If using Self-Rising Flour, omit baking powder, soda and salt.

FAVORITE COFFEE CAKE

    1½ cups Gold Medal Flour* (regular or Wondra)
    ¾ cup sugar
    ¾ teaspoon salt
    2½ teaspoons baking powder
    ¼ cup soft shortening
    ¾ cup milk
    1 egg
    Topping (below)

Heat oven to 375°. In large mixing bowl, blend all ingredients except Topping thoroughly with fork. Beat vigorously 30 seconds. Pour into greased round layer pan, 9x1½ inches, or square pan, 8x8x2 inches. Sprinkle with Topping. Bake 25 to 30 minutes, or until wooden pick inserted in center comes out clean. Serve warm. *8 or 9 servings.*

If using Self-Rising Flour, omit baking powder and salt.

Topping

Mix ⅓ cup brown sugar (packed), ¼ cup Gold Medal Flour (regular or Wondra), ½ teaspoon cinnamon and 3 tablespoons firm butter or margarine until crumbly.

Streusel-filled Coffee Cake: Follow recipe for Favorite Coffee Cake (above) except—spread half the batter in greased round layer pan, 9x1½ inches. Mix ½ cup brown sugar (packed), 2 teaspoons cinnamon, ½ cup finely chopped nuts and 2 tablespoons butter or margarine, melted; sprinkle half of mixture over batter. Repeat with remaining batter and mixture.

DANISH PUFF

An elegant coffee cake that is a cream puff topper baked on a flaky pastry crust. Guests will think they're eating Danish pastry, but you'll know how much easier this is to make!

1 cup Gold Medal Flour (regular or Wondra)
½ cup butter
2 tablespoons water
½ cup butter
1 cup water
1 teaspoon almond extract
1 cup Gold Medal Flour (regular or Wondra)
3 eggs
Confectioners' Sugar Glaze (below)
Chopped nuts

Heat oven to 350°. Measure 1 cup flour into bowl; cut in ½ cup butter. Sprinkle 2 tablespoons water over mixture; mix with fork. Round into ball; divide in half. On ungreased baking sheet, pat each half with hands into a strip, 12x3 inches. Strips should be about 3 inches apart.

In saucepan combine ½ cup butter and 1 cup water; heat to boiling. Remove from heat; stir in almond extract. Beat in 1 cup flour, stirring quickly to keep it from lumping. When smooth add eggs, one at a time, beating after each addition until smooth. Divide batter in half; spread each half evenly over strips.

Bake about 60 minutes, or until topping is crisp and nicely browned. Frost with Confectioners' Sugar Glaze and sprinkle generously with nuts. Slice diagonally to serve. *10 to 12 servings.*

Individual Danish Puffs: Follow recipe above except—pat dough into 3-inch circles, using about 1 teaspoon pastry dough for each. Spread about 1½ tablespoons batter over each circle, extending it just beyond edges of circle. (Topping will shrink slightly when baked.) Bake 40 to 45 minutes. Frost with Confectioners' Sugar Glaze and sprinkle generously with nuts. *Makes 2 dozen puffs. (Pictured on page 121 with French Chocolate.)*

Confectioners' Sugar Glaze

Mix 1½ cups confectioners' sugar, 2 tablespoons soft butter or margarine, 1½ teaspoons vanilla and 1 to 2 tablespoons water until smooth. Tint with food coloring, if desired.

ORANGE-NUTMEG COFFEE CAKE

A quickie to remember for neighborhood parties.

2 cups Bisquick
¼ cup sugar
1 egg
2 tablespoons salad oil or melted shortening
¾ cup milk
1 to 2 tablespoons grated orange peel
Nutmeg Topping (below)

Heat oven to 400°. Grease a round layer pan, 9x1½ inches. Mix all ingredients except Nutmeg Topping; beat vigorously with spoon 30 seconds. Spread in prepared pan. Sprinkle with Nutmeg Topping. Bake 20 to 25 minutes. Serve warm. *8 servings.*

Nutmeg Topping

Mix ¼ cup sugar, 2 tablespoons Bisquick, 2 tablespoons soft butter or margarine and ½ teaspoon nutmeg with fork until crumbly.

PINEAPPLE PIZZA

1½ cups Bisquick
¾ cup granulated sugar
3 tablespoons shortening
1 egg
¾ cup milk
1 teaspoon vanilla
3 tablespoons butter or margarine, melted
⅔ cup brown sugar (packed)
1 can (1 pound 4½ ounces) crushed pineapple, well drained
½ cup finely chopped walnuts or pecans

Heat oven to 350°. Grease and flour a 12-inch pizza pan.* Mix Bisquick and granulated sugar; add shortening, egg and ¼ cup of the milk. Beat 1 minute medium speed on mixer or vigorously by hand. Then blend in the remaining milk and the vanilla. Beat ½ minute longer. Pour into prepared pan. Bake about 25 minutes or until nicely browned. Mix butter, brown sugar, pineapple and nuts. Drop by small spoonfuls over top of cake; with tines of fork gently distribute filling over top. (Cake is delicate; be careful not to tear it.)

Set oven control to broil and/or 550°. Broil cake 6 inches from heat 2 to 3 minutes or until golden brown. Serve slightly cooled. Cut into wedges. *8 servings.*

Two 8- or 9-inch pie pans may be used.

CHOCOLATE SWIRL SQUARES

Marbled with chocolate and topped with coconut. Pictured at left.

⅓ cup flaked coconut
¼ cup chopped nuts
¼ cup sugar
1 tablespoon butter or margarine, melted
2 cups Bisquick
¼ cup sugar
2 tablespoons shortening
¾ cup milk
1 egg
⅓ cup semisweet chocolate pieces, melted

Heat oven to 400°. Grease a square pan, 8x8x2 inches. Mix coconut, nuts, ¼ cup sugar and the melted butter; set aside. Mix Bisquick, ¼ cup sugar, the shortening, milk and egg; beat vigorously with spoon 30 seconds. Spread in prepared pan. Spoon chocolate over batter; run knife through batter to marble. Sprinkle coconut mixture over top. Bake 25 to 30 minutes. Cut into squares. *9 servings.*

ORANGE-GROVE CINNAMON ROLLS

Cinnamon swirls baked in a fresh orange sauce that permeates the rolls, baba fashion. You won't be able to resist serving these with coffee, and again for tea or a salad luncheon.

½ cup sugar
2 tablespoons grated orange peel
½ cup orange juice
¼ cup butter or margarine
2 cups Bisquick
⅔ cup milk
¼ cup sugar
½ teaspoon cinnamon

Heat oven to 425°. Mix ½ cup sugar, the orange peel, juice and butter in saucepan. Heat to boiling; boil 2 minutes, stirring occasionally. Keep sauce warm over very low heat. Mix Bisquick and milk with fork. Beat vigorously 20 strokes until stiff but sticky. Knead 8 to 10 times on lightly floured cloth-covered board. Roll into a rectangle, 12x9 inches. Mix ¼ cup sugar and the cinnamon; sprinkle over dough. Beginning at long side, roll up tightly. Pinch edge into roll. Cut into 12 slices. Spoon about 1 tablespoon hot orange sauce into each of 12 large muffin cups. Place a slice of rolled dough cut side down in each muffin cup. Bake 15 to 20 minutes. Turn pan upside down so sauce runs down over rolls. Serve warm. *Makes 12 rolls.*

JIFFY JAM STICKS

2 cups Bisquick
¾ cup light cream or ½ cup milk plus ¼ cup butter or margarine, melted
2 tablespoons sugar
1 jar (12 ounces) apricot preserves
Creamy White Glaze (page 115)

Heat oven to 450°. Grease a large baking sheet. Stir Bisquick, cream and sugar with fork to form a soft dough. Beat vigorously 20 strokes. Turn onto prepared baking sheet. Pat or roll into rectangle, 14x10 inches, forming a slight edge around the outside. Spread preserves evenly over rectangle. Bake 10 to 15 minutes or until delicately browned. While hot drizzle Creamy White Glaze over top. Cut in half lengthwise and then crosswise into 6 strips. Serve warm. *Makes 12 strips.*

BLUEBERRY PUFFS

Prepare muffins as directed on our wild blueberry muffin mix package except—bake batter in tiny muffin cups 12 to 15 minutes. Mix ½ cup sugar and 1 teaspoon cinnamon. Roll hot muffins in ½ cup melted butter, then in cinnamon-sugar mixture. *Makes about 24 small muffins.*

CRANBERRY-ORANGE NUT BREAD

Terrific for a holiday coffee party.

¾ cup sugar
1 egg
1 tablespoon grated orange peel
1¼ cups orange juice
3 cups Bisquick
¾ cup chopped nuts
1 cup chopped fresh or frozen cranberries*

Heat oven to 350°. Grease well a loaf pan, 9x5x3 inches. Mix sugar, egg, orange peel, juice and Bisquick; beat vigorously with spoon 30 seconds. (Batter may still be lumpy.) Stir in nuts and cranberries. Pour into prepared pan. Bake 55 to 60 minutes, or until wooden pick inserted in center comes out clean. (Crack in top is typical.) Remove from pan; cool before slicing. *Makes 1 loaf.*

Do not thaw frozen cranberries before using.

DATE BREAD

1 package of our date bar mix
½ cup hot water
3 eggs
¼ cup Gold Medal Flour (regular or Wondra)
1 teaspoon baking powder
½ cup chopped walnuts

Heat oven to 350°. Grease a loaf pan, 9x5x3 inches or 8½x4½x2½ inches. Mix date filling from date bar mix with the hot water. Add crumbly mixture, eggs, flour and baking powder; mix thoroughly. Stir in walnuts. Pour into prepared pan. Bake 50 to 55 minutes, or until wooden pick inserted in center comes out clean. Remove from pan; cool. Wrap and store overnight before slicing. *Makes 1 loaf.*

MUFFIN MINIATURES

Tiny frosted muffins—delightfully rich.

2 cups Bisquick
¼ cup sugar
3 tablespoons soft butter or margarine
1 egg
¾ cup milk
Creamy White Glaze (page 115)
Toasted coconut or coarsely chopped
    macadamia nuts

Heat oven to 400°. Grease tiny muffin cups. Stir together Bisquick and sugar; cut in butter. Add egg and milk; beat vigorously with spoon 30 seconds. Fill muffin cups ⅔ full. Bake 12 to 15 minutes or until golden brown. While warm, frost with Creamy White Glaze; sprinkle with coconut or nuts. *Makes 3 to 4 dozen tiny muffins.*

Banana Muffins: Follow recipe above except—omit milk; stir 1 cup mashed very ripe banana into batter.

Pineapple Muffins: Follow recipe above except—stir ½ cup well-drained crushed pineapple into batter.

CRANBERRY MUFFINS

1 cup fresh or frozen cranberries, halved
½ cup sugar
2 cups Gold Medal Flour* (regular or Wondra)
2 tablespoons sugar
3 teaspoons baking powder
1 teaspoon salt
1 egg
1 cup milk
2 tablespoons salad oil or melted shortening
1 tablespoon grated orange peel

Heat oven to 400°. Grease bottoms of 12 muffin cups. Combine cranberries and the ½ cup sugar; set aside. In mixing bowl, stir dry ingredients together; make a "well" in mixture. In another bowl beat egg with fork; stir in milk, salad oil, cranberries and grated orange peel. Pour all at once into dry ingredients; stir just until flour is moistened. (Batter should be lumpy. Do not overmix.) Fill muffin cups ⅔ full. Bake 20 to 25 minutes or until golden brown. Muffins will have gently rounded and pebbled tops. Loosen immediately with spatula. *Makes 12 medium muffins.*

If using Self-Rising Flour, omit baking powder and salt.

COFFEE

Be sure to start with the correct grind of fresh coffee, freshly drawn cold water and a clean coffee maker. For additional tips as well as directions for quantity coffee, see page 98.

Always measure coffee and water to insure desired strength. For medium coffee, use 1½ tablespoons coffee to each ¾ cup water.

Automatic Coffee Maker: Follow manufacturer's directions for selecting grind of coffee, measuring and brewing the coffee and holding the coffee at serving temperature.

Drip Method: Preheat coffeepot by rinsing with very hot water. Measure drip-grind coffee into filter section; place upper container of pot over the filter section. Measure fresh boiling water into upper container. Cover. When dripping is completed, remove upper container and the filter section; stir and serve.

Percolator Method: Measure fresh cold water into percolator; heat to boiling. *Remove from heat.* Measure regular-grind coffee into the basket; place in percolator and cover. Set on low heat; percolate slowly 6 to 8 minutes. Remove basket; serve.

Vacuum Method: Measure fresh cold water into lower bowl; place on heat. Place filter in upper bowl; add fine or drip-grind coffee. When water boils, lower heat and insert upper bowl with a slight twist. Let water rise into upper bowl; stir. Remove from heat. Coffee should return to lower bowl in no more than 3 minutes. Then remove upper bowl and serve.

HOT COCOA

⅓ cup sugar
⅓ cup cocoa
¼ teaspoon salt
1½ cups water
4½ cups milk

Mix sugar, cocoa and salt. Add water. Heat to boiling, stirring constantly. Boil and stir 2 minutes. Stir in milk; heat to scalding, but do not boil. Add ¼ teaspoon vanilla, if desired. Just before serving, stir until smooth or beat until frothy with rotary beater. Serve hot. *6 to 8 servings.*

FRENCH CHOCOLATE

Very fancy! Scalding hot milk is poured over fluffs of chocolate whipped cream. Pictured below with Individual Danish Puffs.

¾ cup semisweet chocolate pieces
½ cup light corn syrup
⅓ cup water
1 teaspoon vanilla
2 cups whipping cream
2 quarts milk

In saucepan combine chocolate pieces, syrup and water; heat over low heat, stirring constantly, until chocolate is melted. Stir in vanilla. Cover and refrigerate until cool. In large mixer bowl beat cream on medium speed, gradually adding the cooled chocolate syrup. Continue beating until mixture mounds when dropped from a spoon. Turn into bowl; chill. Just before serving, heat milk to scalding. Pour milk into heated coffeepot or carafe. Fill serving cups half full of chocolate whipped cream. Pour in hot milk; mix gently. *16 to 18 servings.*

Come for Dessert and Coffee

A dessert and coffee party scheduled for some convenient time after dinner is a nice idea for any hostess, but presents special plusses for the girl with a job or for the young couple with a tiny kitchen (and perhaps an equally tiny budget). It's also ideal for week-night entertaining because such a party generally breaks up early and leaves the hostess with a minimum of cleanup.

Here's how it works. The night before the party prepare a dessert spectacular. And most of the work is already done! On party night you only have to put the finishing touches on your dessert and make the coffee. Serve as soon as the group has assembled. A tea cart will lend a bit of drama to your presentation. Wheel it into the living room with the whole menu aboard—dessert and coffee, perhaps nuts and mints, on the top shelf; cups, plates and silver on the lower one.

Dessert, coffee and conversation are the perfect ingredients for a party that will be enjoyed by one and all. Try it and see.

MOCHA BROWNIE TORTE

1 package (1 pound) of our fudge brownie mix
¼ cup water
2 eggs
½ cup chopped nuts
1½ cups whipping cream
⅓ cup brown sugar (packed)
1 tablespoon instant coffee
Shaved chocolate

Heat oven to 350°. Grease two round layer pans, 9x1½ inches. Blend brownie mix, water and eggs. Stir in nuts. Spread batter into prepared pans. Bake 20 minutes. Cool 5 minutes in pans; turn onto racks to cool thoroughly. Whip cream until it begins to thicken. Gradually add sugar and instant coffee; continue beating until stiff. Fill layers with 1 cup whipped cream mixture. Frost sides and top with remaining whipped cream mixture. Sprinkle shaved chocolate over top. Chill at least 1 hour before serving. *10 to 12 servings.*

LEMON GOURMET CAKE

Add sour cream to the frosting mix for delightful flavor tang! You'll want to try all of our mix-matched variations.

In small mixer bowl, chill ⅔ cup dairy sour cream and 1 package of our lemon velvet frosting mix (dry) at least 2 hours. Bake our lemon velvet cake mix in layer pans as directed on package. Cool. Blend ¼ cup soft butter and sour cream mixture; beat on low speed 1 minute. Do not overbeat as this will thin frosting. Fill layers and frost cake. Chill.

Chocolate Gourmet Cake: Follow recipe for Lemon Cake (above) except—use our creamy white frosting mix and devils food cake mix.

Yellow Gourmet Cake: Follow recipe for Lemon Cake (above) except—use our dark chocolate fudge frosting mix and yellow cake mix.

White Gourmet Cake: Follow recipe for Lemon Cake (above) except—use our chocolate fudge frosting mix and white cake mix.

Marble Gourmet Cake: Follow recipe for Lemon Cake (above) except—use our dark chocolate fudge frosting mix and marble cake mix.

Dark Chocolate Gourmet Cake: Follow recipe for Lemon Cake (above) except—use our dark chocolate fudge frosting mix and dark chocolate cake mix.

CHOCOLATE ALMOND TORTE

Whipped cream is the shortening in this super-rich chocolate cake. Towered with more whipped cream, it's a luscious torte.

1⅔ cups whipping cream
3 eggs (½ to ⅔ cup), well beaten
3 squares (3 ounces) unsweetened chocolate, melted and cooled
1 teaspoon almond extract
2¼ cups Gold Medal Flour* (regular or Wondra)
1½ cups granulated sugar
2¼ teaspoons baking powder
½ teaspoon salt
2 cups whipping cream
1½ teaspoons almond extract
½ cup confectioners' sugar
Chocolate shot
Blanched almonds

Heat oven to 350°. Grease and flour two round layer pans, 8 or 9x1½ inches. Whip 1⅔ cups whipping cream until stiff. Fold in eggs, chocolate and 1 teaspoon almond extract. Stir together flour, granulated sugar, baking powder and salt; fold gently into cream-egg mixture until blended and batter is uniformly brown. Pour into prepared pans. Bake 9-inch layers 30 to 35 minutes, 8-inch layers 35 to 40 minutes, or until wooden pick inserted in center comes out clean. Cool. Split cake to make 4 layers. (Mark with wooden picks and cut with serrated knife.) Whip 2 cups whipping cream with 1½ teaspoons almond extract and the confectioners' sugar until stiff. Fill layers and frost top of cake, using a fourth (about ¾ cup) of the whipped cream for each. Sprinkle a ring of chocolate shot around top edge of cake; decorate with almonds. Chill.

*If using Self-Rising Flour, omit baking powder and salt.

DARK CHOCOLATE MINT CAKE

A delightful combination of colors and flavors. Our darkest chocolate cake is swirled with a delicate mint-green frosting, then gloriously garnished with chocolate leaves. Pictured below.

**1 package of our dark chocolate fudge cake mix
1 package of our fluffy white frosting mix
¼ teaspoon peppermint extract
Few drops green food coloring
Chocolate Leaves (below)**

Bake cake in layer pans as directed on package. Cool. Prepare frosting mix as directed on package except—thoroughly blend in peppermint extract and tint with green food coloring. Fill and frost cake. Decorate with Chocolate Leaves.

Chocolate Leaves

Wash and dry 1 dozen leaves of various sizes and shapes. Melt 1 square (1 ounce) semisweet chocolate or ¼ cup semisweet chocolate pieces with ½ teaspoon butter. Paint chocolate onto backs of leaves, spreading chocolate about ⅛ inch thick and just to edges. Freeze until very firm. Quickly peel off real leaves and arrange the chocolate leaves on cake.

FRENCH RIBBON CAKE

**1 package of our marble cake mix
1 cup whipping cream
¼ cup confectioners' sugar
1 package of our dark chocolate fudge flavor
  frosting mix**

Prepare cake mix batter as directed on package except—pour half of the yellow batter into one of the prepared round layer pans. Add marbling mixture to remaining batter; blend thoroughly. Pour into other pan. Bake and cool as directed on package. Split cake to make 4 layers. Whip cream with sugar; fill layers, alternating yellow and chocolate layers. Prepare frosting mix as directed on package; frost sides and top of cake. Refrigerate.

LEMON VELVET CREAM CAKE

Pictured below.

Bake our lemon velvet cake mix in 9-inch layers as directed on package. In small mixer bowl combine 2 cups of our lemon velvet frosting mix, 1½ cups whipping cream and 1 teaspoon vanilla; chill. Split cooled cake to make 4 layers. Whip chilled frosting mixture on medium speed until stiff; spread between layers. Spread top of cake with Thin Icing (below), allowing some to drizzle down sides. Sprinkle top of cake with chopped nuts, if desired. Chill.

Thin Icing

Blend remaining frosting mix, 2 to 3 tablespoons hot water and 1 tablespoon light corn syrup. Beat until smooth. Add 1 to 2 teaspoons water, if necessary.

PETAL CAKE

A lovely frosting treatment. Pictured at right.

Bake any flavor of our angel food or layer cake mix in tube pan or layer pans as directed on package. Cool. Combine 1½ cups whipping cream with 1 package of our fluffy white frosting mix (dry) in small mixer bowl; refrigerate 1 hour. Beat until stiff. Tint with food coloring, if desired. To frost cake with petal design, scoop about 1 teaspoon frosting on tip of small flexible spatula. Beginning at base of cake and holding spatula blade frosting-filled side down, press against side of cake. Repeat for each petal. Form petals in rows around cake, overlapping petals slightly. Make larger petals on top of cake. Refrigerate.

ANGEL ALEXANDER

Ever so elegant—and in such an effortless way.

Bake our angel food cake mix in tube pan, 10x4 inches, as directed on package. Cool. About 2½ hours before serving, combine 2 tablespoons light cream with ½ cup dark crème de cacao. With a 5-inch wooden skewer, make many holes of varying depths in cake. Pour half of crème de cacao mixture into holes; let cake stand in pan 2 hours. Just before serving, invert cake onto serving plate. Make more holes in top and pour in remaining crème de cacao mixture. Whip 1½ cups whipping cream with ¼ cup confectioners' sugar just until stiff. Frost cake; garnish with shaved chocolate, if desired.

PRALINE SHORTCAKE

A different kind of shortcake—brown sugar and pecans add rich flavor.

1½ cups Gold Medal Flour* (regular or Wondra)
3 teaspoons baking powder
½ teaspoon salt
¼ teaspoon soda
½ cup brown sugar (packed)
⅓ cup shortening
½ cup coarsely chopped pecans
1 egg
¾ cup milk
3 to 4 cups sliced fresh strawberries or peaches, sweetened
1 cup dairy sour cream
½ cup brown sugar (packed)

Heat oven to 375°. Grease a round layer pan, 8x1½ inches. Stir together flour, baking powder, salt and soda. Cut in ½ cup sugar and the shortening. Stir in pecans. Combine egg and milk; stir into flour mixture just until blended. Spread in prepared pan. Bake 20 to 25 minutes, or until wooden pick inserted in center comes out clean. Split cake into 2 layers. Fill and top with fruit. Mix sour cream and ½ cup sugar; serve as topping. *6 to 8 servings.*

*If using Self-Rising Flour, omit baking powder and salt.

MOCK CHEESECAKE

A can of ready-to-spread frosting is the convenience ingredient in this fast and fabulous cheesecake. It's party-pretty, too. Pictured below.

1¼ cups graham cracker crumbs
  (about 16 crackers)
2 tablespoons sugar
¼ cup butter or margarine, melted
1 can of our lemon satin ready-to-spread frosting
1 cup creamed cottage cheese (small curd)
1 cup dairy sour cream

Heat oven to 350°. Mix graham cracker crumbs and sugar in bowl. Add butter; mix thoroughly. Reserve 3 tablespoons for topping. Press remaining mixture firmly and evenly on bottom of square pan, 9x9x2 inches. Bake 10 minutes. Cool. In small mixer bowl, combine frosting, cottage cheese and sour cream. Beat on high speed until blended, about 1 minute. Pour into crumb-lined pan; sprinkle with reserved crumbs. Freeze overnight. If desired, garnish with strawberries, peaches, small bunches of seedless green grapes or other fruit. *9 to 12 servings.*

Chocolate Cheesecake: Follow recipe above except—substitute our chocolate satin ready-to-spread frosting for the lemon frosting and omit the garnish.

CHERRY CHEESECAKE

½ cup fine zwieback or graham cracker crumbs
1 tablespoon sugar
¼ teaspoon <u>each</u> cinnamon and nutmeg
5 eggs, separated
1 cup sugar
2 packages (8 ounces each) cream cheese, softened
1 cup dairy sour cream
2 tablespoons flour
1 teaspoon vanilla
Cherry Glaze (below)

Heat oven to 275°. Butter a 9-inch springform pan or tube pan, 10x4 inches. Stir together crumbs, 1 tablespoon sugar, the cinnamon and nutmeg. Dust sides and bottom of pan with crumb mixture.

Beat egg yolks until thick and lemon colored; gradually beat in 1 cup sugar. Break cream cheese into small pieces and add to egg-yolk mixture; beat until smooth. Add sour cream, flour and vanilla; beat until smooth. Wash beaters to remove all traces of yolk. Beat egg whites until stiff, but not dry. Gently fold egg whites into cheese mixture; pour into prepared pan. Bake 70 minutes. Turn off oven and leave cheesecake in for 1 hour. Do not open oven door during this time. Remove from oven; cool. Spread Cherry Glaze over top; chill. Remove from pan just before serving. *16 to 20 servings.*

Cherry Glaze

Add enough water to reserved liquid from 1 can (1 pound) red tart pitted cherries to make 1 cup. Stir together ½ cup sugar and 2 tablespoons cornstarch in small saucepan. Stir in cherry liquid. Cook, stirring constantly, until mixture thickens and boils. Boil and stir 1 minute. Remove from heat; stir in cherries and, if desired, few drops red food coloring. Cool.

Almond Cheesecake: Follow recipe for Cherry Cheesecake (above) except—omit Cherry Glaze and spread 1 cup dairy sour cream over cheesecake. Sprinkle with ⅓ cup toasted blanched slivered almonds. Bake at 450° for 5 minutes.

SUNDAE BUBBLE CROWN

An impressive frozen "crown" of cream puffs. Pictured above.

Miniature Cream Puffs (right)
1 package of our chocolate fudge flavor frosting
   mix
2 tablespoons light corn syrup
3 tablespoons butter or margarine
⅔ cup milk
2 quarts vanilla ice cream

Prepare cream puffs. To prepare fudge sauce, combine frosting mix, corn syrup and butter in top of double boiler. Gradually stir in milk. Heat over rapidly boiling water 5 minutes, stirring occasionally. Cool.

Place a layer of cream puffs in a tube pan, 10x4 inches, with a removable bottom. (Place pan on piece of aluminum foil—it is easier to handle and the ice cream that may melt through will be "caught.") Stir 1 quart of the ice cream just to soften; spread over cream puffs in pan. Repeat with another layer of puffs, ice cream and puffs. With a teaspoon, drizzle part of fudge sauce over top layer of puffs. (Cover and refrigerate remaining fudge sauce.) Place crown in freezer until firm, preferably overnight; remove 15 minutes before serving. Remove crown from pan by running spatula around outside edge of mold; push bottom up and out. With two large spatulas, lift crown from bottom and place on serving plate. Cut into slices and serve with remaining fudge sauce. *16 servings.*

Miniature Cream Puffs

1 cup water
½ cup butter or margarine
1 cup Gold Medal Flour (regular or Wondra)
4 eggs

Heat oven to 400°. Heat water and butter to rolling boil in saucepan. Stir in flour. Stir vigorously over low heat until mixture forms a ball, about 1 minute. Remove from heat. Beat eggs in thoroughly, one at a time. Beat until smooth. Drop dough by slightly rounded teaspoonfuls onto ungreased baking sheet. Bake about 25 minutes or until puffed, golden brown and dry. Remove from baking sheet and allow to cool. *Makes about 70 puffs.*

Other Ice Cream and Sauce Variations

• Substitute pistachio and black cherry ice cream for the vanilla ice cream.
• Substitute Butter Brickle and vanilla-almond for the vanilla ice cream and add 2 teaspoons instant coffee to the dry frosting mix when making sauce.

CREAM PUFF BOWL

1 cup water
½ cup butter or margarine
1 cup Gold Medal Flour (regular or Wondra)
4 eggs
1 quart vanilla ice cream
2 cups whipping cream
½ cup confectioners' sugar
Chocolate Sauce (below)

Heat oven to 400°. Heat water and butter to a rolling boil in saucepan. Stir in flour. Stir vigorously over low heat until mixture forms a ball, about 1 minute. Remove from heat. Beat in eggs thoroughly, one at a time. Beat until smooth. Drop dough by teaspoonfuls onto ungreased baking sheet. Bake 25 to 30 minutes. Allow puffs to cool slowly away from drafts. Cut off tops with sharp knife. Scoop out any filaments of soft dough; fill each generously with ice cream. Place in freezer at least 1 hour.

Whip cream with confectioners' sugar until stiff. Remove puffs from freezer; place half the puffs in a 4-quart bowl. Spoon half the whipped cream over puffs; fold gently to combine puffs and cream. Repeat with remaining puffs and whipped cream. Pour puff-cream mixture into 3-quart serving dish or punch bowl. Drizzle Chocolate Sauce over top; swirl to give marbled effect. Serve remaining sauce separately. *12 to 14 servings.*

Chocolate Sauce

Heat ½ cup light cream and 1½ bars (4 ounces each) sweet cooking chocolate in top of double boiler over boiling water until chocolate melts. Beat until smooth; cool.

PINEAPPLE WAFER DESSERT

1½ cups crushed vanilla wafers
1½ tablespoons butter or margarine, melted
½ cup soft butter
1 cup confectioners' sugar
1 egg
1 can (1 pound 4½ ounces) crushed pineapple,
    well drained
1 cup whipping cream, whipped

Mix half of the wafer crumbs and the melted butter; press firmly and evenly on bottom of square pan, 8x8x2 inches. Beat ½ cup soft butter, the confectioners' sugar and egg until light and fluffy. Spread over crumbs in pan. Fold pineapple into whipped cream. Spread over butter-sugar mixture. Sprinkle with remaining crumbs. Refrigerate 12 hours or longer. Cut into squares. *9 servings.*

Note: Refrigerate any leftover dessert immediately.

CHERRY-BERRIES ON A CLOUD

Tangy cream cheese, tiny marshmallows, whipped cream and a delicate meringue base mellow together as dessert refrigerates.

6 egg whites
½ teaspoon cream of tartar
¼ teaspoon salt
1¾ cups sugar
2 packages (3 ounces each) cream cheese, softened
1 cup sugar
1 teaspoon vanilla
2 cups whipping cream, whipped
2 cups miniature marshmallows
Cherry-Berry Topping (below)

Heat oven to 275°. Grease an oblong pan, 13x9x2 inches. Beat egg whites, cream of tartar and salt until frothy. Gradually beat in 1¾ cups sugar. Beat until very stiff and glossy, about 15 minutes. Spread in prepared pan. Bake 60 minutes. Turn off oven and leave meringue in until cool, about 12 hours or overnight. Mix cream cheese with 1 cup sugar and the vanilla. Gently fold in whipped cream and marshmallows. Spread over meringue; refrigerate 12 hours or overnight. Cut into serving pieces and top with Cherry-Berry Topping. *10 to 12 servings.*

Cherry-Berry Topping

Stir 1 can (1 pound 5 ounces) cherry pie filling and 1 teaspoon lemon juice into 2 cups sliced fresh strawberries or 1 package (1 pound) frozen strawberries, thawed.

STANDARD PASTRY FOR ONE- AND TWO-CRUST PIES

PASTRY FOR 9-INCH ONE-CRUST PIE

1 cup Gold Medal Flour* (regular or Wondra)
½ teaspoon salt
⅓ cup plus 1 tablespoon shortening or
   ⅓ cup lard
2 tablespoons water

Stir flour and salt together. Cut in shortening thoroughly. (Crumbs should be size of tiny peas.) Sprinkle water over mixture, one tablespoon at a time, mixing with fork until flour is moistened (1 to 2 teaspoons water may be added if needed). Mix until dough almost cleans sides of bowl. Press dough into ball; shape into flattened circle. Roll on lightly floured cloth-covered board 2 inches larger than inverted pie pan. Roll dough evenly in all directions from center to outside. Keep rounding edge of pastry with hands. If pastry breaks apart, pinch broken edges together while rolling. Fold in half; transfer to pie pan; unfold. Lift and pat pastry gently to ease into pan; do not stretch. Fold and roll pastry under. Flute edge. Fill and bake as directed.

If using Self-Rising Flour, omit salt.

9-INCH BAKED PIE SHELL

Follow recipe for One-crust Pie (above) except—do not fill. Prick with fork. Bake 8 to 10 minutes in 475° oven. Cool. Fill as directed.

PASTRY FOR 9-INCH TWO-CRUST PIE

2 cups Gold Medal Flour* (regular or Wondra)
1 teaspoon salt
⅔ cup plus 2 tablespoons shortening or
   ⅔ cup lard
¼ cup water

Stir flour and salt together. Cut in shortening thoroughly. (Crumbs should be size of tiny peas.) Sprinkle water over mixture, one tablespoon at a time, mixing with fork until flour is moistened (1 to 2 teaspoons water may be added if needed). Mix until dough almost cleans sides of bowl. Press dough into ball. Divide in half; shape each half into flattened circle. Roll one part on lightly floured cloth-covered board 1½ inches larger than inverted pie pan. Roll dough evenly in all directions from center to outside. Keep rounding edge of pastry with hands. If pastry breaks apart, pinch broken edges together while rolling. Fold in half; transfer to pie pan; unfold. Lift and pat pastry gently to ease into pan; do not stretch. Fill. Trim overhanging edges ½ inch from edge of pan.

Roll out other part of pastry 2 inches larger than pan. Fold into fourths, making several slits near center. Place on filling; unfold. Trim 1 inch from edge of pan. Fold and roll edge of top pastry under edge of lower pastry, pressing to seal. Flute edge. Place 2- to 3-inch strip aluminum foil around edge to prevent excessive browning during baking. Bake as directed. Remove foil 15 minutes before end of baking time.

If using Self-Rising Flour, omit salt.

SILHOUETTE PARFAIT PIE

A medley in black and white is this new ice-cream pie. For exciting holiday variations, see below.

> **3 egg whites**
> **¼ teaspoon cream of tartar**
> **¾ cup sugar**
> **3 tablespoons cocoa**
> **9-inch Baked Pie Shell (page 129)**
> **1 quart vanilla ice cream**
> **Favorite fudge sauce**

Heat oven to 325°. Beat egg whites until frothy. Sprinkle with cream of tartar; beat until soft peaks form. Gradually add sugar, beating until meringue is stiff but not dry. Sift cocoa evenly over meringue; carefully fold in cocoa with a flexible spatula. Spread evenly in baked pie shell, sealing *over* fluted edge. Bake 25 minutes. (Meringue will be soft.) Cool thoroughly. Just before serving, fill with scoops of ice cream; top with fudge sauce. (If desired, you may scoop ice cream ahead of time, pile into bowl and return to freezer.)

Valentine Heart Pie: Follow recipe above except—stir in 1 teaspoon cinnamon with cocoa before sifting over meringue. Top with fudge sauce; sprinkle with small red cinnamon candies.

Washington Jubilee Pie: Follow recipe above except—top with *Bing Cherry Sauce:* Drain 1 can (1 pound) pitted Bing cherries, reserving syrup. Mix 1 tablespoon sugar and 1 tablespoon cornstarch in saucepan. Stir in ½ cup reserved syrup. Cook, stirring constantly, until mixture thickens and boils. Cool; stir in 1½ teaspoons rum flavoring and the cherries.

Shamrock Pie: Follow recipe above except—substitute green peppermint or pistachio ice cream for vanilla ice cream. Top with marshmallow sauce and dot with green shamrock candies. (*Pictured at left.*)

Father's Day Favorite: Follow recipe above except—when making baked pie shell, add 1 square (1 ounce) semisweet chocolate, grated, to the flour. Top ice cream with *Chocolate-Peanut Butter Sauce:* Mix ¼ cup peanut butter, ¼ cup chocolate syrup and ¼ cup corn syrup.

Christmas Peppermint Pie: Follow recipe above except—substitute pink peppermint ice cream for vanilla ice cream. Top with fudge sauce and sprinkle with crushed peppermint candy. If desired, several candy canes may be used to trim center of pie. (*Pictured at left.*)

GRASSHOPPER PIE

Minted fluff in a chocolate shell.

1½ cups chocolate wafer crumbs
¼ cup butter or margarine, melted
3 cups miniature marshmallows or 32 large
   marshmallows
½ cup milk
¼ cup crème de menthe
3 tablespoons white crème de cacao
1½ cups whipping cream, whipped
Few drops green food coloring, if desired

Heat oven to 350°. Mix wafer crumbs and butter thoroughly in 9-inch pie pan; press evenly on bottom and sides. Bake 10 minutes. Cool.

Combine marshmallows and milk in saucepan; cook over low heat, stirring constantly, until marshmallows melt. Cool thoroughly and add liqueurs. Fold marshmallow mixture into whipped cream. Fold in food coloring. Pour into crumb-lined pan. Sprinkle grated semisweet chocolate over top, if desired. Chill at least 4 hours.

Alexander Pie: Follow recipe above except—substitute ¼ cup dark crème de cacao for crème de menthe and 3 tablespoons brandy for crème de cacao.

CHOCOLATE PIE DELUXE

For an added touch, pass a bowl of red-and-white peppermint candies to enhance the chocolate flavor.

1¼ cups graham cracker crumbs (16 crackers)
2 tablespoons sugar
¼ cup butter or margarine, melted
1½ cups miniature marshmallows or
   16 large marshmallows
½ cup milk
1 bar (9¾ ounces) milk chocolate
1 cup whipping cream, whipped
Toasted slivered almonds

Heat oven to 350°. Mix graham cracker crumbs and sugar in bowl. Add butter; mix thoroughly. Press crumb mixture firmly and evenly on bottom and sides of 9-inch pie pan. Bake 10 minutes. Cool.

In saucepan, combine marshmallows, milk and chocolate; cook over low heat, stirring constantly, until chocolate and marshmallows are melted and blended. Chill until mixture mounds slightly when dropped from spoon. Fold chocolate mixture into whipped cream. Pour into crumb-lined pan; sprinkle with almonds. Chill several hours or until set. To serve, cut into small wedges. *12 servings.*

FROSTY LEMON PIE

½ cup fine graham cracker crumbs (6 crackers)
3 eggs, separated
½ cup sugar
2 teaspoons grated lemon peel
¼ cup lemon juice
1 cup whipping cream, whipped

Sprinkle half of crumbs over bottom and sides of well-greased 9-inch pie pan. Beat egg whites until frothy. Gradually beat in sugar, beating until stiff and glossy. Beat egg yolks until thick and lemon colored. Fold into egg white mixture. Fold lemon peel and juice into whipped cream. Fold into egg mixture; pour into crumb-lined pie pan. Sprinkle remaining crumbs over top. Freeze. Remove from freezer 5 to 10 minutes before serving. *6 to 8 servings.*

BAKED ALASKA SPUMONI PIE

1 of our pie crust sticks
1 pint each hard strawberry, pistachio and
   chocolate ice cream
3 egg whites
¼ teaspoon cream of tartar
6 tablespoons sugar

Prepare 8-inch Baked Pie Shell as directed on inside wrapper. Cool and then chill. Working quickly, pack ice cream into pie shell. Freeze several hours.

Just before serving, heat oven to 500°. Beat egg whites with cream of tartar until frothy. Gradually beat in sugar; beat until stiff and glossy. Do not underbeat. Quickly cover ice cream with meringue, being careful to seal meringue to edge of crust. Place pie pan on a dampened wooden board; bake 3 to 5 minutes, or until meringue is a delicate golden brown. Serve immediately. *8 to 10 servings.*

ICE-CREAM DATE PIE

¼ cup soft butter or margarine
1 package of our date bar mix
½ cup hot water
1 pint vanilla ice cream

Heat oven to 400°. Mix butter and crumbly mix from date bar mix with fork. Spread in oblong pan, 13x9x2 inches. Bake 10 minutes. Do not overbake. Remove from oven; stir crumbly mixture with spoon. Reserve ½ cup for topping. Press remaining mixture on bottom and sides of 9-inch pie pan. Cool. Add hot water to date filling mix. Cool. Spoon ice cream into pie shell and spread with the date filling. Sprinkle reserved crumbly mixture over pie. Serve immediately or freeze.

Snacks—At Five or Midnight

Tops in easy entertaining for both hostess and guest is the snack party. It may be held at cocktail hour or as the midnight finale to an evening of movies, bridge or just TV and talk.

The menu may consist of two or three or more little finger foods put together with an eye to variety in texture, temperature and color. Balance a creamy dip with the crunch of potato chips or raw vegetables; play off ice-cold shrimp against sizzling little meatballs; color-contrast pale cheese with dark ripe olives or bright red caviar.

Or, you can make a light supper of snacks by increasing their number to smorgasbord proportions and featuring one or two of the heartier examples —platters of ham and cheese or chafing dish meatballs.

Whether you're serving a few nibblers or a more substantial meal, remember two rules of thumb: concentrate on pick-up foods and bite-size portions that can be handled with the fingers or speared with wooden picks; and emphasize savory or spicy nibblers, not sweet ones. Incidentally, many of these snacks convert readily to the first course for a party dinner.

DIPSY DEVIL

Keep a jar of cheese and a can of deviled ham on your shelf, and you'll be ready to whip up this dip at the drop of a hat.

1 jar (5 ounces) cream cheese with pimiento
1 can (2¼ ounces) deviled ham
¼ cup mayonnaise or salad dressing
2 tablespoons minced parsley
1 tablespoon minced onion
4 drops Tabasco
Dash monosodium glutamate

Combine all ingredients in small mixer bowl. Beat until creamy. *Makes 2 cups.*

GREEN GODDESS DIP

Originally served as a salad dressing in San Francisco. As a dip it is delightful with relish dunkers— crisp celery and carrot sticks, radishes, cuts of cucumber or raw zucchini.

¾ cup dairy sour cream
¾ cup mayonnaise or salad dressing
1 can (2 ounces) anchovy fillets, drained and finely chopped
⅓ cup snipped parsley
3 tablespoons snipped chives
1 tablespoon vinegar
1 clove garlic, crushed
¼ teaspoon salt
⅛ teaspoon pepper

Combine all ingredients; cover and refrigerate overnight to mellow flavors. *Makes 2 cups.*

LOBSTER FONDUE DIP

2 tablespoons butter or margarine
2 cups shredded sharp process American cheese (8 ounces)
2 drops Tabasco
⅓ cup dry white wine
1 can (5 ounces) lobster, drained and broken into small pieces

Melt butter in small saucepan. Gradually stir in cheese over low heat until cheese melts. (Cheese-butter mixture may appear separated at this point.) Add Tabasco; slowly add wine, stirring until mixture is smooth. Add lobster; stir until heated through. Serve hot in chafing dish. *Makes about 1½ cups.*

Delectable Dippers

Serve these favorite party dips with our Bugles, Whistles and Daisy*s, with potato chips, assorted crackers or crisp and crunchy vegetable relishes.

GUACAMOLE

A dip with a flavor wallop. Serve in a gay Mexican-style bowl or use the avocado shells to hold dip.

2 avocados, peeled and pitted
1 medium onion, finely chopped
2 green chili peppers, finely chopped
1 tablespoon lemon juice
1 teaspoon salt
½ teaspoon coarsely ground pepper
1 medium tomato, peeled and finely chopped
Mayonnaise or salad dressing
Corn chips or Bugles

Mash avocados; add onion, peppers, lemon juice, salt and pepper. Beat until creamy. Fold in tomato. Spread top with thin layer of mayonnaise. Cover and chill. Just before serving, stir gently to mix. Serve as a dip for corn chips or Bugles. *Makes about 2 cups.*

POLYNESIAN SHRIMP DIP

Cut a 1-inch slice from top of pineapple, leaving green leaves on top. With a knife remove fruit, leaving a ½-inch wall. Remove core from fruit and cut remaining pineapple into bite-size pieces. Place a pitted ripe olive in curve of cooked shrimp; skewer together with a plastic pick. Repeat with additional shrimp (you will need about 1 cup shrimp). Place pineapple pieces on picks. Attach shrimp and pineapple in spiral design to shell of pineapple.

Place custard cup of Curry Dip (below) in pineapple; cover with pineapple top. Serve immediately or cover completely with plastic wrap and refrigerate. *6 servings.*

Curry Dip

Stir together 1 cup dairy sour cream, ¾ teaspoon curry powder and ¼ teaspoon salt.

FROSTED PÂTÉ

1 pound liverwurst
1 clove garlic, crushed
½ teaspoon crushed basil leaves
3 tablespoons minced onion
Cream Cheese Topping (below)
Red or black caviar or 3 tablespoons
    anchovy paste
Parsley
Crisp crackers

Mash liverwurst with fork; mix in garlic, basil and onion thoroughly. Place on serving plate; shape mixture into loaf with rounded top. Chill. Spread Cream Cheese Topping over loaf. Cover and refrigerate overnight. Before serving, ring caviar or anchovy paste around cheese topping. Garnish with parsley. Serve as a spread for crackers.

Cream Cheese Topping

Soften 1 package (8 ounces) cream cheese; mix with 1 teaspoon mayonnaise or salad dressing, 1 clove garlic, crushed, and ⅛ teaspoon Tabasco.

TRIO-CHEESE BALL

1 package (8 ounces) cream cheese, softened
¼ pound blue cheese, crumbled
1 cup shredded sharp Cheddar cheese (4 ounces)
1 small onion, minced
1 tablespoon Worcestershire sauce
½ cup chopped pecans
Finely snipped parsley
Small crisp crackers

Beat cheeses in mixer bowl on medium speed until fluffy, scraping sides and bottom of bowl often. Beat in onion and Worcestershire sauce. Stir in pecans. Cover and chill 3 to 4 hours. Mold cheese mixture into one large ball or into 30 to 36 small balls, each about 1 inch in diameter; roll in parsley. Place on serving plate; cover and chill until firm, about 2 hours. Arrange a variety of crackers on plate around cheese ball; serve as a spread. Or insert colored wooden picks in center of small balls and serve with crackers. *1 large ball or 2½ to 3 dozen small balls.*

BRAUNSCHWEIGER SPREAD

10 ounces Braunschweiger
2 cups dairy sour cream
1 package (1⅜ ounces) dry onion soup mix
½ teaspoon Worcestershire sauce
Crisp crackers

Mix Braunschweiger, sour cream, soup mix and Worcestershire sauce; cover and refrigerate. Serve as a spread for crackers. *Makes 3⅓ cups.*

CAVIAR BUFFET

Mound dairy sour cream into one compartment of a three-sectioned dish or a small bowl. Spoon red caviar and snipped chives in second and third compartments or in other bowls. Serve with melba toast rounds or toasted snack rye bread. Guests help themselves to toast, spread it with sour cream and sprinkle with caviar and chives.

NUTTY CEREAL MIXIN'S

1½ cups Kix
1 cup Cheerios
2 cups small cheese crackers
2 cups thin pretzel sticks
½ pound mixed nuts
¼ cup butter, melted
½ teaspoon Worcestershire sauce
¼ teaspoon garlic salt
¼ teaspoon celery salt

Heat oven to 250°. Combine cereals, crackers, pretzel sticks and nuts in oblong pan, 13x9x2 inches. Mix the butter with the remaining ingredients; pour over cereal mixture. Stir and salt lightly to taste. Bake 30 minutes, stirring carefully after 15 minutes. *Makes about 6 cups.*

PARMESAN GLAZED WALNUTS

1½ cups walnut halves
1 tablespoon butter, melted
¼ teaspoon hickory smoked salt
¼ teaspoon salt
¼ cup shredded Parmesan cheese

Heat oven to 350°. Spread walnuts in shallow pan; toast in oven 10 minutes. Stir together butter, hickory salt and salt; toss lightly with walnuts. Sprinkle cheese over top; stir. Return to oven and toast 3 to 4 minutes, or until cheese melts. *Makes 1½ cups.*

CHEESE PENNIES

A jar of cheese spread, shortening and flour—for the fastest cheese pastries ever! Take your choice of cheese flavors and shaping variations.

**1 jar (5 ounces) pasteurized process sharp
American cheese spread***
¼ cup shortening
⅔ cup Gold Medal Flour (regular or Wondra)

In small mixer bowl, mix all ingredients on medium speed 20 to 30 seconds. On lightly floured surface, mold into two 8-inch rolls, 1 inch in diameter. (Dough will be soft but not sticky.) Wrap in waxed paper; refrigerate 2 hours or overnight.

Heat oven to 375°. Cut into ⅛-inch slices; place on ungreased baking sheet. Bake 12 to 15 minutes or until slightly browned. *Makes about 6 dozen.*

*Pasteurized process cheese spread with bacon, garlic or with added hickory flavor may be substituted.

Penny Surprises: Follow recipe for Cheese Pennies (above) except—flatten roll into oblong, 1½ to 2 inches wide. Place choice of small pimiento-stuffed olives, anchovies, cocktail wieners or ¼-inch salami strips down center of oblong. Mold into roll. Wrap, refrigerate, slice and bake as directed above.

Cheese Strips: Follow recipe for Cheese Pennies (above) except—heat oven to 350°. After mixing dough, fill cookie press. Form strips on ungreased baking sheet, using star plate. Cut into 3-inch lengths. Bake 20 minutes or until lightly browned. Remove immediately to cooling rack. *Makes about 2 dozen.*

SESAME SEED SQUARES

Just three ingredients! Tiny cubes of cream cheese are coated with toasty sesame seed and spiked with soy sauce. Easy to make, different to serve!

Heat oven to 350°. Sprinkle 2 tablespoons sesame seed on baking sheet; toast in oven about 10 minutes or until golden. Cool. Cut 1 package (3 ounces) cream cheese into 12 squares. Roll each cheese square in sesame seed; dip into soy sauce. Refrigerate. At serving time, dip squares again into soy sauce. Garnish each with a parsley sprig, if desired. Serve with wooden picks. Or serve squares on picks pegged in a large orange. *Makes 12 cheese squares.*

TOASTED ONION CANAPÉS

20 two-inch bread rounds
¾ cup minced onion
½ cup mayonnaise or salad dressing
¼ cup grated Parmesan cheese

Set oven control at broil and/or 550°. Place bread rounds on baking sheet and toast one side under broiler *just* until golden brown. Mix onion, mayonnaise and cheese; spread on untoasted side of bread rounds. Broil 3 inches from heat 2 to 3 minutes or until golden brown. *Makes 20 canapés.*

BAMBINOS

Heat oven to 400°. Spread 4 dozen Melba rounds or round cheese crackers with ¾ cup pizza flavor catsup. Sprinkle 1 cup shredded mozzarella cheese over catsup; top with ⅛ pound thinly sliced pepperoni or sausage. If desired, sprinkle with crushed oregano leaves. Bake 3 to 5 minutes, or until cheese melts. *Makes 4 dozen canapés.*

TOAST CANAPÉ BASES

Remove crust from close-textured bread. Slice thinly (⅛ to ¼ inch). Cut slices with round, star or crescent cutter. Toast on *one side only* in small amount butter in hot skillet over low heat until nicely browned. About 30 minutes before serving, cover untoasted side with a spread or decorate (below).

Green Leaf Canapés

Soften 2 packages (3 ounces each) cream cheese; place in blender with 2 ounces blue cheese, 2 teaspoons light cream and 2 to 3 drops green food coloring. Mix until smooth. Spoon mixture into decorators' tube with a leaf point attached. Press about three leaves onto each Canapé Base. Garnish with capers or tiny pearl onions, if desired. *Makes 1 cup.*

Note: Cream cheese and blue cheese may be put through a fine sieve, then combined with electric mixer.

Rosette Canapés

Soften 2 packages (3 ounces each) cream cheese; place in blender with 1 tablespoon anchovy paste and 2 to 3 drops red food coloring. Mix until smooth. (Use electric mixer, if desired.) Spoon mixture into decorators' tube with rosette point attached. Press a rosette onto each Canapé Base. Garnish with sprig of mint, if desired. *Makes 1 cup.*

CHAFING DISH MEATBALLS

1 pound ground beef
½ cup dry bread crumbs
⅓ cup minced onion
¼ cup milk
1 egg
1 tablespoon snipped parsley
1 teaspoon salt
⅛ teaspoon pepper
½ teaspoon Worcestershire sauce
¼ cup shortening
1 bottle (12 ounces) chili sauce
1 jar (10 ounces) grape jelly

Mix ground beef, crumbs, onion, milk, egg and next 4 seasonings; gently shape into 1-inch balls. Melt shortening in large skillet; brown meatballs. Remove meatballs from skillet; drain fat. Heat chili sauce and jelly in skillet until jelly is melted, stirring constantly. Add meatballs and stir until coated. Simmer 30 minutes. Serve hot in chafing dish. *Makes 5 dozen meatballs.*

Saucy Sausages: Follow recipe above except—substitute 4 jars (4½ ounces each) cocktail sausages for the meatballs and simmer 20 minutes.

MUSHROOMS ROYALE

1 pound medium mushrooms (about 3 dozen)
3 tablespoons butter or margarine
¼ cup finely chopped green pepper
¼ cup finely chopped onion
1½ cups soft bread crumbs
½ teaspoon salt
½ teaspoon ground thyme
¼ teaspoon turmeric
¼ teaspoon pepper
1 tablespoon butter or margarine

Heat oven to 350°. Wash, trim and dry mushrooms thoroughly. Remove stems; finely chop enough stems to measure ⅓ cup. Melt 3 tablespoons butter in skillet. Cook and stir chopped mushroom stems, green pepper and onion in butter until tender, about 5 minutes. Remove from heat; stir in remaining ingredients except mushroom caps and 1 tablespoon butter. Melt 1 tablespoon butter in shallow baking dish. Fill mushroom caps with stuffing mixture; place mushrooms filled side up in baking dish. Bake 15 minutes.

Set oven control at broil and/or 550°. Broil mushrooms 3 to 4 inches from heat 2 minutes. Serve hot. *About 3 dozen appetizers.*

RUMAKI

Oriental Sauce (below)
6 chicken livers, cut in half
1 can (5 ounces) water chestnuts, drained and cut into 12 slices, or use 12 slices fresh water chestnuts
6 slices bacon, cut in half
¼ cup brown sugar

Pour Oriental Sauce over chicken livers and water chestnuts in baking dish. Cover dish with plastic wrap; refrigerate 4 hours.

Set oven control at broil and/or 550°. Remove chicken livers and water chestnuts from marinade. Wrap 1 liver and water chestnut slice in each piece bacon; secure with wooden pick. Roll in brown sugar. Broil 3 inches from heat 10 minutes, turning occasionally, until bacon is crisp. *Makes 12 appetizers.*

Oriental Sauce

¼ cup soy sauce
¼ cup salad oil
2 tablespoons catsup
1 tablespoon vinegar
¼ teaspoon pepper
2 cloves garlic, crushed

Mix all ingredients. *Makes about 1 cup sauce.*

QUICK LORRAINE TARTS

Fun and fancy—and these little appetizers can be made ahead to avoid last-minute flurry.

2 of our pie crust sticks
1 tablespoon poppy seed
1⅓ cups coarsely shredded Swiss cheese
⅔ cup chopped salami
⅓ cup sliced green onions
4 eggs, slightly beaten
1⅓ cups dairy sour cream
1 teaspoon salt
1 teaspoon Worcestershire sauce

Heat oven to 375°. Prepare pastry for Two-crust Pie as directed on inside wrapper except—stir poppy seed into dry crumbled mix. Roll pastry 1/16 inch thick on lightly floured board; cut into 3-inch rounds. Fit rounds into 2½-inch muffin pans. Combine cheese, salami and onion; spoon into pastry-lined muffin pans. Stir together eggs, sour cream, salt and Worcestershire sauce; pour about 1 tablespoon sour cream mixture into each muffin pan. Bake 20 to 25 minutes or until lightly browned. Cool in pans 5 minutes. *Makes 36 tarts.*

Do-ahead Note: Tarts may be baked in advance, cooled and wrapped in aluminum foil. At serving time, heat in 350° oven 10 minutes.

SNACK BRIOCHES

These filling appetizers are just right when guests are too hungry for only chips and olives.

1 package (8 ounces) frozen brioches, thawed
1 can (2¼ ounces) deviled ham
1 tablespoon drained pickle relish
1 tablespoon light cream

Heat oven to 350°. Cut around topknot of each brioche; remove. With a fork, scoop out centers and reserve bread. Crumble reserved bread; stir together with the remaining ingredients. Fill brioches; replace tops. Return to foil package; heat uncovered 10 minutes or until warm. *6 servings.*

Chicken Filling: Stir together 1 can (2¼ ounces) chicken spread, 1 tablespoon toasted diced almonds, 1 tablespoon sherry, 3 pimiento-stuffed olives, sliced, ⅛ teaspoon poultry seasoning and the reserved crumbs.

Liver Pâté Filling: Stir together 1 can (3 ounces) liver pâté, 1 tablespoon minced onion, 1 tablespoon light cream and 3 pitted ripe olives, cut into wedges. Stir in the reserved crumbs.

RYE RIBBON ROUND

A sandwich torte towered with layers of deviled ham, blue cheese and crabmeat. Slice into wedges, serve with chips and relishes for a snack supper.

2 cans (4½ ounces each) deviled ham
1 teaspoon instant minced onion
¼ cup chopped pitted ripe olives
1 package (3 ounces) cream cheese, softened
2 ounces blue cheese
1 drop green food coloring
1 can (7¾ ounces) crabmeat, drained and cartilage removed
1 jar (5 ounces) pasteurized Neufchâtel cheese with pineapple
¼ cup chopped celery
1 round loaf (2 pounds) rye bread, about 8 inches in diameter (unsliced)*
3 cartons (4 ounces each) whipped cream cheese, softened
¼ cup slivered blanched almonds, toasted
½ cup sliced pitted ripe olives

Combine deviled ham, minced onion and chopped olives; cover. With electric mixer, blend cream cheese, blue cheese and green food coloring; cover. Flake the crabmeat; stir in cheese with pineapple and the chopped celery; cover. Remove crust from loaf; cut horizontally into 4 slices. Spread bottom slice with ham filling; top with second slice. Spread with blue cheese mixture; top with third slice. Spread with crabmeat mixture; top with fourth slice. Cover loaf tightly with plastic wrap; refrigerate several hours or overnight. An hour before serving, frost loaf with whipped cream cheese. Press almonds and olives into cheese frosting around side and top of loaf. Refrigerate until serving time. Cut into wedges. *8 to 10 servings.*

*Available on special order from a bakery.

PARTY PIZZA

¾ cup chopped onion
1 clove garlic, crushed
1 can (15 ounces) tomato sauce
1 cup sliced pepperoni or cooked Italian sausage
½ teaspoon salt
¼ teaspoon pepper
1 package active dry yeast
¾ cup warm water (105 to 115°)
2½ cups Bisquick
2½ cups shredded mozzarella cheese or
   2 packages (6 ounces each) sliced mozzarella
   cheese, cut into thin strips
3 to 4 teaspoons crushed oregano leaves

Mix onion, garlic, tomato sauce, meat, salt and pepper; set aside.

Heat oven to 425°. Dissolve yeast in warm water. Add Bisquick and beat vigorously. Turn dough onto well-floured surface. Knead until smooth, about 20 times. Allow dough to rest a few minutes. Divide dough into 4 parts. Roll each part very thin into a circle about 10 inches in diameter. Place on ungreased baking sheets. Pinch edge of dough to make rim. Spread meat mixture over circles. Sprinkle with shredded cheese or arrange cheese strips on top. Sprinkle with oregano. Bake 15 to 20 minutes, or until crust is brown and filling hot and bubbly. Cut into wedges; serve immediately. *4 servings.*

Hamburger Pizza: Follow recipe above except—substitute 1 pound browned ground beef and ½ cup chopped green pepper for the pepperoni or sausage.

OLIVE-CHEESE BALLS

So popular for hostessing. And no wonder. These surprise cheese balls are make-aheads!

2 cups shredded sharp Cheddar cheese (8 ounces)
1¼ cups Gold Medal Flour* (regular or Wondra)
½ cup butter or margarine, melted
1 jar (2 ounces) pimiento-stuffed small olives
   (about 36)

Work cheese and flour together until crumbly. Add butter and mix well with fork. (If dough seems dry, work with hands.) Mold 1 teaspoon dough around each olive; shape into ball. Place 2 inches apart on ungreased baking sheet. Cover and chill 1 hour or longer.

Heat oven to 400°. Bake 15 to 20 minutes. Serve hot. *Makes about 3 dozen balls.*

Do not use Self-Rising Flour in this recipe.

TRIPLE-CHEESE APPETIZER WHEEL

1 cup Gold Medal Flour* (regular or Wondra)
½ cup shredded Swiss cheese
½ teaspoon salt
⅓ cup plus 1 tablespoon shortening
2 tablespoons water
Cheese Filling (below)

Heat oven to 475°. Stir flour, cheese and salt together. Cut in shortening thoroughly. Sprinkle water over mixture, 1 tablespoon at a time, mixing with fork until flour is moistened. Gather into a ball; divide dough in half. Roll one half into 9-inch circle. Place on baking sheet; turn under ½ inch all around. Crimp edge and prick with fork. Bake 8 to 10 minutes or until lightly browned. Roll out other half to 7-inch circle; place on baking sheet. Score into 16 sections, cutting only part way through pastry. Cut around rim of each section to form scalloped edge. Cut a 2-inch hole in middle. Bake about 10 minutes or until golden brown. Cool. Just before serving, spread Cheese Filling evenly to edge of 9-inch circle; place scalloped circle on top. Candles may be inserted in Cheese Filling around scalloped circle, if desired. Garnish with parsley and olives, if desired. To serve, cut into wedges.

If using Self-Rising Flour, omit salt.

Cheese Filling

Soften 4 ounces cream cheese; beat with 2 ounces blue cheese and 1 tablespoon horseradish until fluffy and smooth. Add 1 tablespoon milk; beat until fluffy. Fold in ¼ cup sliced pimiento-stuffed olives.

HAM PUFFS PETITE

1 recipe Miniature Cream Puffs (page 127)
3 cans (4½ ounces each) deviled ham
1 tablespoon horseradish
¾ teaspoon onion salt
¾ teaspoon pepper
⅓ cup dairy sour cream

Prepare Miniature Cream Puffs. When ready to serve, cut off tops with sharp knife; remove filaments of soft dough. Blend deviled ham, horseradish, onion salt, pepper and sour cream; fill each puff with slightly rounded teaspoonful of mixture. *Makes 6 dozen puffs.*

Midnight Snack Supper

Lobster Bisque
Assorted Crackers   Cheese Straws
Pickle Buffet
French Ribbon Cake (page 124)   Coffee

A snack party at the cocktail hour calls for a handsome spread of nibblers; at midnight it means a more formal and more filling meal. This menu offers an elegant ending for a dress-up evening at a play or concert. The last-minute preparations are all super-simple and can be safely handled in your prettiest party clothes. Just heat the soup and pop the Cheese Straws in the oven—supper will be on the buffet table just minutes after you step through the door.

Serving suggestions: Arrange everything, including cake and coffee, on the buffet so your guests can help themselves. Then relax and enjoy yourself—your company will.

PLAN FOR PREPARATION

Day before (or morning of party): 1. *Bake cake.* **2.** *While cake bakes, prepare Cheese Straws; wrap and refrigerate.* **3.** *Chill pickles.* **4.** *Fill and frost cake.*

Just before serving: 1. *Heat soup; add lobster and sherry.* **2.** *Bake Cheese Straws.* **3.** *Prepare coffee.* **4.** *Arrange crackers in basket.* **5.** *Arrange pickles on tray.*

LOBSTER BISQUE

2 cans (11¼ ounces each) condensed
    green pea soup
2 cans (11 ounces each) condensed bisque of
    tomato soup
1 soup can milk
2 cups light cream
1 teaspoon salt
½ teaspoon pepper
1 teaspoon Worcestershire sauce
3 cans (5 ounces each) lobster meat, drained
⅓ cup dry sherry

In large saucepan combine all ingredients except lobster meat and sherry with rotary beater; heat through. Stir in lobster meat and sherry; heat. *6 to 8 servings.*

PICKLE BUFFET

On a large divided tray or plate, arrange a variety of chilled pickles. Select pickles of various shades of green and in different shapes such as: crinkle-cut candied dill slices, bread and butter-type pickles, tiny sweet gherkins, watermelon pickles, pickled green beans and marinated artichoke hearts.

CHEESE STRAWS

1 of our pie crust sticks
½ cup shredded Cheddar cheese (2 ounces)
Salt
Caraway or poppy seed
Paprika

Heat oven to 450°. Prepare pastry as directed on inside wrapper except—add cheese with the water. Roll out on lightly floured cloth-covered board into an oblong, 13x10 inches. Place on baking sheet. With a sharp knife, cut dough lengthwise into thirds. Cut each piece of dough crosswise to make 15 strips. (Do not separate strips; they will bake apart.) Sprinkle with salt, caraway or poppy seed and paprika. (At this point, pastry may be covered and refrigerated, if desired.) Bake 8 to 10 minutes or until brown. Serve hot. *Makes about 45 straws.*

Happy Holiday Specials

There's something especially lighthearted about a holiday party; even adults have a day-off-from-school feeling. And if you're the kind of hostess who enjoys theme-ing a party, this is your chance to go all out. The nearest dime store will have the gay seasonal paraphernalia you'll need, or, if you prefer, you can make your own decorations. In either case, choose invitations symbolic of the occasion, deck your door with a bit of welcoming decor, have a centerpiece and place favors, games and prizes in the tradition of the particular day.

Let your menu say happy holiday too—in the foods you choose and the way you present them. Use your cookie cutters to make bell-shaped or heart-shaped or shamrock-shaped cookies or sandwiches. Sculpt Easter or Christmas motifs or messages with your pastry tube. Garnish cakes or pies with candies of the season—tiny cinnamon hearts, corn candies, little peppermint candy canes. Above all, don't be afraid to be a little nostalgic, a bit sentimental. That's what holidays are all about.

The parties and decorating ideas that follow are keyed to individual fete days, but they can all be easily translated for other occasions as well.

New Year's Buffet, Chinese Style

Sweet 'n Sour Pork   White Rice
Chinese Pea Pods
Sesame Sticks   Oriental Relishes
Cherry Freeze   Almond Butter Cookies   Tea

By the end of the holiday season most of your friends are likely to have eaten a good deal of turkey, drunk as many eggnogs as they care to and had their fill of holly and tinsel and carols. So why not change the pace completely with a New Year's Eve supper that borrows some of the delicious foods and colorful customs of the Chinese? Begin with a bit of Oriental decoration—a set of wind chimes hung over the table or some Chinese good luck symbols stitched on the tablecloth. Or you can make up "fortunes" for the new year and bake them into the cookies. The menu, styled after the type originally eaten with chopsticks, requires no knives; thus it's ideal for buffet service. And the piquant food is just right for early evening or midnight.

Serving suggestions: Have everything except the dessert on the buffet. Keep hot foods hot in chafing dishes, over warmers or on an electric hot tray.

SWEET 'N SOUR PORK

3¾ pounds pork shoulder, cut into 1-inch cubes
¾ cup Gold Medal Flour (regular or Wondra)
1 tablespoon plus 1 teaspoon ginger
½ cup salad oil
2 cans (13½ ounces each) pineapple chunks, drained (reserve syrup)
½ cup vinegar
½ cup soy sauce
1 tablespoon Worcestershire sauce
¾ cup sugar
1 tablespoon salt
¾ teaspoon pepper
2 small green peppers, cut into strips
1 can (1 pound) bean sprouts, drained
2 cans (5 ounces each) water chestnuts, drained and thinly sliced
2 tablespoons chili sauce
White Rice (right)

Trim any excess fat from pork. Combine half the flour and the ginger in paper bag. Place a few pieces of pork at a time in bag; shake well to coat meat. Heat oil in large heavy skillet or Dutch oven; brown pork on all sides, removing pieces as they brown. Add water to reserved pineapple syrup to measure 1¾ cups liquid; gradually stir in remaining flour. Stir flour mixture, vinegar, soy sauce and Worcestershire sauce into pork drippings. Heat to boiling, stirring constantly. Boil 1 minute. Stir in sugar, salt, pepper and meat; cover and simmer 1 hour or until meat is tender, stirring occasionally. Add pineapple and green pepper; cook uncovered 10 minutes. Stir in bean sprouts, water chestnuts and chili sauce; cook 5 minutes longer. Serve over rice. *8 servings.*

WHITE RICE

Heat oven to 350°. Combine 2 cups uncooked regular rice, 2 teaspoons salt and 4 cups boiling water in 3-quart casserole or oblong baking dish, 13½x9x2 inches; mix thoroughly. Cover dish tightly with casserole lid or aluminum foil. (Lid or foil cover must be tight enough to prevent escape of steam.) Bake 25 to 30 minutes, or until liquid is absorbed and rice is tender. Fluff and spoon into bowl to serve. *8 servings.*

CHINESE PEA PODS

Prepare 3 packages (10 ounces each) frozen Chinese pea pods as directed on package for boiling method. *8 or 9 servings.*

SESAME STICKS

For this meal, bake the rice 45 minutes before serving; remove (keep covered) and increase oven temperature to 450° for the breadsticks.

Heat oven to 450°. Melt ⅓ cup butter or margarine in oblong pan, 13x9x2 inches. Stir 2 cups Bisquick and ⅔ cup milk to a soft dough with fork. Beat vigorously 20 strokes until stiff but sticky. Roll dough around on lightly floured cloth-covered board. Knead gently 8 to 10 times. Roll into rectangle, 10x6 inches. Cut in half lengthwise. Cut each half into 12 strips, about 3x¾ inch. Roll each stick in the melted butter and arrange in pan. Sprinkle with ¼ cup sesame seed. Bake 10 to 15 minutes. *Makes 24 sticks.*

ORIENTAL RELISHES

1 jar (8 ounces) preserved kumquats
1 package (1 pound) frozen melon balls
1 unpared cucumber, thinly sliced
½ teaspoon salt
⅛ teaspoon pepper
¼ cup vinegar

Chill kumquats. Thaw melon balls as directed on package. Place cucumber slices in bowl; sprinkle with salt and pepper. Pour vinegar over slices. Cover and refrigerate about 1 hour. Drain. Just before serving, drain kumquats and melon balls; arrange with cucumber slices in a three-sectioned dish.

CHERRY FREEZE

1 package of our fluffy white frosting mix
1½ cups whipping cream
1 cup flaked coconut
⅓ cup well-drained finely chopped maraschino cherries
2 drops red food coloring

Prepare frosting mix as directed on package except— use ½ cup *cold* water. Beat frosting until fluffy, about 3 minutes. On high speed gradually beat in whipping cream. Continue beating until mixture is the consistency of whipped cream. Fold in coconut, cherries and food coloring. Divide mixture among 12 pink paper baking cups set in muffin pan. Sprinkle with additional coconut and garnish each with a maraschino cherry half, if desired. Cover with plastic wrap; freeze. Thirty minutes before serving, transfer to refrigerator to soften. *12 servings.*

ALMOND BUTTER COOKIES

½ cup soft butter or margarine
¼ cup sugar
½ cup finely chopped blanched almonds
1 teaspoon almond extract
1 cup Gold Medal Flour* (regular or Wondra)
Blanched whole almonds

Heat oven to 350°. Cream butter and sugar thoroughly. Stir in chopped almonds and almond extract. Mix in flour; work with hands until dough is smooth and well blended. Shape scant teaspoonfuls of dough into balls. Place on ungreased baking sheet. Flatten with greased bottom of glass dipped in sugar. Press whole almond into center of each cookie. Bake 9 to 10 minutes or until slightly browned. *Makes about 3 dozen.*

Do not use Self-Rising Flour in this recipe.

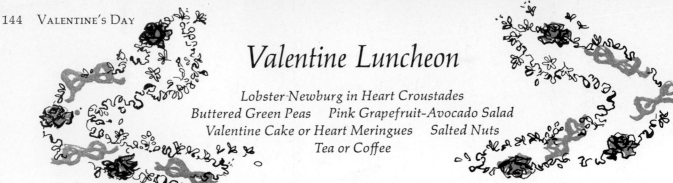

Valentine Luncheon

Lobster Newburg in Heart Croustades
Buttered Green Peas   Pink Grapefruit-Avocado Salad
Valentine Cake or Heart Meringues   Salted Nuts
Tea or Coffee

LOBSTER NEWBURG

1 can (6 ounces) sliced mushrooms, drained
   (reserve liquid)
1 tablespoon minced onion
1 tablespoon minced parsley
¼ cup butter or margarine
2 tablespoons flour
1 teaspoon salt
Dash cayenne pepper
Dash nutmeg
¾ cup liquid (mushroom liquid and water)
2 egg yolks, slightly beaten
1½ cups dairy sour cream
1 can (5 ounces) lobster or 1 can (7¾ ounces)
   crabmeat, drained and cartilage removed
2 tablespoons sherry

Cook and stir mushrooms, onion and parsley in the butter over low heat 5 minutes. Remove from heat. Blend in flour, salt, cayenne pepper and nutmeg. Cook over low heat, stirring constantly, until mixture is bubbly. Remove from heat. Stir in the liquid. Heat to boiling, stirring constantly. Boil 1 minute. Remove from heat. Blend egg yolks and sour cream; stir into hot mixture with the lobster and sherry. Heat through, stirring constantly. *6 servings.*

HEART CROUSTADES

Heat oven to 375°. Trim crust ends from 1-pound 8-ounce unsliced loaf sandwich bread. Cut into 6 slices, 2 inches thick. With cookie cutter or heart-shaped cardboard pattern, cut slices into heart shapes. Cut out center of each heart, leaving ½-inch-thick wall on bottom and sides. Brush tops and sides of hearts with melted butter. Bake 12 to 15 minutes or until golden brown. *Makes 6 croustades.*

VALENTINE CAKE

Heat oven to 350°. Grease and flour two heart-shaped pans, 8 inches wide at widest part and 1½ inches deep. Prepare 1 package of our white cake mix as directed except—pour into prepared heart-shaped pans. Bake 30 to 35 minutes, or until top springs back when touched lightly with finger.

Prepare 1 package of our fluffy white frosting mix as directed. Tint frosting pink with red food coloring. Fill and frost cake. If desired, decorate around edge with cherries or heart candies.

TWIN HEARTS CAKE

Bake two heart cakes as in recipe above. Prepare 2 packages, one at a time, of our fluffy white frosting mix as directed. Tint frosting pink with red food coloring. Fill and frost cakes. On a pretty tray, arrange frosted cakes so they are just touching at wide end. Trim tray with flowers and place a net bow at top of hearts, if desired.

HEART MERINGUES

A medley in pinks—lovely for Valentine's Day. Remember also as an appropriate dessert when entertaining for bridal occasions.

3 egg whites
¼ teaspoon cream of tartar
1 cup sugar
1 quart strawberry or vanilla ice cream
Sliced fresh strawberries

Heat oven to 275°. Beat egg whites and cream of tartar until frothy. Gradually beat in sugar; beat until very stiff and glossy. Tint pink with 5 or 6 drops red food coloring, if desired. Make 8 mounds, dropping ⅓ to ½ cup meringue for each on heavy brown paper on baking sheet; shape each into heart shape with back of spoon. Bake 55 minutes. Turn off oven; leave meringues in oven until cool. Just before serving, fill shells with ice cream. Garnish with strawberries. *8 servings.*

Red, White and Pink Say "Happy Valentine's Day"

Your Table

• Use a delicate lace tablecloth to carry out the sentimental theme of the day, or bring out lace or cutwork place mats for service on card tables or individual trays. • Cover the table with a red or pink cloth and use lacy white place mats. • Stitch red felt hearts on a delicate pink runner. Show it off on a plain white tablecloth.

Your Centerpiece

• Any arrangement of pink, white and red flowers will be perfect. • Make a table-size holiday tree (see page 148). Trim with red paper hearts of varying sizes, pink and red bows and/or decorated heart-shaped cookies and candies. Tuck in tiny artificial flowers here and there.

Your Food

• Cut your favorite sugar cookies into heart shapes and decorate with red decorators' sugar. • Serve heart-shaped tea sandwiches for a festive tea or lunch. • Use heart-shaped molds for aspic, or serve red molded fruit salads. • For dessert, fill baked Heart Meringues (page 144) with strawberries and ice cream. • Valentine Heart Pie (page 130) is perfect for a party or family dessert. • Use your imagination! Practically anything touched with red or pink or cut into a heart shape will help you say "Be my Valentine."

Easter Sunday Brunch

Bouquet Fruit Cup
Scrambled Eggs with Avocado   Crisp Bacon
Easter Egg Rolls   Butter Curls (page 71)
Coffee

BOUQUET FRUIT CUP

Sherbet glasses encircled with lace doilies and mounded with fruit resemble old-fashioned nosegays. They'll set the pace for a springtime brunch.

For each sherbet glass, fold a 6- to 8-inch paper doily into fourths. At tip of fold, cut out an arc large enough to allow the doily to fit sherbet glass about 1 inch from top. (You will need to experiment for exact size.) Slip doily up over base of glass; secure in place with cellophane tape. Fill sherbet glass with chunks of fresh, frozen or canned pineapple and whole or halved fresh strawberries. Tuck in a few sprigs of mint or watercress for leaves of the "bouquet."

SCRAMBLED EGGS WITH AVOCADO

8 eggs
½ cup light cream
1 teaspoon salt
¼ teaspoon pepper
1 avocado, peeled and cubed (about 1 cup)
2 tablespoons butter or margarine

Mix eggs, cream, salt and pepper with fork. Add avocado. Heat butter in skillet just until hot enough to sizzle drop of water. Pour in egg mixture; reduce heat enough to cook egg quickly. When mixture starts to set at bottom and sides, lift cooked portions with spatula and turn gently to cook evenly. Avoid constant stirring. Cook until eggs are thickened throughout but still moist. *6 to 8 servings.*

EASTER EGG ROLLS

Tiny rolls in a pie pan "nest," frosted and decorated in Easter egg fashion. Pictured below.

Prepare 1 recipe Sweet Dough (page 113). Divide dough into 24 pieces; form into small balls and place evenly in greased 9-inch pie pan. Let rise until double, about 30 minutes.

Heat oven to 375°. Bake rolls 20 to 25 minutes or until nicely browned. Cool; do not separate. Prepare 1 recipe Creamy White Glaze (page 115); tint with food coloring as desired. Frost rolls with icing. Decorate "eggs" with remaining icing and with candies to make names, borders, bows and flowers, leaving some rolls undecorated for contrast. *Makes 24 rolls.*

Company Favorites for Easter Time

MINIATURE EASTER BONNETS

Bake cupcakes as directed on 1 package of our white or yellow cake mix; cool and remove papers. Prepare our creamy white frosting mix as directed on package; divide into 4 parts. Keep one part white; tint the remaining portions pink, yellow and green with food colorings. Place cupcakes upside down in centers of flattened paper baking cups or doilies. Frost sides and top of each cupcake to resemble crown of hat, using a color to match or contrast with the paper "brim." Decorate with one of the following: Row of chocolate pieces, red cinnamon candies or pillow mints around base of crown to form hatband.... Coconut or colored decorators' sugar sprinkled over hat.... Gumdrops or nuts cut or shaped to resemble flower petals. *Makes about 30 bonnets.*

EASTER EGG COOKIES

Charming hand-painted "eggs."

1½ cups confectioners' sugar
1 cup butter or margarine
1 egg
1 teaspoon vanilla
½ teaspoon almond extract
2½ cups Gold Medal Flour* (regular or Wondra)
1 teaspoon soda
1 teaspoon cream of tartar
Egg Yolk Paint (below)

Cream sugar and butter. Mix in egg, vanilla and almond extract. Stir dry ingredients together; blend into creamed mixture. Refrigerate 2 to 3 hours.

Heat oven to 375°. Using half the dough at a time, roll dough ⅛ inch thick on floured cloth-covered board. Cut with egg-shaped cutter made by bending and shaping open end of a 6-ounce juice can. Decorate with Egg Yolk Paint. Bake about 7 minutes. *Makes 5 dozen.*

*If using Self-Rising Flour, omit soda and cream of tartar.

Egg Yolk Paint

Blend well 1 egg yolk and ¼ teaspoon water. Divide mixture among several small custard cups. Add food coloring to each cup to make bright colors. Paint designs on cookies with small paintbrushes. If paint thickens on standing, add a few drops water.

GREEK EASTER BREAD

Greek holiday bread baked in a three-petaled loaf to represent the Trinity. The finished loaf is decorated with cherries and almonds arranged like petaled flowers. The bread is sliced across each of the petals.

2 packages active dry yeast
½ cup warm water (105 to 115°)
½ cup lukewarm milk, scalded then cooled
½ cup sugar
1 teaspoon salt
2 eggs
½ cup shortening
1 cup currants or 2 teaspoons grated lemon peel
4½ to 5 cups Gold Medal Flour* (regular or Wondra)
Confectioners' Sugar Glaze (page 118)
Blanched whole almonds
Red candied cherries, sliced

In mixing bowl dissolve yeast in warm water. Add milk, sugar, salt, eggs, shortening, currants or the peel and half the flour. Mix with spoon until smooth. Add enough remaining flour to handle easily; mix with hand. Turn onto lightly floured board; knead until smooth and elastic. Round up in greased bowl; turn once to bring greased side up. Cover. Let rise in warm place (85°) until double, about 1½ hours. Punch down; divide dough into 6 parts. Shape each into a round bun. Place 3 buns about ½ inch apart in cloverleaf shape on greased baking sheet. Let rise until double, about 45 minutes.

Heat oven to 375°. Bake 20 to 25 minutes or until nicely browned. While warm, frost with Confectioners' Sugar Glaze; decorate with petaled flowers made with almonds and cherry slices. *Makes 2 loaves.*

*If using Self-Rising Flour, omit salt.

Special Treats for Easter

Holiday Tree for Easter

To brighten the hall or a corner of the living room, arrange medium-sized tree branches in an attractive bucket or urn. (If you wish, spray the branches with white or metallic paint.) Trim the tree with one or more of the following: Easter cookies, artificial spring flowers, chocolate marshmallow bunnies, beautiful imported novelty candies or decorated Easter eggs. If desired, bank the base with green paper grass.

For a table centerpiece, you can make this same arrangement with smaller branches in a flowerpot or vase.

This tree can be trimmed for any holiday or special occasion—paper shamrocks, green candies and clay pipes for St. Patrick's Day; booties and bows for a baby shower. Just use a little ingenuity.

Elegant Easter Eggs

Beautifully decorated Easter eggs deserve to be displayed. Arranged in a basket or glass bowl, they would make a lovely centerpiece.

It's best to use empty egg shells (they need not be refrigerated as hard-cooked eggs must be) so you can keep the eggs from one year to the next if you store them carefully.

Here are some of our favorite decorating ideas: Glue beads and buttons on alternating rows of gold tape and pink velvet ribbon. • Wind a rubber band around eggs before dyeing. • Glue on rows of ribbons and matching bows; tiny artificial flowers can be stuck on too. • Glue on rickrack and bias tape in any number of geometric patterns; choose elegant Easter colors—pink, green, yellow, purple. • Apply bits of adhesive tape to the eggs before dyeing; when the tape is removed, the white patterns remain. • Make a Ukranian-style design by using a pencil to mark the egg in half lengthwise, then across the center. Divide each of these sections in half. Paint a different geometric pattern in each section. Use many different colors.

Easter Table Runner

Start with a runner in any color (purple is particularly nice for Easter). Make soft, fuzzy terry-cloth bunnies—you can copy them from a child's story book—and appliqué them to the runner. Then appliqué baskets of flowers on either side of the bunnies. The baskets can be made of rickrack and bias tape; the flowers can be formed with a gaily flowered cotton print. Finish the runner with harmonizing stripes of bias tape or rickrack.

Use the same flowered print for matching mother-daughter Easter aprons. Make a basket-shaped pocket and outline it with bias tape.

Polynesian Picnic

Ham-Chutney Rolls
Chilled Curried Chicken   Salad South Pacific
Buttered Rye Buns   Relish Tray of Gay Colors
Macadamia Feast Cake   Aloha Pineapple Punch

Surprisingly, one of the most sophisticated ways to entertain in summer is at a picnic—but not just an ordinary picnic. Make the occasion a real event with this Pacific-island menu, spicily flavored and served very cold. Spread out in a grove, a park, the backyard or on a boat deck it's an ideal prelude to the big events of a holiday weekend.

All the food may be prepared well in advance and refrigerated until take-off time. Then pack everything into picnic coolers, using canned refrigerant, or into metal boxes bedded with dry ice beneath layers of newspaper. For both flavor and safety's sake, don't rely on a few ice cubes to keep these dishes cool.

HAM-CHUTNEY ROLLS

Soften 1 package (3 ounces) cream cheese; spread on 6 thin slices boiled ham. Dot with 2 to 3 tablespoons chutney. Roll slices jelly-roll fashion; place on cutting board seam side down and cut into 1-inch slices. Cover and chill. *Makes about 30 appetizers.*

CHILLED CURRIED CHICKEN

Two 3½- to 4-pound broiler-fryer chickens
¼ cup butter or margarine, melted
4 slices bacon, diced
2 tablespoons flour
1 tablespoon sugar
2 teaspoons curry powder
¼ teaspoon salt
¼ teaspoon onion salt
1 cup water
2 tablespoons lime juice
1 tablespoon bottled steak sauce
1 jar (4¾ ounces) strained apricots (baby food)

Heat oven to 375°. Rinse birds with cold water; drain and pat dry with paper towels. Fasten neck skin to back with skewer. Lift wing tips up and over backs for natural brace. Tie legs securely to tail. Place breast side up on rack in shallow roasting pan. Brush with melted butter. Roast 30 minutes.

In skillet fry bacon until crisp. Blend in flour, sugar, curry powder and salts. Cook over low heat, stirring until mixture is bubbly. Remove from heat. Stir in remaining ingredients. Simmer, stirring constantly, 15 minutes. Spoon part of apricot mixture over chickens. Roast 30 minutes; remove string holding legs together. Continue roasting ½ to 1 hour, or until leg moves easily, basting occasionally. Cool; cover and chill. *6 servings.*

SALAD SOUTH PACIFIC

3 cups fresh or canned pineapple chunks*
2 cups cold cooked rice
½ cup chopped celery
⅓ cup raisins
¼ cup dairy sour cream
¼ cup salad dressing
1 teaspoon salt
½ teaspoon ginger

Combine pineapple, rice, celery and raisins; toss lightly. Stir together remaining ingredients; pour over rice mixture and toss. Cover and chill. Serve in a bowl lined with crisp salad greens, if desired. *6 servings.*

*If using fresh pineapple, sweeten to taste.

RELISH TRAY OF GAY COLORS

Place cherry tomatoes, green pepper sticks, cucumber slices and drained preserved kumquats in individual plastic bags; chill. Just before serving arrange relishes on tray. *6 servings.*

MACADAMIA FEAST CAKE

1⅓ cups Bisquick
¾ cup sugar
3 tablespoons soft butter or shortening
1 egg
¾ cup milk
1 teaspoon vanilla
Broiled Macadamia Topping (below)

Heat oven to 350°. Grease and flour a square pan, 8x8x2 inches, or a round layer pan, 9x1½ inches. Mix Bisquick and sugar. Add butter, egg and ¼ cup of the milk. Beat 1 minute medium speed on mixer or vigorously by hand. Gradually stir in remaining milk and the vanilla. Beat ½ minute longer. Pour into prepared pan. Bake 35 to 40 minutes. Serve with Broiled Macadamia Topping.

Broiled Macadamia Topping

Soften 3 tablespoons butter; mix with ⅓ cup brown sugar (packed), 2 tablespoons light cream, ½ cup flaked coconut and ¼ cup chopped macadamia nuts. Spread on warm baked cake.

Set oven control at broil and/or 550°. Place cake 3 inches from source of heat. Broil until nicely browned, about 3 minutes.

ALOHA PINEAPPLE PUNCH

Slice tops from 6 pineapples. Remove core and fruit from each, leaving a ¾-inch wall around pineapple. Reserve fruit for Salad South Pacific (page 149) or for another use of your choice. Without removing leaves, puncture a hole in top of each pineapple. The hole should be large enough for a straw to pass through. Replace tops. Wrap each pineapple in aluminum foil; chill well. Chill 3 bottles (1 pint 9 ounces each) pink sparkling catawba grape juice.

At serving time, divide chilled grape juice among the pineapples. Replace tops; insert straws through holes. *6 servings.*

Note: For carrying to picnic, well-chilled pineapples can be wrapped in newspaper and packed in a cardboard box. They will stay cold 3 to 4 hours, depending on temperature of the day. To keep 5 hours or longer, fill pineapple shells with ice cubes before wrapping in newspaper.

Make Your Summer Parties Special

Even though you're not eating in the dining room, make your outdoor table just as attractive as the one in your home. • A fabric tablecloth and napkins start you off right. Choose a gay denim or sailcloth in a plain color or a bright print; make sure the napkins harmonize. • Carry out a special theme—Western, Fourth of July, Polynesian or just Summer Fun—with all your picnic paraphernalia. Carry cooked foods safely and serve them with flair from plastic refrigerator dishes decorated with wallpaper, decals or your own hand-painted designs. Repeat the theme on tin or plastic containers that hold fresh fruits and vegetables and on a screw-top jar that holds the salad dressing. • Finish off the party air with paper plates and cups. Your novelty store has them in the most exciting designs this side of the art museum.

Especially for the Fourth

Red, white and blue are everywhere! A blue oilcloth on the picnic table is the beginning. Use pinking shears for a pretty finish or sew alternating bands of red and white rickrack along the edge of the cloth. (Spills won't spoil this pretty cloth!) For napkins, use old-fashioned red and white bandanas. And bring some extras to double as bibs for the children. A gay bowl- or basket-liner can be made from a larger bandana knotted in two corners. It makes a great holder for buns. For your food, bring along your grill and choose your favorites from the selection of barbecue foods on pages 101-104. And for dessert, nothing could be more appropriate than the cupcakes at right that look just like Fourth of July firecrackers.

FIRECRACKERS

Bake cupcakes as directed on 1 package of our devils food cake mix. Cool; remove papers. You will need 24 cupcakes to make 12 firecrackers; use remaining cupcakes as desired.

For icing, blend ½ cup soft butter or margarine and 4½ cups sifted confectioners' sugar. Stir in 2¼ teaspoons vanilla and about ¼ cup light cream until smooth. Reserve ¾ cup; color remaining icing with red food coloring.

To assemble firecracker, seal bottoms of 2 cupcakes together with small amount of red icing. Frost sides about ⅔ of the way around with red icing, leaving an uniced strip for firecracker to rest on. Frost ends with reserved white icing. Insert small red candle in one end to resemble wick. *Makes 12 firecrackers.*

Halloween Punch Party

Goblin Cinnamon Puffs   Black Cat Cookies
"Bobbing Apple" Punch Bowl
Salted Nuts

GOBLIN CINNAMON PUFFS

1 package of our wild blueberry muffin mix
½ cup sugar
1 teaspoon cinnamon
½ cup butter, melted

Prepare muffins as directed on package except—bake batter in tiny muffin cups 12 to 15 minutes. Mix sugar and cinnamon. Roll hot muffins in melted butter, then in cinnamon-sugar mixture. *Makes about 24 small muffins.*

BLACK CAT COOKIES

Bake Sugar Cookies as directed on page 35 except—do not sprinkle with granulated sugar. As soon as cookies come from oven, place a chocolate peppermint wafer in the center of each. Arrange 2 semisweet chocolate pieces next to mint for head, 1 piece for tail. Lift cookies onto cooling rack as chocolate melts. With wooden pick, shape melted chocolate pieces into head and tail of a cat. *Makes 5 dozen 2- to 2½-inch cookies.*

"BOBBING APPLE" PUNCH BOWL

A favorite with children, teenagers and adults. Pictured below.

1 gallon apple cider
2 teaspoons whole cloves
2 teaspoons whole allspice
2 sticks cinnamon (3 inches each)
⅔ cup sugar
2 whole oranges, washed
Whole cloves
3 medium red apples, washed

Heat cider, 2 teaspoons cloves, the allspice, cinnamon and sugar to boiling; cover and simmer 20 minutes. Stud oranges with cloves. Strain punch and pour into punch bowl.* Float oranges and apples in punch bowl. *Makes 32 half-cup servings.*

*If using a glass punch bowl, first pour in warm water to heat bowl.

Traditional Thanksgiving Dinner

Harvest Celebration Cup
Roast Turkey with Stuffing
Buttered Mashed Potatoes   Giblet Gravy
Creamed Onions Almondine   Lima Beans with Mushrooms
Corn Sticks   Cranberry Relish Mold
Choice of Two Pumpkin Pies   Coffee

Thanksgiving dinner is probably the most traditional holiday party of the year. But traditions vary from one part of the country to another and even from one family to another. Of course there'll be turkey, but how will it be stuffed? We present five marvelous choices, including popular regional favorites. And pumpkin pie is a must, but just which kind? Again we offer five exciting variations, from a tangy cheesecake type to a spectacular Baked Alaska Pumpkin Pie.

Because the major emphasis in this celebration is on the food, Thanksgiving dinner usually requires a good deal of attention, both the days-ahead kind and the last-minute variety. With such a menu, convenience foods must come to the aid of the cook. The salad, a make-ahead mold, gets off to an easy start with a package of frozen cranberry relish. The vegetables are from the freezer too, but each is enhanced with a gourmet touch. The potatoes, made from our mashed Potato Buds, are also timesaving—and delicious.

Since this is the most family oriented of feasts, a hostess needn't feel reluctant to accept any assistance that's offered. If there's a teen-age daughter in the family, she can do yeoman's service all along the way. If not—or even in addition—a sister, cousin, aunt or niece can be a very welcome help on Thanksgiving Day morn.

PLAN FOR PREPARATION

Day before: 1. *Prepare salad.* **2.** *If turkey is frozen, thaw as directed on wrapping.* **3.** *Prepare pies (except for Old-fashioned Pumpkin Pie which should not be baked until Thanksgiving morning).*

Thanksgiving Day: 1. *Bake Old-fashioned Pumpkin Pie, if desired.* **2.** *Wash and clean turkey.* **3.** *Prepare stuffing; stuff and roast turkey.* **4.** *Cook giblets.* **5.** *Thaw fruit for appetizer.* **6.** *Set table.* **7.** *Unmold salad; refrigerate.* **8.** *When turkey is done, remove from oven; let "set."* **9.** *Prepare appetizer; serve.* **10.** *Prepare and bake Corn Sticks.* **11.** *Prepare coffee.* **12.** *Cook beans.* **13.** *Prepare our mashed Potato Buds; cover to keep warm.* **14.** *Prepare gravy.* **15.** *Cook onions.* **16.** *Pour water.*

HARVEST CELEBRATION CUP

Thaw 2 packages (12 ounces each) frozen mixed fruit as directed on packages; *do not drain.* Spoon ⅓ cup fruit with syrup into each of 8 punch cups. Pour about ¼ cup chilled pink sparkling catawba grape juice into each cup; stir once. Serve immediately. *8 servings.*

ROAST TURKEY

When buying turkeys under 12 pounds, allow ¾ to 1 pound per serving (ready-to-cook weight). For heavier birds, 12 pounds and over, allow ½ to ¾ pound per serving. (For 8 generous servings, plus some left over, choose a 10- to 12-pound turkey.)

Heat oven to 325°. Rinse bird with cold water; drain and pat dry. Fold wings, bringing the wing tips onto the back. Fill neck cavity lightly with Bread Stuffing (right), if desired. Fasten neck skin to back with skewer. Stuff body cavity lightly; do not pack, as stuffing will expand while cooking. (Rub cavity of bird lightly with salt if bird is not stuffed.) Push drumsticks under band of skin at tail or tie drumsticks to tail.

Place turkey breast side up on rack in shallow roasting pan. Brush skin with fat. If meat thermometer is used, insert it so the bulb is in the center of the inside thigh muscle or the thickest part of the breast meat. Be sure bulb does not touch bone. Roast turkey, basting occasionally with pan drippings. When turkey is ⅔ done (see timetable right), cut band of skin or cord at drumsticks so heat can reach inside of thighs. Cover turkey *loosely* with tent of heavy-duty aluminum foil, if necessary, to prevent excessive browning, or place pieces of foil over browned areas.

Allow turkey to stand 20 to 30 minutes to "set" before carving.

How to Carve Turkey

1. Place turkey in front of host with legs to the right. Starting at nearest side, cut leg from body, first bending it back with left hand. Lift to auxiliary plate; sever thigh from drumstick. Slice meat from leg.

2. With fork astride breast, cut down sharply on joint connecting wing to body. Starting at point where wing had been attached, cut thin slices of breast meat, working up to breast bone.

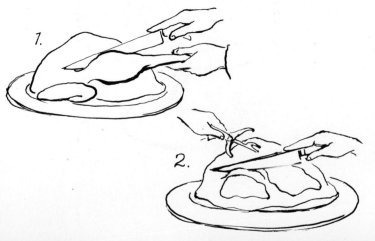

BREAD STUFFING

¾ cup minced onion
1½ cups chopped celery (stalks and leaves)
1 cup butter or margarine
9 cups bread cubes
2 teaspoons salt
1½ teaspoons crushed sage leaves
1 teaspoon crushed thyme leaves
½ teaspoon pepper

In large skillet cook and stir onion and celery in butter until onion is tender. Stir in about ⅓ of the bread cubes. Turn into deep bowl. Add remaining ingredients; toss lightly. Stuff turkey just before roasting. *Makes 9 cups—enough for a 12-pound turkey.*

New England Oyster Stuffing: Follow recipe for Bread Stuffing (above) except—decrease bread cubes to 8 cups. Drain 2 cans (8 ounces each) oysters; chop and toss with stuffing.

Far-west Apple Stuffing: Follow recipe for Bread Stuffing (above) except—decrease bread cubes to 7 cups and increase salt to 1 tablespoon. Add 3 cups finely chopped apples and ¾ cup raisins with remaining ingredients.

Midwest Corn Stuffing: Follow recipe for Bread Stuffing (above) except—decrease bread cubes to 8 cups and add 1 can (12 ounces) whole kernel corn, drained, and ½ cup chopped green pepper with the remaining ingredients.

Southern Pecan Stuffing: Follow recipe for Bread Stuffing (above) except—decrease bread cubes to 8 cups and butter to ¾ cup. Add 2 cups coarsely chopped pecans with the remaining ingredients.

Timetable for Turkey

This chart gives the approximate time required to roast stuffed fresh or completely thawed birds. (Time will be slightly less for unstuffed turkeys.)

Ready-to-cook Weight	Oven Temperature	Approximate Roasting Time	Interior Temperature
6 to 8 pounds	325°	2 to 2½ hours	185°
8 to 12 pounds	325°	2½ to 3 hours	185°
12 to 16 pounds	325°	3 to 3¾ hours	185°
16 to 20 pounds	325°	3¾ to 4 hours	185°
20 to 24 pounds	325°	4½ to 5½ hours	185°

GIBLET GRAVY

Giblets and neck from turkey
1 celery stalk, cut up
1 onion, sliced
1 large carrot, cut up
1 small bay leaf
1 teaspoon salt
6 cups water
½ cup Gold Medal Flour (regular or Wondra)
1½ teaspoons salt
½ teaspoon poultry seasoning
¼ teaspoon monosodium glutamate
¼ teaspoon pepper

Wash giblets and neck; refrigerate liver. Place gizzard, heart and neck in saucepan with vegetables, bay leaf, 1 teaspoon salt and the water. Heat to boiling; simmer 2½ to 3 hours, or until gizzard is fork tender, adding the liver the last 20 minutes. (Refrigerate giblets and broth unless used immediately.) Strain broth; discard neck and vegetables. Coarsely chop giblets; set aside.

When turkey has been removed to warm platter, pour the drippings (meat juice and fat) into a bowl, leaving brown particles in the pan. Let fat rise to top of drippings; skim off fat. Place ½ cup fat in roasting pan. Blend in flour. Cook over low heat, stirring until mixture is smooth and bubbly. Remove from heat. Measure giblet broth; add meat juice, if necessary, to measure 4 cups. Stir broth into flour mixture. Heat to boiling, stirring constantly. Boil 1 minute. Stir in giblets, 1½ teaspoons salt, the poultry seasoning, monosodium glutamate and pepper. Heat through. *Makes 4½ cups.*

CREAMED ONIONS ALMONDINE

In one large pan, prepare 3 packages (9 ounces each) frozen onions in cream sauce as directed on package except—substitute sherry for ⅓ of the liquid. Turn into serving dish; sprinkle with ¼ cup toasted slivered blanched almonds. *8 or 9 servings.*

LIMA BEANS WITH MUSHROOMS

Prepare 2 packages (10 ounces each) frozen small lima beans as directed on package. Drain 1 can (6 ounces) sliced mushrooms. Add mushrooms and 3 tablespoons soft butter or margarine to the drained beans; toss. *6 to 8 servings.*

CORN STICKS

1⅓ cups Bisquick
⅔ cup cornmeal
2 tablespoons sugar
⅔ cup milk
2 eggs

Heat oven to 450°. Grease corn stick pans; place in oven to heat. Stir together all ingredients; beat vigorously 30 seconds. Fill heated pans ⅔ full. Bake 12 to 15 minutes. (If corn sticks are baked ahead, wrap in foil and heat in oven just before serving.) *Makes 16 corn sticks.*

Note: For quick and easy Corn Sticks, prepare 2 packages of our corn muffin mix as directed on package except—fill corn stick pans half full.

CRANBERRY RELISH MOLD

1 package (3 ounces) lemon-flavored gelatin
1 cup boiling water
1 package (10 ounces) frozen cranberry-orange relish
1 can (8¾ ounces) crushed pineapple (undrained)
1 unpared red apple, chopped
½ cup chopped celery
Crisp salad greens

Dissolve gelatin in boiling water. Stir in frozen relish, fruit (with syrup) and celery, stirring until relish is thawed. Pour into 1-quart mold; chill until set. Unmold on salad greens. *6 to 8 servings.*

OLD-FASHIONED PUMPKIN PIE

Pastry for 9-inch One-crust Pie (page 129)
2 eggs, slightly beaten
1 can (1 pound) pumpkin
¾ cup sugar
½ teaspoon salt
1 teaspoon cinnamon
½ teaspoon ginger
¼ teaspoon cloves
1⅔ cups evaporated milk or light cream

Heat oven to 425°. Prepare pastry. Mix remaining ingredients; pour into pastry-lined pie pan. (To prevent spills, fill pie shell on oven rack or on open oven door.) Cover edge with 2- to 3-inch strip aluminum foil to prevent excessive browning. (Remove foil 15 minutes before end of baking time so edge will brown slightly.) Bake 15 minutes.

Reduce oven temperature to 350°; bake 45 minutes longer, or until knife inserted in center comes out clean. Cool. Top with sweetened whipped cream, if desired.

SURPRISE CHIFFON PIE

Under fluffy pumpkin chiffon is a layer of rich mincemeat—a splendid choice for those who can't decide between the two traditional favorites!

9-inch Baked Pie Shell (page 129)
1⅓ cups mincemeat
2 teaspoons unflavored gelatin
½ cup brown sugar (packed)
¼ teaspoon <u>each</u> salt, ginger, cinnamon and nutmeg
¾ cup canned or mashed cooked pumpkin
2 egg yolks
⅓ cup milk
2 egg whites
¼ teaspoon cream of tartar
⅓ cup granulated sugar

Prepare pie shell. Spread mincemeat on bottom and sides of cooled pie shell. Mix gelatin, brown sugar, salt, spices, pumpkin, egg yolks and milk in saucepan. Heat to boiling over medium heat, stirring constantly. Remove from heat; place pan in cold water. Cool until mixture mounds slightly when dropped from a spoon. Beat egg whites with cream of tartar until frothy. Gradually beat in sugar. Continue beating until stiff and glossy. Fold in pumpkin mixture. Pour into mincemeat-lined crust. Chill until set.

Note: Refrigerate any leftover pie immediately.

BAKED ALASKA PUMPKIN PIE

Following "the big dinner," pass a dish of mints and postpone this spectacular dessert until evening. Such a pumpkin pie deserves its own show...and a hungry audience!

1 of our pie crust sticks
1 egg, slightly beaten
2 egg yolks, slightly beaten
1 can (1 pound) pumpkin
¾ cup sugar
½ teaspoon salt
1 teaspoon cinnamon
½ teaspoon ginger
¼ teaspoon cloves
1⅔ cups evaporated milk
1 pint vanilla, Butter Brickle or butter-pecan ice cream
Brown Sugar Meringue (below)

Heat oven to 425°. Prepare pastry for 9-inch One-crust Pie as directed on inside wrapper. Mix remaining ingredients except ice cream and Brown Sugar Meringue. Pour into pastry-lined pie pan. Cover edge with 2- to 3-inch strip aluminum foil to prevent excessive browning. (Remove foil 15 minutes before end of baking time so edge will brown slightly.) Bake 15 minutes.

Reduce oven temperature to 350°; bake 45 minutes longer, or until knife inserted in center comes out clean. Soften ice cream slightly; press into waxed paper-lined 8-inch pie pan. Freeze solid. Meanwhile, chill cooled baked pie at least 1 hour.

Heat oven to 550°. Just before serving, unmold ice cream onto pie, removing waxed paper. Cover completely with Brown Sugar Meringue. Bake 2 to 3 minutes or until golden brown. Serve immediately.

Brown Sugar Meringue

Beat 2 egg whites and ¼ teaspoon cream of tartar until soft peaks form. Add ⅓ cup dark brown sugar (packed) and ½ teaspoon vanilla. Beat until meringue is stiff and glossy.

PUMPKIN-CHEESE PIE

A happy "cross" between a cheesecake and a pumpkin pie.

1 of our pie crust sticks
1 package (8 ounces) cream cheese, softened
¾ cup sugar
2 tablespoons flour
1 teaspoon cinnamon
¼ teaspoon <u>each</u> nutmeg and ginger
1 teaspoon grated lemon peel
1 teaspoon grated orange peel
¼ teaspoon vanilla
3 eggs
1 can (1 pound) pumpkin
Sour Cream Topping (below)

Heat oven to 350°. Prepare pastry for 9-inch One-crust Pie as directed on inside wrapper. In large mixer bowl blend cream cheese, sugar and flour. Add the next 8 ingredients and beat at medium speed until smooth. Pour into pastry-lined pan. Cover edge with 2- to 3-inch strip aluminum foil to prevent excessive browning. (Remove foil 15 minutes before end of baking time so edge will brown slightly.) Bake 50 to 55 minutes, or until knife inserted in center comes out clean. Immediately spread top of pie with Sour Cream Topping. Cool. Refrigerate at least 4 hours. Serve well chilled.

Sour Cream Topping

Blend ¾ cup dairy sour cream, 1 tablespoon sugar and ¼ teaspoon vanilla.

PUMPKIN ICE-CREAM PIE

1 of our pie crust sticks
1 pint vanilla ice cream
2 to 3 tablespoons cut-up crystallized ginger
1 cup canned or mashed cooked pumpkin
1 cup sugar
1 teaspoon pumpkin pie spice
½ teaspoon ginger
½ teaspoon salt
½ cup chopped walnuts
1 cup whipping cream, whipped

Prepare 9-inch Baked Pie Shell as directed on inside wrapper. Cool. Stir ice cream to soften. Quickly fold in crystallized ginger and spread in pie shell. Freeze until ice cream is solid. Stir together pumpkin, sugar, pumpkin pie spice, ginger, salt and walnuts. Fold in whipped cream. Pour over ice cream in pie shell. Freeze at least several hours. Just before serving, remove from freezer and place in refrigerator a few minutes to soften.

Centerpieces for Your Thanksgiving Table

Gilded Fruit Centerpiece

You'll need a compote or footed candy dish, gold spray, aluminum foil, a fresh pineapple, a variety of nuts and fresh fruit (bananas, pears, apples, lemons) and greens.

Protect the pineapple leaves by wrapping them in aluminum foil, then spray the pineapple and the other fruits and nuts gold. Allow them to dry. Remove foil from pineapple leaves.

Spread greens in center of table; place compote or candy dish on the greens. (You can use a block of wood as the pedestal.) Place the pineapple in the compote; arrange the fruits and nuts around it, building them up from the table to the pineapple. Make sure the centerpiece looks well from all sides.

This beautiful piece will keep a week or more. After Thanksgiving, use it to grace a side table.

Fall Flower Showpiece

Start with a white compote (or use a cake stand topped with a shallow white bowl). Cover a piece of plastic water-retaining material with chicken wire and place in compote.

Choose Fuji mums, pompon mums and daisies in shades of yellow and white and arrange in compote. Place bunches of green grapes near the base of the flowers, allowing the grapes to hang over the edge of the compote. Complete the arrangement with lemon leaves.

Make your turkey a companion piece. Circle shiny green leaves around the turkey; tuck in a few tiny mums and daisies and several small bunches of green grapes. Remove the garnishes before carving.

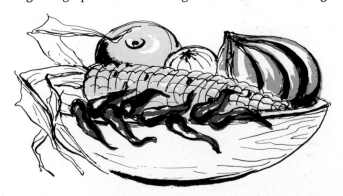

Fruits of the Harvest Arrangements

• Arrange shiny fresh fruits and vegetables, gourds or ears of corn in a china pitcher, cut-glass bowl or other attractive container. • Show off dark green acorn squash, amber winter onions, dried red peppers and white or yellow daisies in a low wooden bowl. • Tuck graceful sprays of wheat into an arrangement of chrysanthemums. An antique iron mortar makes a stunning and unusual container for such a display.

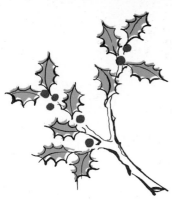

Merry Christmas Dinner

Cranberry Frost
Roast Ducklings with Wild Rice Stuffing
Mashed Rutabagas with Green Peas
Holiday Salad   Hot Rolls
Steamed Date Pudding with Butter Cream Sauce
Coffee

Make Christmas dinner the happy high point of a best-loved holiday with a menu as pretty and festive as it is delicious. Every course—from the cranberry appetizer to the holly-circled dessert—is gaily garnished in Christmas reds and greens to blend merrily with your own very special holiday centerpiece or tablecloth.

Red and green greet the guests as soon as they sit down—already in place are the appetizers and the apple and avocado salads. Place the platter of ducklings, with its gay Christmas garnish, before the host. He has the honor of carving and serving. Later, bring on the traditional Steamed Date Pudding and serve it at the table.

~~~~ PLAN FOR PREPARATION ~~~~

Christmas Day: 1. *Prepare stuffing.* **2.** *Wash and stuff duck-lings; roast.* **3.** *Set table.* **4.** *Prepare and steam pudding.* **5.** *Prepare sauce.* **6.** *Wrap rolls in foil; set aside.* **7.** *Spoon lemon sherbet into cups; freeze.* **8.** *Cook rutabagas.* **9.** *Arrange salads.* **10.** *Heat rolls.* **11.** *Prepare coffee.* **12.** *Cook peas.* **13.** *Mash rutabagas with potatoes.* **14.** *Pour water.* **15.** *Pour cranberry cocktail over sherbet; serve.*

CRANBERRY FROST

Divide 1 quart lemon sherbet among 8 small glass cups or footed goblets; freeze until serving time. Just before serving, pour 1 quart cranberry cock-tail over sherbet. *8 servings.*

ROAST DUCKLINGS
WITH WILD RICE STUFFING

4 cups boiling water
1 cup uncooked wild rice
2 ready-to-cook ducklings (4 to 5 pounds each)
2 jars (4½ ounces each) whole mushrooms, drained (reserve liquid)
3 beef bouillon cubes
1 cup long-grain white rice
1¾ teaspoons salt
¼ teaspoon pepper
½ cup chopped onion
½ cup chopped celery
¼ cup butter or margarine
½ cup coarsely chopped Brazil nuts
¼ teaspoon marjoram
½ cup honey

Pour boiling water over wild rice; cover and let stand 20 minutes. Drain. Wash ducklings; dry thoroughly. Fasten neck skin to back with skewers. Lift wing tips up and over back for natural brace. Add hot water to reserved mushroom liquid to measure 3 cups. Add bouillon cubes to this liquid in large skillet; heat until bouillon cubes dissolve. Add white and wild rice, salt and pepper; stir until mixed. Heat mixture to boiling; reduce heat and cover. Simmer about 14 minutes, or until rice is tender. Fluff rice with fork; cover and steam 5 minutes. Cook and stir onion and celery in butter until onion is tender. Stir onion mixture, mushrooms, nuts and marjoram into rice mixture; toss lightly.

Heat oven to 325°. Stuff body cavity of each duckling with rice mixture. *Do not pack.* Secure openings with skewers and string. Roast ducklings 2 to 2½ hours. Brush with honey during last 15 minutes. Arrange ducklings on platter. *6 to 8 servings.*

MASHED RUTABAGAS WITH GREEN PEAS

4 pounds rutabagas, pared and cut into 1½-inch cubes
8 cups water
1 teaspoon salt
2 packages (10 ounces each) frozen green peas
Enough of our mashed Potato Buds (dry) for 4 servings
1 teaspoon salt
¼ teaspoon pepper

In large saucepan cook rutabagas in salted water until tender, about 30 minutes. Cook peas as directed on package. Prepare mashed Potato Buds as directed on package for 4 servings except—omit milk and butter. Drain rutabagas; combine with mashed potatoes. Add 1 teaspoon salt and the pepper; mash thoroughly. Spoon into bowl or onto platter, leaving an indentation in center. Fill center with peas. *8 servings.*

HOLIDAY SALAD

Have 1 large red apple well chilled; quarter apple and cut into ⅛-inch slices. Peel 2 ripe avocados; remove pits and cut into ¼-inch slices. Sprinkle apple and avocado slices liberally with lemon juice. (If desired, cover and refrigerate.) Arrange endive on 8 salad plates; arrange apple and avocado slices on greens. Sprinkle with pomegranate seeds; drizzle with bottled fruit salad dressing. *8 servings.*

HOT ROLLS

Wrap 1 dozen baked crescent rolls or other favorite dinner rolls in aluminum foil. Heat in 325° oven 15 minutes. *12 rolls.*

Permanent Party Gear

Poultry shears make carving a duckling, chicken or any game bird very simple. And what an inspired Christmas present for a hard-to-buy-anything-for husband!

STEAMED DATE PUDDING WITH BUTTER CREAM SAUCE

½ cup hot water
1 package of our date bar mix
2 eggs
½ cup finely chopped nuts
½ teaspoon mace
½ teaspoon cinnamon
¼ teaspoon nutmeg
Butter Cream Sauce (right)

Mix water and date mixture thoroughly. Add the crumbly mix, eggs, nuts and spices; mix well. Pour into well-greased 3-cup oven-proof glass bowl. Cover bowl with aluminum foil. Place rack in saucepan and pour boiling water into pan up to level of rack. Place bowl of pudding on rack. Cover saucepan; keep water boiling over low heat to steam pudding 2 hours. (If it is necessary to add water during steaming, lift lid and quickly add boiling water.) Remove foil and let pudding stand about 5 minutes before removing from bowl. If desired, place pudding in center of plate garnished with holly. Serve warm, cut into wedges. Pass Butter Cream Sauce. *8 servings.*

Butter Cream Sauce

1 cup sugar
1 cup light cream
¼ cup butter
1 egg yolk, beaten
1 teaspoon vanilla

Combine sugar, cream and butter in saucepan. Cook, stirring constantly, 3 to 4 minutes. Remove from heat. Stir at least half the hot mixture into egg yolk. Return egg mixture to saucepan and cook, stirring constantly, 1 minute. Remove from heat. Blend in vanilla. Serve warm. *Makes about 1½ cups.*

Company Favorites for the Christmas Season

CANDY CANE COFFEE CAKE

1 recipe Sour-cream Yeast Dough (page 116)
1½ cups finely chopped dried apricots
1½ cups finely chopped drained maraschino
    cherries
Butter or margarine
Decorators' Icing (below)

Heat oven to 375°. Divide dough into 3 parts. Roll each third into a rectangle, 15x6 inches. Place on greased baking sheet. Make cuts, 2 inches deep, from edge of 15-inch sides at ½-inch intervals.

Combine apricots and cherries. Spread ⅓ of fruit mixture down center of each rectangle. Crisscross strips over filling. Stretch cane to 1½ times its length (22 inches). Curve dough to form cane. Bake 15 to 20 minutes or until golden brown. While warm, brush with butter and drizzle with Decorators' Icing. Decorate with cherries, if desired. *Makes 3 canes.*

Decorators' Icing

Blend 2 cups sifted confectioners' sugar with about 2 tablespoons water. If too stiff, add few drops water.

DELLA ROBBIA MINCE PIE

Pastry for 9-inch Two-crust Pie (page 129)
1 jar (29 ounces) mincemeat (3 cups)*
1½ cups chopped apple
Della Robbia Wreath (below)

Heat oven to 425°. Prepare pastry. Stir together mincemeat and apple. Pour into pastry-lined pie pan. Cover with top crust as directed. Bake 40 to 45 minutes. Serve slightly warm, garnished with Della Robbia Wreath.

*If packaged mincemeat is used, prepare as directed on the package.

Della Robbia Wreath

Shape small apples and pears of process American cheese and "blush" with red sugar. With these "cheese fruits," dates and green and red maraschino cherries, form a small wreath on top of pie.

BÛCHE DE NOËL

French Yule Log Cake for Christmas Eve.

2 cups Gold Medal Flour* (regular or Wondra)
1⅓ cups sugar
2½ teaspoons baking powder
¾ teaspoon salt
1½ teaspoons rum flavoring
⅔ cup shortening (half butter)
1 cup milk
6 egg yolks
French Silk Frosting (below)
Mocha Icing (below)

Heat oven to 350°. Grease and flour a loaf pan, 9x5x3 inches. In large mixer bowl stir together dry ingredients; blend in rum flavoring, shortening, milk and egg yolks. Beat 3 minutes medium speed on mixer or 450 vigorous strokes by hand. Pour batter into prepared pan. Bake 65 to 70 minutes, or until wooden pick inserted in center comes out clean. Cool 10 minutes in pan; turn onto rack to cool completely.

Trim off edges and top of cake to make a rounded log shape; save trimmings. Cut cake lengthwise into 4 layers. Reassemble log, filling layers with French Silk Frosting. With some of the trimmings, make a "branch," 3 inches long and 1 inch in diameter; secure on top of log with French Silk Frosting. Frost ends of log and "branch" with Mocha Icing. With fork, make circular markings on ends of log. Spread remaining French Silk Frosting on top and sides of log, rounding it while spreading. With a fork, make markings lengthwise to resemble bark. Garnish with pistachio nuts, green icing or gumdrop leaves to resemble a vine on the log, if desired. Store cake in refrigerator.

*Do not use Self-Rising Flour in this recipe.

French Silk Frosting

Melt 3 squares (3 ounces) unsweetened chocolate; cool. In mixer bowl, beat 4 cups sifted confectioners' sugar, 1 cup soft butter or margarine, 1 egg, the melted chocolate and 1 teaspoon vanilla until smooth and fluffy.

Mocha Icing

Dissolve 1 teaspoon instant coffee in 1 tablespoon hot water; stir in 1 cup sifted confectioners' sugar until smooth. Add a few drops water, if necessary, for spreading consistency.

Pictured from top to bottom: Candy Cane Coffee Cake, Della Robbia Mince Pie, Bûche de Noël.

A Merry Christmas All Through the House

Unusual Tree Trims

• Artificial fruits and nuts on a white-flocked tree. Tie the fruits on with red velvet or satin bows; fill in with red ball ornaments. • Make your tree old-fashioned with popcorn balls, candy canes and strings of cranberries and popcorn. • Hang decorated Christmas cookies on the tree with ribbon. • Attach artificial red roses on the boughs of your tree. If you prefer an artificial tree, use red or pink roses on a white tree, pale blue roses on a green or blue tree.

Wreaths for Your Table or Door

• *Candy and Cookie Wreath:* Use bright ribbons to tie individually wrapped (in plastic wrap) cookies, candies and nuts onto a wire coat hanger that has been shaped into a circle. Curl the loose ribbon ends and tuck in sprigs of holly or greens. Finish off with a big bow. • *Cone and Leaf Wreath:* Gather leaves and pine cones in the autumn; save them for this lovely piece. Cut two large doughnut shapes from corrugated cardboard and staple together for the base of the wreath. (Make the base 16 inches in diameter, 3 inches wide.) Gild the leaves, a few of the pine cones and some walnuts and hazelnuts with gold paint. Paste the leaves on the surface of the wreath, using linoleum paste. Paste on cones, placing them in different directions. (You may want to dip the cones in wood preservative before pasting them on.) Fill in with the nuts. To add a touch of color, paste on red ball ornaments (dip the hook end into paste). Allow the wreath to dry overnight. • *Wreath of Roses:* For a base, purchase an imitation Christmas wreath from the novelty store. Using florists' wire and white paste, cover the wreath completely with paper roses (or other flowers). Fill in with tiny ball ornaments.

Apple Tree Centerpiece

For the base, cut a 10-inch circle from strong cardboard. Glue a 5-inch piece of broom handle or wooden dowel to the center of round. This is the candle support. Then cut a 13-inch circle from pliable cardboard. Cut away ⅓ of the circle. With the remaining piece, form a cone, overlapping edges about ½ inch (sew or staple together) so the center hole is large enough to fit over the candle support. Slip cone over candle support and tape securely to base.

Wrap 24 medium apples in 10-inch squares of red cellophane, tying each at stem end with strong string. Leave ends of string about 5 inches long. Arrange one row of apples around edge of base and tie together tightly. Add a second and third row of apples. Attach a 12-inch red candle to the top of the support with florists' clay. Fill in empty spaces between apples with small sprays of greens.

Make smaller trees for card-table centerpieces or to place at either side of the large tree. For each tree, cut a 3½-inch circle from strong cardboard. Attach a 12-inch red candle to the center with florists' clay. Wrap 4 medium apples as directed above; arrange around candle, tying as directed above. If necessary, prop up apples with florists' clay so string ends are next to candle. Fill in with greens.

Jingle Bells Bread Basket

Use a narrow ribbon to tie 5 or 6 colored bells onto your bread basket. Passing the bread makes a happy, typically Christmas sound.

Gay Christmas Runner

Sew green ball fringe around the edge of a length of red and white striped fabric. This runner is particularly gay on a red or white tablecloth.

For a matching apron, use the same striped fabric; sew the ball fringe on the bottom. For the pocket, cut a Christmas-tree shape out of green felt.

Subject Index

Names of menus are listed in **boldface** type.

Recipe Index